W9-ALU-650

IT TOOK
HEROES

To Larry Hampfling,
Best wishes and
God's blessings!

Claude Newby
14 May '99

IT TOOK HEROES

One Chaplain's Story and Tribute to Vietnam Veterans and Those Who Waited for Them

CLAUDE D. NEWBY

Copyright © 1998 by Claude Newby

All Rights Reserved.

No part of this book may be reproduced in any form whatsoever, whether by graphic, visual, electronic, filming, microfilming, tape recording, or any other means, without prior written permission of the author, except in the case of brief passages embodied in critical reviews and articles.

ISBN: 1-55517-392-6

v.11 L14C

Published by: **Bonneville Books**
Distributed by:
925 North Main, Springville, UT 84663 • 801/489-4084

Cedar Fort, Incorporated
CFI Distribution • CFI Books • Council Press • Bonneville Books

Cover Design and Page Layout by Corinne A. Bischoff
Printed in the United States of America

Contents

Preface

"It doesn't take a hero to order men into battle. It takes a hero to be one of those men who goes into battle," said General H. Norman Schwarzkopf. He knew first hand of what he spoke, and this book is about those of whom he spoke, as I knew them.

My Vietnam memoirs began as part of my autobiography. Sometime before 1995, I listed several good reasons for writing my life story. These reasons included a desire to leave a chronicle of my life that my posterity may "know" me, gain some advantage from the lessons life taught me, and cherish their heritage. I also wanted to pay tribute to and give credit to key people for their influence in my life. Deeper inside me, though, something gnawed at me, some motivation these stated reasons failed to satisfy. Do I crave recognition? Yes, at some level of human weakness, but this answer doesn't assuage the gnawing.

In November 1972 a military man wrote me: "The Vietnam War is over, and it's time to forget it. Please quit telling war stories, and let's leave the war behind us." These well-intended words pained me deeply — the gnawing increased. *If even military people want to bury and forget the faithful sacrifices rendered in Vietnam, does anyone care? Can we forget the event and still remember those who served and sacrificed so much?* — There was a connection between Vietnam and the gnawing inside me, but I missed it.

In 1969 President Richard M. Nixon began pulling combat forces out of Vietnam. By 1973 the process was complete except for a few advisors, and "peace with honor" was declared. We Army Chaplains in Europe, where I then served, were ordered to celebrate the peace with special religious services. *"No!"* I declared. "Rather, I will conduct a final memorial service for the soldiers and civilians who died and will yet die — on both sides — in Vietnam, and for their grieving loved ones," I wrote.

So in memorial services and on countless other speaking engagements, I shared my memories of many of the heroes who went into battle in Vietnam. As I shared these memories, the gnawing inside me eased. Finally, in 1995, I recognized the connection.

My serendipitous awakening occurred the day I finished the first draft of the chronicle of my tours in Vietnam. Suddenly, a great weight lifted from me — a mental, emotional, spiritual burden of near tangible proportions. That's when I first realized the gnawing had been there all along because I needed to preserve "the rest of the story" in writing.

Thus, with my war memories on paper and in the computer — making up two-thirds of almost a thousand pages of double-spaced manuscript, the gnawing almost ceased for the first time in more than a quarter of a century, and I felt free of a vague melancholy. It was as if I'd been properly relieved from some lonely guard post, of some awesome burden, which burden I never fully appreciated until it lifted off of me. *I don't have to remember anymore. Now, whatever happens to me, the story is preserved, lest we forget.*

As for American involvement in the Vietnam War, my strong feelings are — should they show through — incidental. This is about heroes, about whole life spans compressed into months, days, hours. It is about grunts, a tribute to them and to those who supported them up close and personal. As a chaplain in Vietnam, I served no war, just or unjust. I served soldiers — heroes — faithful souls who stepped forward when called upon by their country, while others received accolades for refusing to serve. It took a special kind of hero to step forward in the decade of the sixties. And I owe those special heroes for much more than memories. I owe them my life, literally.

This book is not about tenets of religion or points of religious doctrine. However, considering its source, an Army chaplain (retired), it is occasionally necessary to refer to my own and other chaplains' and soldiers' faith and religious affiliation. To do otherwise and remain true to the facts and context of the events and people described is impossible. A "prime directive" of each of America's military chaplaincies is that the chaplain will not attempt to win soldiers from other religious denominations to his or her own. While retirement released me from this "rule of engagement," I adhere to it in the pages of this book because my purposes are quite non-denominational. By the way, adherence by chaplains to the prime directive is not a sellout, because their commission is to provide or coordinate spiritual and religious support for soldiers and their families without regard to one's religious affiliation or lack thereof. In other words, the role of a military chaplain, in most respects, is an institutional one rather than an ecclesiastical one. Of course, each chaplain must be endorsed to serve by a church or group of religious bodies, and he or she must be ordained in whatever way that church or body of churches describes. A chaplain is not required to violate the tenets of his religious vows or faith to support the soldier. However, he is expected to do all in his power to bring to bear those resources that are necessary to meet those spiritual needs of the soldier that he cannot personally provide. In this way, I was as responsible for the Baptist and athiest as I was for those of my own faith.

The chronology of this memoir rests firmly on my personal journal, which provides the framework and foundation for the memories. I augmented these by interviewing fellow soldiers, by personal and official journals, and by other sources. Not to brag, but my memory is verifiably exceptional, especially for directions, lay-of-the-land and chronology. This ability I've validated through research and revisits to places of long ago. Almost always, my recollections of sites and events are accurate as to geographic orientation. And usually sites and layouts are the way I remembered them — schools, houses, farms, streams, roads, and dates and sequences. This holds true back to when I was a toddler, before I knew of compass directions. Apparently, this talent is inborn in me, perhaps a psychological need to know where — and when — I am. Whatever its source, my gift served me well in combat and in writing this memoir.

The hardest thing about writing this book has been stopping, because every action and story has as many facets and perspectives as there were individuals involved in it. I've discovered that every veteran I contact adds detail that helps clarify and clear up seeming inconsistencies, and deserves at least a chapter of his own. I hope I didn't stop writing too soon. I trust I'll be forgiven by my grunts, medics, LRRPs (rangers) and scouts, aviators and former leaders when my memories, notes and perspective differ from theirs, for I have been faithful to my memories and journal and strove to verify and validate every detail and name whenever I could.

Foreword

I am honored to give my endorsement for Claude Newby's book, *It Took Heroes*. I have known Claude for more than a quarter of a century, and he has been a hero/son to me.

I have known him professionally in his role as a distinguished military chaplain during these years. The book, *It Took Heroes*, is written with absolute truth, honor and integrity. It will give every reader a lump in his throat, a tear in his eye and a pride in his heart for the thousands of brave young men who served and gave their lives for all of us. "No greater love hath any man than this."

It Took Heroes dead and alive to make this book possible. Their voices are heard as if coming from the dust. We need to place this book in an honored place among the treasures we accrue for our posterity.

— *Lucile Johnson*

Family Therapist, Speaker and Author,
Recipient of the Bob Hope Five Star Civilian
Award in miniature for service to her country

June 23, 1967

Ambush! screamed my brain the instant geysers of dirt began sprouting up on the right shoulder of the road ahead of the jeep. A fraction of a second later, my ears confirmed what my eyes saw. An AK-47 on full automatic was kicking up those geysers. The enemy had hit us when we were about 200 feet from where the road curved left at the top of the hill.

One enemy gunner had opened up as we entered the kill zone, firing ahead of our jeep — leading us — and no doubt expecting us to try to speed away from the kill zone as quickly as possible. Had we sped up as expected, we would have driven straight into almost certain death. Martinez, however, reflexively slammed on the brakes and brought the chugging, laboring jeep to an instant halt, sparing our lives.

As Martinez hit the brakes, I leaped from the jeep and down a bank into the elephant grass. A fraction of a second later, Preacher landed almost on top of me. Almost simultaneously, Martinez threw himself down across the seat I'd just vacated, beating by a fraction of a second a burst of machine-gun fire from a second concealed position straight ahead, where the road curved to the left. Three bullets tore through the windshield and dash and passed on, missing Martinez. Other rounds punctured the radiator and a tire.

With the AK-47 and machine gun blazing away, Martinez slithered from the jeep and joined us in the grass. Hot lead cracked continually over our heads. My first thought was *the gunners will keep us pinned down while others sneak up and frag us. We've got to move away from the road!*

chapter one

Marching as to War

(From the hymn "Onward Christian Soldiers")

Braniff Airline Charter Flight W243B departed Travis Air Force Base, California, at 2:38 p.m. September 14, destination South Vietnam with stops on the way in Alaska and Japan. As the airplane plunged forward toward whatever awaited, my pained thoughts hung tightly to the wife and five children I left behind. I could hardly believe I was here, an Army chaplain headed into war.

The final leg of this journey really began a year and a half earlier on a Sunday evening in February 1965. Helga was already in bed when I decided to visit Alan Smith, a fellow seminary teacher and neighbor. During the visit I informed Smith that I had tendered my resignation from my teaching position, effective at the end of the current school year.

"Why don't you return to the Army as a chaplain?" Smith asked.

"No thanks," I snapped, "I've had enough of the Army." Between 1952 and 1958 I had been an enlisted soldier and was currently a medic on a Special Forces A-team in the National Guard.

Not to be put off by my reflexive response, Smith referred me to an article in the latest edition of the *Deseret News*. The piece announced that for the first time since the Korean War, the military services were accepting chaplaincy applications from Latter-day Saint men. By an agreement worked out between the military services and the LDS Church, acceptable applicants could enter the chaplaincy under an educational waiver of the requirement that all chaplains have 90 hours of graduate credit and a divinity-school degree. This requirement was an almost impossible barrier for LDS candidates because their church had neither divinity schools nor professional clergy. For Mormons, a bachelor's degree would henceforth be sufficient. So read the announcement — I had one of those!

Though I'd reflexively rejected Alan's suggestion about the chaplaincy, I had second thoughts as I walked home from his house. For one thing, being in the National Guard, I knew American involvement was heating up in Vietnam, and experienced soldiers would soon be in demand. With my Army background, I reasoned,

I'd have an edge in understanding soldiers' lives and challenges and in serving those of all faiths. And I'd earn at least $500 per month as a lieutenant, before taxes.

At home, my mind swirling, I crawled into bed next to Helga and nudged her until she acknowledged my intrusion into her dreams. "What is it?"

"How would you like to go back in the Army and earn five hundred dollars a month?" I asked.

In response, Helga mumbled something that I chose to interpret as agreement and fell back to sleep. She doesn't remember this conversation.

Moments later, in the living room, I penned a letter to apply to become a chaplain. The letter highlighted those aspects of my background that I believed would make my application stand out. I expressed preference for the Army and infantry and added that I had received the Good Conduct Medal as an enlisted man.

I seriously doubted I'd be accepted for the chaplaincy. After all, my seminary-teaching career was less than spectacular. An ecclesiastical leader, upon learning of my intentions, advised me to not get my hopes up because he had failed to be selected to be a chaplain, despite his having much better credentials than I had. But I tried and dared hope, with nothing to lose. Meanwhile, to be on the safe side, I continued to seek employment elsewhere for the coming summer and school year.

*

Excitement reigned in our home the day we were called to come for an interview at church headquarters in Salt Lake City. I was the first of a hundred applicants to be interviewed because we had planned to be in Tennessee come June, the scheduled time for the interviews.

Elder Boyd K. Packer, a general or church headquarters-level leader, interviewed me alone, and then Helga and me together. During the private interview, Elder Packer asked, in effect, "Have you ever done anything that would cause you to be unworthy to represent the church as a chaplain," a pause while my life flashed before my eyes, "since you joined the church?"

"No," I answered honestly.

We left Elder Packer's office quietly convinced we'd better keep looking elsewhere for employment, which conviction we shared with each other a few nights later during a drive-in movie date.

*

In May 1965, I accepted the junior position in a two-teacher school in Kiana, Alaska. Kiana is situated on the banks of the Kobuk River, 40 miles north of the Arctic Circle and 80 miles inland from the frigid Bering Sea. The boys and I looked eagerly toward Alaska. Helga and Jeannie looked forward with dread and trepidation. But wonderful companion that she was, is, Helga prepared resolutely for two years in the cold north wilderness. The reprieve, when it came, was very welcome.

*

Upon returning home from our June trip to Tennessee, we solidified plans for the move to Alaska and readied ourselves to receive the packers. That's when the telephone rang. We received the call on a wall telephone in our small kitchen. Helga came close when she heard me say, "Elder Packer." Standing face to face with her, I heard him say:

"I regret to inform you (pause for effect), you've been selected to be a chaplain in the Army. Do you accept?"

With barely controlled emotions and feigned dignity, I accepted. *The Army, my first choice!*

The main business attended to, Elder Packer instructed me to attend an orientation meeting at church headquarters where I would receive further instructions.

Helga's beautiful eyes sparkled with joy as she interpreted my side of the conversation. Cool dignity dissolved as I hung up the telephone; Helga did a little dance of glee as we melted joyfully into each other's embrace. We were in, we thought. Little did we suspect the obstacles between the telephone call and *being in*.

*

War clouds loomed heavy when, on July 25, 1965, we eleven endorsed candidates gathered at church headquarters. Infantry divisions were going to Vietnam, screamed the headlines that day — the next step in Secretary of Defense Robert McNamara's policy of limited war and gradual escalation, a policy obviously doomed in the opinion of many professional soldiers.

As part of a daylong orientation, Elder Packer said, looking straight at me, "You were not selected for the chaplaincy because you are necessarily the best qualified applicants. You were selected because you are who the Lord wants." These words would motivate me for more than a quarter of a century.

Upon completion of the orientation, H. Richard Thomas gave to each candidate a set of military application forms and a formal military letter. My letter, dated 29 July 1965, authorized me to obtain an Army physical examination at the nearest military induction center. I was further instructed to send my application and physical exam results to the Office of the Army Chief of Chaplains. Once I had active-duty orders in hand, I was to return to church headquarters and be set apart (an LDS ordinance similar to ordination in many churches). The process of "getting in" seemed simple enough.

※

I reported to Fort Douglas, Utah, for a physical examination on August 2, 1965, and flunked it because of high-frequency deafness in both ears. How could that be? I'd passed hearing tests to enter and exit the Army, to become a correctional officer at Alcatraz, to be a police officer, and within the past year to enlist in the National Guard. But the previous hearing tests each consisted of a doctor clicking coins together and asking me if I heard it, which I always had. This time, the Army had tested my hearing with me inside an electronic box and declared me unfit for military service.

Reluctantly, sorrowfully, I returned and shared the sad news with Helga. She was wonderful. First, she assured me the Lord was aware of us, that He was bound to bless us because we faithfully paid an honest tithe, and we tried to keep His commandments. "And," she reflected, "do you really have to have perfect ears to be a chaplain?" Perhaps not.

A letter dated 11 August 1965 informed me that my request for a waiver of my hearing disability had been forwarded to the Office of the Surgeon General of the Army with a recommendation that it be approved. The chaplain who signed the letter promised to cooperate with me in every possible way, and said, "I trust whatever the news may be, it will be God's will for you."

The waiver was approved in late August. "Commissioning and active duty awaits only completion of a security check on you. You should be on active duty by early September [1965]," said an official letter.

※

Meanwhile, times were getting very tight, financially. We'd canceled the move to Alaska, and almost three months had passed since our last paycheck. Even the monthly National Guard drill pay had ended in May due to my impending move to Alaska, and that, alas, just before I was to have attended paratrooper training at Fort Benning, Georgia. To make matters worse, I couldn't find decent employment without being dishonest. For example, Sears declined to hire me because I "might" enter the Army soon. Other potential employers turned me away because I was "overqualified."

September came and went without any further word from Washington. We were desperate. With little money for house payments, utilities, food, we were falling deeper and deeper in debt. Between June and October we racked up more than $3,000 in medical bills alone, a fortune even had paychecks been regular. Fortunately, with the new school year came the opportunity to earn a little — about $500 over four months — as a substitute teacher.

Our financial condition became so bad that by late fall I was forced to seek help from our bishop. He gave us food orders to be filled at the Bishop's Storehouse. Thus, I continued to feed my family, though the mortgage payments and other bills were very difficult to meet. In exchange for help from the church — between substitute teaching and job hunting — I helped out at a church welfare warehouse, cannery and dairy and delivered coal to churches. Doing her part and more, Helga did ironing and sewing jobs assigned to her by the bishop. Thus, we kept our dignity by earning the assistance we received.

*

About mid-October, having heard nothing from Washington, I called on H. Richard Thomas, the Servicemen Committee secretary at church headquarters. He greeted me with, "Hello, Brother Newby. I'm glad you are here, but I have bad news for you."

The chaplaincy had rejected my application, along with another one, Thomas said. I, like the other candidate, would not be allowed to enter the chaplaincy on an education waiver because I lacked a master's degree and hadn't completed a full-time, two-year LDS mission. The mission requirement was in lieu of 60 of the required 90 hours of graduate study — though it had not been listed as a prerequisite.

The Army, Thomas said, had to deny me an appointment to maintain the quality of chaplains and to keep the chaplaincies from being swamped with unqualified clergy. Thomas added that the Servicemen Committee had received notification of my rejection by telephone and had been assured my application was in the mail, marked *"disapproved."*

Never in my life had I felt so low, so dejected. Words can't describe how I dreaded to face Helga with this news — our dream was dashed for sure this time. Still, I approached home with this faint glimmer of hope that she, with her unshakable faith, would again restore my spirits.

I gave Helga the disappointing news while we stood by the wall telephone in the kitchen, in the same spot where months before we had heard that we had been selected as candidates for the Army chaplaincy. This time, for the first time, Helga cried, but only for a moment. Then, leaning her head and shoulders away from my embrace, she said, "Claude, I don't know what will happen. But we've done our best, and now it is God's problem. He will cause things to work out for us, somehow."

Then, in an instant, Helga's grieved, anxious demeanor changed. She went silent and seemed to stare through me for a moment, dry-eyed and deep. "Besides," she said, "I still believe *we* will be chaplains." I believed her, though reason shouted that the dream was over, that the chaplaincy was out of the question for us. Her faith and confidence rang louder though, stronger and infectious. The dreaded rejection letter from the Army never came.

*

November arrived. I was substitute teaching in a science class — trying to explain the *big bang theory of creation* — at the Brigham City Indian School. The principal or his assistant stuck his head in the classroom. "You must call your wife during the next break. It is very important."

Helga's excitement radiated from the telephone as she informed me I was to return a call to Chaplain (Lieutenant Colonel) Will Hyatt through Operator Two in Washington, D.C.

I called Washington. Chaplain Hyatt opened with, "First of all, Reverend Newby, don't get excited. Everything is all right." He explained I was approved for the chaplaincy and asked if I accepted the appointment. I accepted.

"A letter is on the way," Chaplain Hyatt said, "instructing you to report immediately to Fort Ord, California. Please ignore those instructions and wait for orders directing you to report to Fort Hamilton, New York, for the Chaplain Officer Basic Course ... on or about 3 January 1966, en route to your assignment at Fort Ord, California." Helga was ecstatic, but not very surprised!

*

A few days later, resplendent in my new Army uniform with silver first lieutenant bars on each shoulder, I reported with my family, unannounced, to the Servicemen Committee. Surprise was all over H. Robert Thomas' face, like *what is Newby, the reject, doing in uniform?* Thomas' surprise turned to consternation when I produced official orders. "I'm here to be set apart, according to instructions," I said.

Shocked now, Thomas studied my orders. "This cannot be. You were rejected. The Army told me so, personally. Something is wrong here."

He stared at the orders in silence, trying, I presumed, to make sense of the incongruence between what he knew and what he saw. Finally, with, "I don't know what to do," he called Elder Gordon B. Hinckley, his superior on the committee.

Thomas' side of the telephone conversation went pretty much this way. "Newby is here with Army orders to active duty, to be set apart. ... Yes, I have the orders in my hands. ... Yes, they appear to be in order. ... Yes ... Yes sir." He hung up and said, "Elder Hinckley knows this can't be. We are to come to his office."

Helga and the children waited with Elder Hinckley's secretary while I entered his office with Thomas, confidently at first because I knew my orders were all right. Soon, though, my confidence wavered because, apparently, one whom I believed to be one of the Lord's anointed thought something about me wasn't *kosher*.

With reserved demeanor, Elder Hinckley acknowledged my presence as he took the orders from Thomas. After a moment he repeated Thomas' earlier denial. "This just can't be. He was rejected."

"Are you certain these are in order?" Elder Hinckley asked me.

"Yes," I responded and explained the telephone call from Chaplain Hyatt. "I've already been sworn in by a duly qualified U.S. Army officer. I'm a commissioned first lieutenant."

Elder Hinckley hesitated. To Thomas, he said in essence, "This can't be. I'm not sure what to do. I'd better ask President Lee."

Elder Hinckley dialed Harold B. Lee, his superior in the leadership of the church. After explaining the purpose of the call, Elder Hinckley continued in essence with, "Yes ... They appear in order. ... Yes sir."

Hanging up the telephone, Elder Hinckley said to Thomas, "President Lee said to set Newby apart. I know it isn't right, but that's what we will do."

Elder Hinckley invited my family in. Helga and the children took seats on the northwest side of his office. Elder Hinckley turned a chair around and I sat in it.

With reluctance obvious in voice and countenance, Elder Hinckley placed his hands on my head, and everything changed. In a voice flowing with warmth and acceptance, he pronounced a wonderful blessing upon me and through me upon my family. I knew all his earlier doubts were gone, which he confirmed publicly less than a year later in far-off Saigon and again six months after that in Fujiyama, Japan; but those stories come later. The impossible had happened. We were in!

*

For the first three months of 1966, I trained at Fort Hamilton, Brooklyn, New York, where I had served as a military policeman 10 years previously. Following training I reported with my family to Fort Ord, California. There I served from late April to mid-August, first as a chaplain to basic trainees and then as chaplain to the Reception Station, where draftees from Berkeley and other exotic — often vocally antiwar — places were processed into the Army prior to beginning basic training. In August, I volunteered for Vietnam.

*

I was ill when we left Fort Ord for Utah and for most of the trip there, I believed due to one or more of several shots I received the day before we departed — injections for plague, typhus, tetanus, all sorts of shots. Fortunately, I felt much better by the time we reached Ogden, Utah, though my arms and shoulders were still sore.

We drove straight through Ogden to the home of the Dallas and Joan Murdoch family in Grace, Idaho. There we left the children, and Helga and I returned to Ogden to find a temporary home. Soon we were settled in a rented home, received our household goods and brought the children down from Idaho. The next priority was to reexamine our personal affairs, insurance, wills and such. I intended to make sure Helga and the children could get along without me, if necessary. I wanted her to feel free to remarry if I should die, yet free from marrying out of fiscal necessity.

*

To create good family memories, we played, fished, and water-skied with the Murdochs in Idaho and visited Yellowstone National Park for the first time.

As my departure drew near I became increasingly contemplative — not that I had premonitions or was scared. But I couldn't help thinking what the future might be like for Helga and the children should I be killed or dismembered, which were distinct possibilities if I served with the infantry as I hoped to do.

I especially wanted to serve with the 1st Air Cavalry Division, a new-type division much in the news, which I figured needed a chaplain who was infantry at heart, who wanted to be with the soldiers who had it hardest and hurt the most.

*

Many members of the LDS Church place great trust in blessings by the laying on of hands. Several Vietnam-bound LDS servicemen of my acquaintance each sought a promise of a safe return from war via this medium. Though I appreciated this practice and approved of soldiers seeking special blessings on the eve of war, I sought no such blessing and assurance for myself for valid spiritual reasons, I thought.

I reasoned that only by sharing the soldier's existence and sense of uncertainty about survival could I fully comprehend and appreciate his immediate and urgent needs. Only in this way could I understand how to reach him. In other words, I believed that to be effective as a chaplain I must voluntarily share the danger, discomfort, and uncertainty the infantryman endured. I reasoned he would, because I was beside him, respond with increased faith in what I represented and with deeper trust in my words, actions, and counsel. Thus, I hoped to better provide the spiritual comfort the soldier would so desperately need. Only Dallas and Joan Murdoch, Helga and two other officers knew how I felt about a personal "pre-combat" blessing.

The children would grow and develop in my absence. Milestones would pass. Joyful "firsts" and "once onlys" would come and go. One such passage would be the twelfth birthday of James, my oldest. With his birthday two months hence would come eligibility for a religious ordination, a special rite of passage. Another would ordain him in my stead.

Helga and I clung to each other emotionally and spiritually as "D-day" approached. We yearned to block out all but each other, while giving the children the attention they also needed. From such fleeting moments as a picnic for two on our last Saturday together, I increased my reserves of courage for what lay ahead, and I think Helga did also. On September 11 we attended church together, not for the last time, we hoped.

Mom, Dad and my sister Beulah called Sunday evening. I gathered from their emotional comments that they expected me to die in Vietnam. My reassurances were less than convincing because I couldn't promise what was beyond my control — things like life and death.

As our last social act together, Helga and I called on the wife of Air Force Captain Layne. Mrs. Layne elicited my promise, freely given, to try to visit her husband, who was already in Vietnam. This promise I wanted to keep because I understood the value of intermediory contacts between a soldier and his loved ones.

✳

September 13 had passed in a blur, hastened on by our efforts to wring every ounce of joy and hope from each moment. Mostly, I remember the day for overwhelming feelings of melancholy and homesickness — even before we departed for the airport.

I had gathered my family around me after dinner and blessed them one by one, from the eldest to the youngest, and Helga last of all. I'm sure the blessings contained a mixture of assurance, promise, admonition and love, according to my perception of each individual's special needs. As I recall, this was a tearful occasion. With the blessings attended to, Melvin Lunt, a friend from my days on the police force, and his wife, Carol, drove us to the airport.

At the airport, Helga and I tried to reassure one another without violating our covenant of honesty — to not promise outcomes beyond our ability to deliver. I promised Helga I would keep no secrets from her; she promised to do likewise. We were but confirming a long-established compact to share everything so there would be no cause to worry about bad things being held back. The children handled their emotions well, or concealed them. Helga, James and Jeannie were focused and affectionate. John controlled his emotions by focusing his attention on airport activities. Laura maintained an extreme quiet, an almost stone-faced demeanor. Two-year-old Brenda knew something was happening, something she didn't like, and expressed her concern with anxious eyes and tight, clinging hugs.

The dreaded moment arrived, so slowly and all too soon — time seemingly dragging and contracting the way it can only in those rare moments when every nerve and emotion is at peak stimulation. I kissed each child one last time, squeezed James' shoulder, and said to him in effect: "You have the manly responsibilities now. I'm depending on you to look out for the family while I'm gone."

I hugged Jeannie especially tight because I was concerned most for her. She would enter puberty during this year of separation, and Daddy might be especially missed.

After hugging and kissing Helga one last time, I climbed up the ramp and boarded a Boeing 727. It was 9:25 p.m. My dear family waved until the plane had taxied from sight. My somber face stayed glued to the tiny, oval-shaped window long after she and the children were left behind.

*

At 1:30 a.m., I arrived at Travis Air Force Base by bus from San Francisco and checked into a room at the BOQ (Bachelor Officers' Quarters), which I shared for two hours with a Vietnam-bound helicopter pilot. He kept me awake while he searched for a clock he'd forgotten to pack and awakened me an hour or so later when he left to catch his flight.

At 9 a.m., I had checked in at the passenger terminal where I spent the next five hours getting more injections, being ill, writing letters and waiting. A medic jabbed two needles into my left shoulder simultaneously, one-handed. One or more of the shots probably accounted for my feeling sick. In a letter to Helga I tried to convey my love for her, to describe my misery, and to apologize for putting us through all this. Momentarily, I repented for having volunteered for the chaplaincy and for duty in Vietnam. *If I feel so awful, how must the "lowly" privates and draftees feel? They have no choice about going to Vietnam.*

Chapter 2

Hoping for a Cav Assignment

The sun set at 12:45 a.m. September 15 (California time), as we flew west from Anchorage, Alaska, toward the International Dateline. At 2:30 a.m. September 16, following a stop in Japan, we landed at Tan San Nut Air Base in Saigon. After a brief delay to hear a welcome speech, we replacements got off the airplane, collected our luggage and boarded an old U.S. Army bus. A grease gun-armed enlisted airman rode shotgun for the short bus ride to the replacement in-processing center at Camp Alpha. The grease gun and chicken wire-covered bus windows (to deflect grenades) were the only immediate indicators this was a combat zone.

✳

Vietnam impressed itself indelibly on my memory and olfactory nerves with that first glimpse and whiff. The night was hot and muggy, even at 0300 hours. Strange, yet vaguely familiar aromas assaulted my nose — decaying garbage and vegetation and human waste, all mingled with the essences unique to military bases — tents, latrines, machines, oil and disinfectant.

At Camp Alpha, I went exploring in the night. I was too intrigued with my surroundings and pumped up with anticipation to sleep.

Puddles of dirty, stinking water, evidence of a recent downpour, dotted the walkways between and around the hooches we replacements were billeted in. Just beyond the replacement center fence was a small cluster of makeshift shacks. I got a better appreciation of the natives' burden in this war when someone said, "Those are family housing for Vietnamese Air Force officers."

At dawn I cleaned up, dressed and ate my first in-country meal at the air-conditioned Tan San Nut Officers Club — pretty fancy place. I thought it amazing that rear-echelon troops and officers, while living like this, received the same combat pay as infantry.

My assignment came right after breakfast. I had my wish. I was going to the Cav — 1st Cavalry Division (Airmobile) — in the central highlands to serve with infantrymen, I assumed, as I *knew* I should. After all, I had grown up in the hills of Tennessee, where the ideal of serving where one could serve best was instilled in me. I had fed on the lives and exploits of the likes of Sergeant Alvin York during World War I and other heroes such as my uncles and Audie Murphy of World War II and Korea. I honestly believed I was a natural to serve the grunt and that many other chaplains could better serve rear-area support troops because of their pastoral experience and "come to chapel" focus. Well, I was going to the Cav. Now all I had to sweat was where in the Cav I would serve. Later in the morning, in company with two other chaplains, I got a pep talk and a headquarters perspective of the war from the senior USARV (US Army Vietnam) Chaplain.

I slept lightly during my first full night in-country, despite the soothing rhythm of a driving rain on the tin roof a few feet above the top bunk on which I lay — the sheets were clammy in the high humidity, and the required mosquito netting blocked any refreshing breeze.

✳

The next day I teamed up with another chaplain for a bus trip to Long Binh, a major American base northeast of Saigon. On the way we passed palm trees, rice paddies, small businesses, hamlets, and the first real signs of war: a civilian compound filled with burned-out vehicles that the Vietcong (VC) had destroyed three days earlier. We also passed the burned-out shell of an Army truck that had been destroyed by a direct hit from a recoilless rifle.

At the 93rd Evacuation Hospital, the resident chaplain took us to visit a 25th Division (Tropical Lightning) soldier who had just been brought in. The day before, while I explored my new surroundings, he was getting both legs blown off by the mine that destroyed his Armored Personnel Carrier (APC) and killed some of his crew.

Back at Camp Alpha, at about 3 p.m., I wrote to Helga and tried to express my feelings, impressions and experiences. She kept this and all my letters from Vietnam for several years, only to lose them during one of our many Army transfers.

At 2:30 p.m. September 18, after attending services with the LDS Group in Saigon, I boarded a C-130 cargo airplane for the two-hour flight to An Khe. My fellow passengers included about 65 American soldiers and two very attractive Vietnamese women, wives of ARVN soldiers. In flight, I casually examined the women. They each had beautiful eyes and features and appeared quite serene. Traditional Vietnamese dresses enhanced their beauty. Upon closer examination, though, the ladies' eyes belied their composed demeanor — stress was there and tension and fear. This was as I expected. These women and their husbands were engaged in a long, bloody war without the hope American soldiers shared, of leaving the war behind after a year.

The Vietnamese women and several soldiers off-loaded at Pleiku. Other soldiers took their places, and we continued on to An Khe, flying at treetop level with the rear-loading ramp open, which gave me a bird's-eye view of the jungles I anticipated spending the next twelve months in. Naturally, I was all eyes.

*

We landed about 5:30 p.m. on an airstrip called the Golf Course, at Camp Radcliff, the 1st Cav base camp. The camp, which supported some 20,000 soldiers, was named after the first American to be killed there. The airstrip was called the Golf Course because the general in charge of replacing the jungle with it had ordered that it be made "as smooth as a golf course." Some said the VC "named" the airstrip by placing eighteen holes in it — mortar craters, that is.

The weather here, unlike the heat and high humidity of Saigon, was hot and dry. A two-hour flight had carried me from a hot, wet monsoon to a hot, dry one.

Despite tangled emotions — homesickness, relief at having arrived and anticipation of what awaited me — I had the presence of mind to note that the air terminal, such as it was, sat about midway on the southerly side of the Golf Course. The Golf Course appeared to be about 200 meters wide and two kilometers long and was paved down its center with perforated sheets of steel, called PSP. Several types of aircraft and buildings were visible across the runway, mostly Huey helicopters and aircraft support facilities. Jungle-shrouded mountains stood out in sharp contrast to the east and southeast. The nearest mountain, Hon Cong, appeared to be about a kilometer southwest of the easterly end of the Golf Course.

Hon Cong Mountain sported a gigantic replica of the shoulder patch worn by soldiers of the 1st Cavalry Division. The patch depicted a black horse's head in the upper right corner of a shield-shaped, black-bordered patch of yellow, with a black stripe running diagonally across the yellow from the upper left to the lower right. This brazen symbol of air-cavalry presence reminded me of a novel about a legendary frontiersman and Indian fighter, Bigfoot Spencer, who wore his hair long as a challenge to Indians to take his scalp if they dared. No doubt, the 1st Cav patch up on Hon Cong had something to do with *esprit de corps* and morale, but I think my first impression was nearer the truth. That patch was sort of like the "I-double-dog-dare-you" flaunt I'd heard so often in my youth.

Chapter 3

Assigned to the Medical Battalion

An enlisted representative of the Division Chaplain met me at the airstrip with the unwelcome news that I would be assigned to the 15th Medical Battalion, rather than to an infantry unit. This news so disappointed me that I recall nothing further about my first day with the Cav, except for writing a letter to Helga. According to my journal, I spent the night in the hooch of the Support Command Chaplain — he was away somewhere. I met him the next day.

During the morning of September 19, I in-processed and chatted with Chaplain (Lieutenant Colonel) Webb. He was the Deputy Division Chaplain, and he seemed pleased with my vision of duty — to soldiers, whatever their religious affiliation, preferably infantry soldiers in my case. He hinted that the assignment to the medical battalion would not likely be for my whole tour.

＊

Resigned to my fate, I began searching for ways to make the best of it, to use my assignment to get nearer to the infantry, to go forward. To this end, with little more than in-processing to occupy my time, I spent most of the next two days orienting myself to the structure, mission and operational area of the 1st Cav and to the layout of base camp. Also, I read a lot and wrote several letters to Helga and the children.

On September 19 at about 10 p.m., 2200 hrs in military time, I met my new supervisory chaplain, Major Clinton E. Browne, a supportive, fatherly Baptist. The next day I met Chaplain (Colonel) McGraff, pronounced McGraw, and attended a steak cookout with the officers of Support Command, after which I spent my last night in Chaplain Browne's hooch.

Wednesday, September 21, I moved to the 15th Medical Battalion, commanded by Lieutenant Colonel (Doctor) Henry A. Leighton. I was assigned temporary accommodations in a hooch with one Captain Sparanio and was assured this arrangement was very temporary, as it was understood I required privacy for counseling. Sparanio, who looked like a Mohawk Indian, denied any Indian lineage. He apparently loved and missed his family, and he read the Bible a lot. He was easy to like and get along with.

✳

Headquarters and Headquarters Company of the medical battalion occupied a narrow strip of land between the east-southeast end of the Golf Course and a small stream. The stream was about five feet across at the widest point in the medics' area. Heavy vegetation covered every spot that was not occupied or used as road or walkway, and this more than a year after the Cav arrived and started clearing away the jungle. I would soon discover that the little stream could be quite threatening during the rainy season.

The medics had built enough solid hooches on concrete slabs to house most of the officers. The hooches had tin roofs and were screened all around with heavy shutters, hinged at the top, so they could be swung out for ventilation or closed to keep out the rain.

Some officers and the enlisted men lived in twelve-man Army tents. One tent was designated as the unit chapel. It was furnished with logs for pews, a simple pulpit, and a foot-powered field organ. A wooden mess (dining) building also served as the battalion staff room. Battalion operations were directed out of a tactical operations center (TOC) in a well-sandbagged bunker.

Medical Companies A, B and C were each co-located with one of the combat maneuver brigades in the division. The brigades further broke down each medical company by assigning a platoon to each infantry battalion. Each company operated a medical clearing station at brigade level, and each platoon operated an aid station at battalion level. Individual medics or medical aidmen were attached to infantry companies in support of grunts, up close and personal. All medics in the 1st Cav belonged to the 15th Medical Battalion, regardless of where they served. Those medics attached to infantry units seldom if ever saw their parent unit.

The Medical Battalion staff and Headquarter Company (HHC) operated a four- or five-ward hospital for ill and lightly wounded troopers, in addition to commanding and controlling the rest of the battalion. These wards were housed in Quonset huts and provided backup for the 2nd Surgical Hospital, which was located half a kilometer — half-klick — away, at the base of Hon Cong Mountain.

Each medical company, HHC included, had a Medical Evacuation (Medevac) platoon. These platoons conducted helicopter operations to rescue and evacuate wounded and seriously ill soldiers. Medevac helicopters in the Cav mounted two M-60 machine guns, unlike the unarmed "Dust-Off" Medevac choppers that supported other units in Vietnam.

*

The Division Chaplain expected me to coordinate and ensure division-wide support for soldiers of my own faith, in addition to supporting the medics. His expectations provided legitimacy to my intentions. I quickly realized that my assignment allowed me to get away from base camp and move almost at will across the 1st Cav AO. I could roam almost to Saigon to support a 7th Cav — Garry Owens — battalion on the coast at Phan Thiet. Another medical company operated west of Pleiku near the Cambodian border and Idrang Valley, the site of battles in November 1965 where more men of the 5th Cavalry and 7th Cavalry had died than were killed at the Battle of Little Bighorn under Brevet-General George Armstrong Custer. A third medical company operated at Landing Zone (LZ) Hammond, over the mountains to the east and northwest of the major port city of Qui Nhon and of Phu Cat Air Base.

*

For the remainder of my first week with the Cav, I visited patients in the battalion medical ward, wrote letters, read, scouted out the base camp and visited An Khe for a closer look at how the natives in the area lived. I also got ready to conduct and preach my first in-country general Christian worship service. My chaplain assistant, Pfc. David Berg, prepared to play the field organ for me, which welcome support was not in his job description.

That first Saturday I spoke by invitation in a service for members of the Seventh-Day Adventist faith. Most SDAs were assigned to the medical battalion because members of that faith were also conscientious objectors. That was also the day I first suffered stomach miseries in consequence of taking a large anti-malaria tablet. To lessen our chances of getting malaria, we took a small pill each day and a big one each week. The big pill frequently left me with an upset stomach and diarrhea. To make matters worse, I suffered severely from mail deprivation during the first week or two, or what infantrymen called a shortage of "sugar rations."

The war loomed closer on September 23. We were alerted to prepare to receive 25 wounded soldiers, the expected overflow from the 2nd Surgical Hospital. The wounded troopers arrived, and all of them (10, not 27) were treated at the 2nd Surgical Hospital.

*

Chaplain Browne attended my first Sunday service to support me — he insisted he'd not come to inspect or evaluate my performance.

That afternoon, I attended and spoke at an LDS service in the 2nd Surgical Hospital Chapel, at the invitation of Major Harper, the group leader. I immediately felt a special bond with these young men, many of whom were very valiant in spirit. Friendships developed that continue today, 30 years later. Apparently, these feelings were mutual, considering what some of those men said of me on occasion.

It was during that first LDS service that I became aware of the bane of worship services in rear areas — the diesel-powered electric generator. This noisy contraption made it almost impossible to hear myself speak, and usually it was placed next to wherever worship services were conducted.

*

With the first week and my Sunday duties behind me, I began taking advantage of the dispersion of the medics across the whole divisional areas of operation and making good use of the organic Medevac elements. It quickly dawned on me that I probably had about as good a combination of freedom to set my agenda and mobility to follow it as any officer in the division. I was more free to move about than most commanders were, because I did not have to limit my focus to a company, battalion or brigade area of operations.

To maintain this freedom, I made certain my priorities and agenda were based on doing the right things for the right reasons, and for me this meant effectively supporting American soldiers, first and last. The Sunday morning worship service for headquarters was the only regular external constraint on my movements. And since I had to be in the area anyhow each Sunday, I usually stayed around and attended LDS meetings in the afternoon.

From the start, I got along well with the battalion leaders. Colonel Leighton frequently attended my Sunday worship services. He always treated me cordially and respectfully gave me free rein to operate as I thought best. Only once did he suggest censure or anything less than satisfaction with my performance, and even then he veiled his dissatisfaction.

It happened following the Sunday worship service on October 10, I think it was, as I rode somewhere with Colonel Leighton in his jeep. Earlier during my sermon, I had sensed someone's displeasure with my simple message. As we rode, Leighton referred casually to a less than flattering portrayal of Mormons in Zane Grey's *Riders of the Purple Sage*. "I prefer more profound preaching," he added. *So you are the displeased soul I sensed.*

I took Leighton's veiled criticism as a statement of personal taste and neither rejection nor a personal attack. Never again during 27 years in the chaplaincy did another commander (or chaplain) imply criticism of my sermons. By the way, I found nothing about Mormons in *Riders of the Purple Sage.*

I could have used some of Leighton's tact in criticizing his executive officer. It was during a staff meeting that the XO, a major, threw out God's name in vain in reaction to something. "Sorry about that, Chaplain," he quickly added.

"Why apologize to me? It wasn't my name you used," I replied.

Silence.

Though my retort was accurate, it was thoughtless, and I immediately regretted having upbraided the XO before the staff and commander. The XO was cool toward me after that, but not vindictive.

✳

Routinely, I visited dispersed medical units, staying a night or two at each clearing station to counsel soldiers, take part in helicopter Medevac missions, and generally be available to staffs and patients. Between trips among the dispersed medical companies, I visited the medical wards at headquarters and the hospitals on base and in Qui Nhon and Cam Ranh Bay. Of course, I also attended to the ever-present staff and administrative duties and meetings and scrounged building materials for a combination chaplain's hooch and office.

At least weekly, I reminded Chaplains McGraff and Webb that I was ready for an infantry battalion. Persistence bore fruit after two and a half months. But before telling that tale, I shall here highlight some actions and events that occurred during my 80 days with the medics.

Though it may seem of little significance, my homesickness evolved after about a month from feelings of constant, seemingly unbearable misery into a bearable, low-intensity ache that was interspersed with occasional bouts of acute heart pain.

On September 30, I flew via helicopter to LZ Hammond and joined with some Army doctors and medics to visit a civilian hospital in Phu Cat. At the hospital, I wandered around the area while the docs attended to the wounded and ill. Behind the little facility, near the northeast corner, I came upon a mature Vietnamese woman. She was bare to the waist and engaged in bathing herself by drawing well water in a bucket and pouring it over her head. The woman, engrossed in her personal hygiene efforts, seemed to be unaffected by my presence. Still, I hurried on, intent on giving the woman a degree of privacy, which may have meant more to me than it did to her.

Turning west as I hurried around the southeast corner of the hospital, I came upon the bodies of two infants. They lay unattended on a stretcher between two trees. At first, I thought the bodies were dolls because of the waxy, taut appearance of their skin. The infants had been smothered to death by a smoke bomb the previous night.

Inside the hospital were several female Vietnamese patients, including several new mothers. The patients were lying about on Army cots or atop bloody newspapers on the floor. They shared their beds, pads and newspapers with family members who stayed with them around the clock. Little children played happily in the midst of this scene. I was at once depressed by the conditions of treatment and impressed by the support each patient got from her family.

American medics brought a young woman in for treatment while we were there. She had serious shrapnel (mortar) wounds to her legs and arms.

Later, back at the Medical Clearing Company at LZ Hammond, a little girl was carried in with multiple fragmentation wounds. Her father, a VC, had used the girl and her mother to shield himself from a hand grenade. The blast wounded the little girl and killed her mother. The Americans promptly killed the girl's father and evacuated the newly created orphan.

*

On October 1, near Phan Thiet, I found myself aboard a Medevac chopper, in the right-door seat behind an M-60 machine gun. The trip had started as an administrative run, a non-tactical flight, or ash and trash sortie, in Army jargon. We had a routine flight until an urgent call diverted us to pick up some wounded infantrymen.

This turn of events placed me in a delicate position as a chaplain. Normally a door gunner would sit where I sat, but he had stayed behind, probably because of the intended nature of this flight. Now we were going into an area where infantry troops were fighting and where the VC might fire on the Medevac chopper. We'd been warned the pickup zone was hot, meaning it was still receiving enemy fire. I locked and loaded the M-60 machine gun.

We flew about twenty minutes to reach the contact area (jargon for the place where friendly and enemy forces are engaged in battle), came in fast, flared and hovered for a moment, and settled into a muddy rice paddy on the edge of thick jungle.

Several mud-covered, soaked grunts — the label "grunt" was respectfully reserved for the infantryman — crouched near the tree line beside a buddy who appeared to be dead or unconscious.

Quickly, the four grunts placed their buddy on the chopper. Two walking-wounded climbed aboard and we headed for Phan Thiet.

The LZ hadn't been hot, after all, but had we taken fire, I would have returned it. Officially a combatant or not, I couldn't have, wouldn't have, sat on my hands while wounded grunts and the chopper crew were shot at with impunity. In part, my reaction behind the machine gun — as would be the case often in combat — represented a triumph of training over education. My training and experience during years as a police officer and as a former infantryman and medic often won out over my *education* as a chaplain. Oh yes, the unconscious grunt reached the doctors in very bad shape, but alive.

*

Back during the Chaplain Basic Officer Course in early 1966, we were apprised of an applicable clause in the Geneva Conventions: "Chaplains shall not be *required* to bear arms." (Italics added.) A chaplain, by bearing arms, we were instructed, might endanger the noncombatant, detainee (as opposed to prisoner-of-war) status of any chaplain who falls into the hands of the Vietcong or North Vietnamese forces.

Risks that sounded significant in theory paled in the face of the reality. No American chaplain had survived capture by communist forces during the Korean War, perhaps because the closest thing communist forces had to a chaplain was the party political officer. Perhaps this statistic helps explain why many chaplains on the line in Vietnam placed little stock in the protection spelled out in the Geneva Conventions. Lacking regulatory or statutory prohibitions, each chaplain dealt with the decision whether to take up arms, even in extreme situations, according to his own values, conscience, and the dictates and tenets of his faith or church. Consequently, some chaplains in Vietnam kept a concealed weapon on their persons or kept one near at hand. Occasionally a chaplain was seen carrying a weapon openly — more on that later.

I wrestled with myself before writing of chaplains and weapons. Should I mention the issue at all and risk bringing harm to chaplains on some future battlefield? Should I risk offense to someone's expectations? Or should I be true to things as they were in Vietnam? I chose to write about the issue, to break my 30 years of silence because it is an integral part of the true story of what chaplains wrestled with in a confusing war without front lines or a clear and effective national strategy. Also, I write about the issue because I believe chaplains will, on some future battlefield, have to deal with self-defense issues not considered in the policy-making process, regardless of peacetime theorizing.

In Vietnam, some chaplains refused to keep a personal weapon close at hand, but had no problem with chaplains who did, provided those who did were discreet. Chaplains in this group saw no conflict between chaplains bearing arms and the Geneva Conventions and were often heard to say: "If ever I am in a situation that requires me to fight to defend myself or others, plenty of weapons will be laying around for my use." By this, chaplains implied they might use the weapon of a fallen soldier during a dire emergency.

Some chaplains insisted both the Geneva Conventions and tenets of faith forbade chaplains to take up arms under any provocation. Chaplains in this group generally looked askance upon chaplains of the other groups.

Other chaplains, believing God helps him who helps himself, strictly interpreted the Geneva Conventions to wit: Chaplains shall not be required to bear arms; neither shall chaplains be prohibited from bearing arms.

Several chaplains in the 1st Cav, even some senior ones, kept a personal weapon. One concealed a grease gun in his pack, and another carried a concealed nickel-plated revolver — though privately owned weapons were against regulation for any soldier.

Most field commanders, in my experience, smiled on the chaplain carrying a weapon for his own protection, and some of them on occasion allowed or forbade a chaplain to go into a hot situation, depending on whether the chaplain was prepared to "take care of himself."

While most chaplains dealt privately with the issue of personal weapons, on occasion a chaplain was less than tactful. For example, a national magazine published photographs of a young chaplain as he came "armed to the teeth" out of the jungle onto a firebase. In private conversation, the chaplain insisted he was but helping the grunts carry the many weapons of fallen comrades, lightening the grunts' loads. Whatever the real story, the Army Chief of Chaplains gave the young chaplain a written reprimand, which could have been a career stopper. However, the young chaplain was promoted ahead of his contemporaries, all the way to colonel (0-6). I thought that some of my leaders spoke with a forked tongue on this issue.

What did I do? I carried what I jokingly called my .45-caliber *camera* — for close-up shots. This item of equipment remained discreetly out of sight in my left-front trouser pocket, except on those occasions when none present objected to my possession of it. "Spare film" I kept in an ammo pouch on my pistol belt, naturally.

The issue of chaplains taking up arms would be discussed often following the Vietnam War. Eventually, the Army chaplaincy declared clear policy: Chaplains shall not bear arms. If placed again in Vietnam-like conditions, I would prefer the less restrictive, "Chaplains shall not be required to bear arms."

❋

My first mail from home arrived October 3 and included letters from Helga, James, Jeannie, Laura and my mother. These were items recently touched by my loved ones — a modern miracle, almost too good to believe. Suddenly, the world seemed all right again. The pain of homesickness began to be bearable, almost. Mail!

❋

The rainy monsoon came in earnest to central and northeast Vietnam, bringing the promise of cooler days and seemingly frigid nights in the highlands. Continual torrential rain turned the camp to muck. Low, moisture-laden clouds socked the camp in. Hon Cong Mountain was invisible at times from a hundred feet away.

At about 1630 hours October 4, all available Medevac helicopters and all available doctors and medics were scrambled and headed for the top of Hon Cong Mountain. A CV-2 Caribou, laden with sky troopers, including several wounded grunts, had crashed head-on into the side of the mountain. It had crashed while trying to land on the Golf Course runway, despite redundant on-board and ground-based safety guidance systems. Fortunately, the Caribou could fly at the amazingly slow air speed of 40 miles per hour, which made the difference between life and death for several grunts, but not for the crew of the Caribou.

The mountainside was too steep for the rescue choppers to land at the crash site. So from the man-made flat top of Hon Cong, scores of rescuers, including medical personnel and Medevac crews, tore their way slipping and sliding down the very rugged, jungle-covered slope to the crash site. There, to their amazement, they found more of the crash victims were alive than were dead.

All the survivors were injured, and many of them required immediate, operating room-quality medical attention. So the rescuers formed a human chain and moved the injured up the mountain to the waiting helicopters. Exerting superhuman strength, the rescuers defied gravity to keep each casualty-laden stretcher approximately level on the 50-to-80 degree incline of the mountainside. Though there was nothing funny about the situation, humor appeared, and from an unlikely source.

One of the rescuers on the human-chain wondered aloud why the doctors had bothered sending up one grunt. An M-16 rifle stuck straight upward out of the grunt's abdomen. The violence of the crash had driven the barrel of another grunt's rifle all the way through him.

Looking up at his benefactors from the litter, the grunt said, "They can't accuse me of not taking my weapon with me, can they?"

Based on a medic's description of this trooper's wounds, I expected him to die, despite his sense of humor. But I learned differently in 1969. A sergeant, who was on a second or third tour with the 1st Cav, told me the rest of the story. "Yeah, that was Sergeant [forgot the name]. He was wounded earlier that day during a 'blue-team' operation … He's stationed now at Fort …." Perhaps *Readers Digest* had it right, that *Laughter Is the Best Medicine.*

The commander or executive officer had directed me to remain behind to help medical ward personnel attend to incoming survivors, if any. This order came in response to me asking where I could best help — a mistake I'd not make again. In the future, I would do what I thought best and repent later, if necessary. As it turned out, no crash survivors were brought to our facility.

By evening, routines were continuing as if little or nothing had happened. It's hard to imagine how individuals and units can so quickly fall back into and onto routine following tragedy. This ability, I suppose, is essential to maintaining one's sanity in war.

The next day, I learned that 15 grunts survived the Caribou crash. A day or so later, another survivor showed up. This was probably Pfc. Henry L. Creek, who had been listed as MIA. He had pulled himself from the wreckage before rescuers reached the scene, and despite combat wounds and subsequent crash injuries, had climbed down the mountain. The surprised members of a patrol found him when he staggered from the jungle.

I wondered how prepared or unprepared for eternity those who died had been.

*

Meanwhile, the rains brought relief from the constant dust — of which we got our share, positioned as we were at the end of the airstrip and right next to an active helipad.

The morning of October 6, I struggled with intense yearnings to be with Helga. Then I considered all she meant to me, and my emotions soared. Suddenly, I appreciated my misery, an attitude some soldiers didn't share. Rather, some of them, officer and enlisted alike, saw separation from wife and children as an opportunity to fornicate and "adulterate" without fear of being found out or held accountable. This debasing philosophy was evident by the constant stream of soldiers to Sin City — and to the medics for penicillin.

Sin City was a military-controlled collection of brothels in An Khe, where soldiers could have all their lusts attended to at low prices and with lessened risk of catching a venereal disease. American military police guarded the brothels, and American medics examined the prostitutes weekly, so we were told. *I thank God for the misery I feel when separated from Helga. Thank God Sin City holds no attraction for me.*

These thoughts and feelings I tried to convey to Helga, to assure her of my love and my determination to maintain our high-fidelity marriage.

That evening something occurred that I must relate because it led to many other significant events. While visiting the sick and lightly wounded in the Quonset huts, I noticed a patient was watching me closely. Catching my eye, he asked where I was from. "Tennessee," I answered, though I might have said Utah, my adopted home state.

"Oh," said the slender, dark-haired patient and went silent.

I shrugged the incident off, little suspecting the chain of events that this soldier was about to bring into my life.

---

5 October 1969, 1st Cav. Div., G-1 Journal: 2115 Hours, "MIA: Pfc. Henry L. Creek ... passenger on CV-2 on flight from fwd area ... crashed into mountainside coming in for a landing ... 1/12 Cav [then follows others, same crash]; SFC Armando Ramos, 13 Sig. Bn; Capt. Johnnie L. Daniel, Hq. 1st Bde; 1LT Kenneth W. West, Sp4 John T. Bird, Pfc. Donald A. Smith Jr., A 5/7 Cav; SSG Richard M. Prociv, Hq 1st Bde; Pfc. James G. Litts, 8th Eng; Pfc. Donald E. Lewis, B 1/5; Sgt. Homer L. Pickett, B 1/21.

Chapter 4

"We Are Going to Crash!"

On October 7, during another visit to the medical wards, I greeted the patient who the night before had asked where I was from. After exchanging pleasantries and names — his was David Lillywhite — I asked, "Where are you from?"

"Snowflake, Arizona," he answered.

"That's Mormon country. Are you a Mormon?"

"Yes sir, I am."

"A good Mormon?" I asked.

"I try my best to be."

"I'm LDS, too," I said.

Smiling broadly, Lillywhite said, "I thought you were last night, but I didn't think the Army had LDS chaplains. And when you said you're from Tennessee, I figured you couldn't be a Mormon."

Lillywhite was a draftee, an infantryman, a longtime member of his faith and fairly new member of Bravo Company, 2nd Battalion, 8th Cavalry (2-8 Cav). He was being treated for burns, the results of a plastic bottle containing insect repellant coming open in his pocket. Lillywhite told me of a buddy and fellow member of his faith, Pfc. Danny Hyde. He said Hyde had recently vowed to put his life in spiritual order. "Would I visit his buddy?" Lillywhite asked me. I promised to visit Hyde, assuming I could easily keep the promise because I knew my way around the AO — how to deal with the gatekeepers to units, the sergeants major and first sergeants.

Besides what was about to happen with Danny Hyde, my association with Lillywhite soon involved me in another tragedy. This tragedy, actually an atrocity, led to a chain of events that years later would be written up in the *New Yorker* magazine, published in a book, plagiarized into an award-winning underground film titled *Mau,* and produced as a major Hollywood movie titled *Casualties of War.* This incident would also get me a few lines of favorable mention in a seven-volume history of the U.S. Army Chaplaincy.

＊

At 1645 hours October 9, following Sunday duties at base camp,

29

I flew through driving rain to LZ Hammond. There I spent the night with the Medevac pilots, one of whom I almost decked when he came up behind me unannounced.

Next morning I braved especially sticky, deep, vehicle-churned red mud to reach the 2-8 Cav field trains on the west side of LZ Hammond. There, the battalion Sergeant Major agreed to let me visit Danny Hyde out in Bravo Company, but I'd have to wait until the company got out of a firefight. He wouldn't promise when conditions in Bravo Company would be secure enough to receive a chaplain from another unit. I decided to return and try again the next day.

To make good use of what was left of the day, I returned to the medical company on Hammond in time to accompany a medical team on a visit to a prisoner of war (POW) camp at Phu Cat.

At the POW camp I saw two confirmed VC, a seventeen-year-old female and a VC Master Sergeant (or equivalent rank). The VC sergeant had surrendered to American forces on the condition that he could bring along his family and plow.

While the medics treated enemy patients, I wandered about the camp, but soon wished I hadn't. While passing a building, I looked through a window into an almost empty room. Inside, two ARVN soldiers were interrogating a VC or native suspected of being VC. Wires ran from a hand-cranked generator to the suspect's bare genitals. The Vietnamese interrogators seemed unconcerned about me watching them, which led me to conclude this type of interrogation might be a common practice. One of my great regrets is that I didn't interfere with this interrogation, though I didn't know what to do as it involved natives on a native compound. Apparently, the officer in charge of the medical detail did not know what to do either.

About 2100 hours, back at the An Khe base camp, I sat on a bunker during an alert — the enemy was probing the northwest perimeter. Unknown to me, Chaplain Browne had minutes earlier received a call from the division chaplain: "LDS man critically injured, being evacuated to 85th Hospital. Request Chaplain Newby, LDS chaplain, to proceed."

In the TOC, Colonel Leighton gave me the message from Chaplain Browne and said a chopper would pick me up momentarily at the Medevac pad. Because of the weather, only emergency flights were authorized. The urgent call for a chaplain constituted an emergency.

Before the chopper took off at 2100 hours, I strapped myself into the right-door seat (machine gun position) of a fully loaded Huey (UH10). The other passengers were soldiers going on emergency leave or heading home after completing their tour. They'd been waiting, perhaps praying, for an emergency like this so they could fly out of An Khe. The crew chief checked my safety belt before we took off, the only safety check ever given to me during two Vietnam tours.

✱

We'd just cleared the Medevac pad when I realized I'd left my consecrated oil in the hooch. I took seriously the scriptural admonition to, when any are sick, "call the elders … let them pray … anointing with oil" (James 5:14). *"Never mind*, logic whispered, *the power is not in the oil. Besides, I can probably find some olive oil at the hospital in Qui Nhon.*

Conscience whispered, *yes, but I am supposed to always be ready to do the Lord's work in the Lord's way.*

We were into the clouds and approaching the Deo Mang Pass (often called the An Khe Pass by Americans) at 5000 feet altitude by the time I'd wrestled through all this. Just then, the engine of the chopper began making odd noises, and we went into a sudden dropping U-turn to the left, almost a dive. The crew chief shouted excitedly into my left ear, "We're losing RPM and going down. We'll try to crash inside the perimeter!"

This is my fault. We're crashing because I am not prepared, I thought.

Closing my eyes, I prayed, "Heavenly Father, please don't let these others be hurt or killed because of my failings." A moment later, my prayer completed, I saw the tops of tall, almost bare trees whipping diagonally upward, left to right, past my window.

At just the right moment, the pilot pulled pitch or whatever it was that the emergency called for. The chopper auto-rotated in a controlled crash, hit the ground hard, and came to rest facing uphill on an incline, in the middle of an ammunition dump. The impact crumpled the landing skids on the chopper and caused serious structural damage.

In a flash, the crew chief had my door open and was in my face, inquiring if I were all right. Answering, "I'm okay," I jumped from the chopper and moved away, ducking low to avoid the main rotor blade that continued to spin and was skimming within a few feet of stacked boxes of artillery rounds.

Rescuers located us after about 15 minutes, and one of my Medevac choppers landed to evacuate casualties. There were none, thanks to good fortune, a skilled crew and, perhaps, sincere prayers.

I was the only taker of a proffered lift on the Medevac chopper. The crew of the downed chopper insisted on staying with their ship. "We'll wait for ground transportation, thank you," said the other passengers.

The Medevac chopper dropped me off at my battalion, where I grabbed my consecrated oil, telephoned a report of the crash to Chaplain Browne, and stood by. At 2300 hours, Chaplain Browne called. Captain Dubois, 15th Transportation was providing me another chopper — I'd be the only passenger.

We approached Qui Nhon from the sea, which allowed us to drop from the clouds without risking a crash into a hill, several of which were near the city. Once out of the clouds, I watched green tracer rounds reach upward at us from several points in the Qui Nhon waters. A moment later we landed safely at the airfield, and from there I hitched a ride to the 85th Evac Hospital.

At about 0200 hours October 11, a medic directed me to the bedside of a "black soldier" in the intensive care ward. The nurse who accompanied me said the patient had no chance of survival. A card on the patient's bed identified him as Pfc. Hyde, Danny, Company B 2-8, 1st Air Cavalry Division, Negro; religious preference: LDS. Before me lay the young trooper I'd been called to see. He was also the same trooper I had tried unsuccessfully to visit in the field the previous day.

Immediately, guilt and self-censure inundated me. *I should have stuck around Danny's battalion. Perhaps he wouldn't be here if I had reached him.* Not likely, but *maybe.*

At 1905 hours the previous evening, a claymore mine had traumatically amputated Danny Hyde's left leg and arm, damaged his other appendages, destroyed one eye and severely injured the other one. The blast also burned away all his hair and blackened the front of what was left of his body; thus, he appeared to be a black man.

After the nurse withdrew to give me privacy, I prayed mightily for the spirit to guide me that I might administer to Danny Hyde and convey to him whatever blessing the Lord wanted him to have. Next, I found an undamaged spot on Danny's head, anointed him with oil, sealed the anointing, and blessed him to live and return home to his loved ones. Even as I blessed Danny, I doubted the spiritual source of the promises I gave him.

The ministration completed, the nurse returned and noted on Danny's chart that he was *Caucasian* rather than *Negro,* according to me. Still, she insisted he was obviously a Negro. My feelings of guilt calmed somewhat as I returned to the airfield and during the flight to An Khe.

We departed Qui Nhon at 0400 hours with a send-off of green tracer bullets to match the welcome the VC had given us earlier. Upon landing on the Golf Course, my pilot, a major, said, "Young man, if you want an Army career, you'd better never again demand a helicopter to fly under conditions like this."

"It wasn't me demanding anything," I explained and told him about the urgent message I'd received.

Upon learning the nature of the mission and that I had willingly boarded two other helicopters within minutes of falling from the sky in one, the major said, "You've got more guts than I've got," and walked away.

The previous evening as we were about to crash, I'd felt as the Biblical Jonah must have when he advised the crew of a ship to throw him overboard, lest they all die. And that was before I knew I'd been called to the bedside of Danny Hyde, whom I'd failed to reach a few hours earlier.

In retrospect, it didn't seem reasonable for God to strike down a helicopter just to teach me a lesson, and from this new perspective my intense guilt seemed excessive. Sure, I could have waited all day in the unlikely event I could reach Hyde, but lacking the vision and foreknowledge of God, I had decided, reasonably so, to attend to other duties and try again the next day.

Thus, my feelings of guilt lessened even as I increasingly questioned the source and inspiration for the blessing I had given Danny Hyde. Had I been inspired when I blessed him to live, or had I spoken from misplaced guilt? The latter, I feared.

＊

At 0730 the same morning, I learned from the Division Casualty Office which tracked sick, dead, and wounded soldiers, that Danny yet lived and his condition was unchanged. With this news in hand, I visited the sick ward and told Lillywhite what had befallen his friend. At 0900 hours, I flew to LZ Hammond to get more information about what happened to Hyde.

From the medics and battalion chaplain, Charles Lockie, I learned this. The previous evening, following a battle and while he dug in for the night, Hyde went forward of his foxhole to place a claymore mine. Already, he'd inserted a detonator into the mine and connected the detonating cap by wire to the "clicker" or "clacker" (a hand-held device used to set off the mine, making it a "command-detonated mine"). A buddy had accidentally stepped on the clicker back in the foxhole as Hyde bent over to place the mine.

The medics at the clearing company on LZ Hammond said, though Hyde's were the worst wounds they'd ever seen on a living grunt, he was awake and alert when evacuated to Qui Nhon. He'd asked his buddies to send to his parents the cash he had on hand, but the cash had disappeared after he left the field. I visited Danny at noon. His condition had worsened.

＊

At 1430 hours, after visiting Danny Hyde, I flew to Nha Trang via a C-123 to attend a retreat for chaplains. Two 1st Cav chaplains paled when I walked in and one declared, "You're supposed to be dead!" Someone had concluded I died of injuries suffered in the chopper crash. After all, I had departed the crash site in a Medevac helicopter, been flown to Qui Nhon, but wasn't listed as a living patient in any hospital there.

＊

On October 13, I swung by on the way to An Khe and visited Danny Hyde. His condition was unchanged. By then, I'd almost concluded Hyde's original blessing had come of my guilt, rather than from God, that my administration might be causing Danny unnecessary suffering.

＊

The next day, some Seventh Day Adventist troopers, in a fine Christian gesture, voluntarily poured concrete and prepared a pad for my hooch and office. Later that day I went on two Medevac missions, and at 2000 hours I returned to Qui Nhon and Danny Hyde. He lingered on, barely clinging to life, too badly wounded for evacuation to Japan or the states.

Finding a quiet, private spot, I prayed for understanding and inspiration on Danny's behalf. Then I returned to the ward, pulled the curtains around his bed and placed my hands again upon Danny's comatose head. This time, after waiting for inspiration, I petitioned for Danny's release from the effects of the previous blessing and commended him to God, to live or die according to God's will, not mine. Danny Hyde died at 0400 hours, October 21, 1966. I was thankful I could write to his parents about his recent vow to get his spiritual life in order.

A year later, Danny's parents would approach me as I walked about in uniform on a public square in Salt Lake City and request my help in finding someone who could tell them more about their beloved son's last days and circumstances.

❋

Meanwhile back home my children suffered as much, probably more, than I, which became clearer in a letter I received on October 23. Helga wrote of James having become very agitated recently when he discovered his model airplane in the middle of the bedroom floor, crushed. Somehow, knowing Laura Jane was the culprit, he angrily demanded she be punished and that she replace the model. Helga sought motive. "Because the airplane took my Daddy away," Laura confessed. She wasn't punished.

❋

Back in Vietnam, two days later, a young Vietnamese woman "propositioned" me. Approaching me with an infant on her hip at a market in An Khe where I bartered for materials for my office and hooch, she offered herself to me for ten piasters — a dollar or two as I recall. Instantly, an older woman jumped between us and, pointing at my chaplain insignia, chided the younger woman in very harsh tones. The young woman slunk away, eyes downcast, the image of shame. Obviously, the young mother felt shame, though her standards and circumstances differed greatly from mine. The incident brought to mind the Biblical account of Jesus' response when a woman taken in adultery was brought before him. I wished I could emulate the Savior and admonish the woman in Vietnamese to "go thy way and sin no more [cease prostituting yourself]."

---

10 October 1966, 1st Cav Chaplain Section Journal: 2040 Hrs, request from Hammond. LDS soldier critically injured...request Chaplain Newby ... to proceed to 85th as soon as possible. 2200 Hrs: Major Brandt called to notify that Chaplain Newby's helicopter crash-landed in Song Be. 2300 Hrs: Notified by Cpt. Dubois that 15th TC is providing a plane and Chaplain Newby will be airborne shortly.

Chapter 5

Friendly Fire

Occasionally, one religious denomination or another would hold a conference for its military chaplains. At noon on October 24, I received word that an LDS conference would be held in Nha Trang the following Sunday. This would be for all members, not just chaplains. General church authorities Elders Gordon B. Hinckley and Marion D. Hanks would be attending. This was great news for most LDS troopers, the importance of which other chaplains had difficulty comprehending until I explained just who these were in the hierarchy of the church.

The conference offered a great opportunity for the grunts and support troopers, leaders and privates to worship and learn at the feet of great spiritual leaders. But how, I wondered, do I arrange it in five short days? I'd need several layers of command and staff approval, the cooperation of the Air Force for transportation, and to contact LDS men throughout the division AO. And I must convince scores of small-unit leaders it would be in the best interest of each of their respective units to release each LDS soldier for two days. And I must do all this without experience or after-action reports for reference.

Well, being confident I could cause it to happen, I spent the rest of the day staffing my idea through technical (chaplain) and command channels. To my pleasant surprise, division-level approval came easily, and the U.S. Air Force agreed to provide transportation. By early evening, several others and I were out hunting for troopers who were LDS, which search I continued at LZ Hammond on October 25.

The plan developed quickly: On October 26, a 25-passenger CV-2 Caribou was "laid on" for the conference. By October 27, we had confirmation of 26 attendees, one more than the dedicated airplane could carry. In the next two days, the list of committed attendees grew to 37, 11 too many for the airplane seats available. Major Denver Harper came to the rescue; he would fly his Huey helicopter to the conference. We prayed our flights would not be canceled because of bad weather or increased combat activity.

✳

At 0600, October 30, 34 troopers departed for the conference in Nha Trang. Two hours and 30 minutes later, I sat in meeting with

37

hundreds of soldiers, airmen and a sprinkling of sailors and civilians. Before the meeting, I had visited with Elder Hinckley and was pleased that he remembered me from when he set me apart almost a year earlier. I also became acquainted with Elder Marion D. Hanks; he and I developed a life-long friendship.

Following the conference, after getting the troopers in the air en route back to An Khe, I flew to Saigon aboard an Air Force C-47 in company with Elders Hinckley and Hanks and a few others. Elder Hanks took advantage of the flight to teach us military passengers from the scriptures.

After the conference in Saigon I linked up with a Captain Layne, USAF, thus keeping a promise to his wife to visit him in Vietnam. That evening I rode behind Layne on his Honda motorbike through the chaotic streets of Saigon — a scary, exhilarating experience.

Layne was expected to attend an evening meeting with Elders Hinckley and Hanks in the Brinks Hotel (which served as accommodations for American Officers). As Layne's guest for the night, I accompanied him to the leadership meeting.

✳

The meeting began with about 12 men present, including the general and local church leaders. Elder Hinckley began the meeting by announcing there would be no business conducted. Instead, we were invited to share our thoughts and feelings in turn, beginning on his right and going around the room.

Each impromptu testimony was moving and some were amazing. Layne, for example, told of spending a long, lonely night in his downed jet fighter and of how he sang gospel hymns all night to "keep the VC away."

When my turn came, I told about Danny Hyde, David Lillywhite and grunts like them. In conclusion, I related the events leading up to and during my meeting in Elder Hinckley's office in 1965.

Speaking last, Elder Hinckley apologized to me for having questioned the validity of my orders to active duty. He said, in effect: "I did not mean to question you, Brother Newby, but I knew it was not possible for you to have valid orders. The Army had informed us you, specifically, were not acceptable in the chaplaincy. I knew something was wrong, and I would not have set you apart had President Lee not said, 'If he has orders, set him apart.'"

Continuing, Elder Hinckley said, "I'm sorry I doubted you, Brother Newby, for when I placed my hands on your head, the Lord revealed to me it was right, that you were in the chaplaincy because the Lord wanted you there … which just goes to show, brethren, what the Lord wants to happen will happen, military regulations notwithstanding."

Elder Hinckley may never appreciate in mortality how supporting his words were to me there in that crowded room in the Brinks Hotel. So often over the next quarter of a century, his words reinforced and comforted me during dark hours and influenced me to continue in the chaplaincy for 13 years beyond when I could have retired.

✳

The next day I used faked flight orders, provided by Layne, to return to the Cav. I was glad to escape from rear-area trappings and conditions, which I thought were silly and out of place in a combat zone — air conditioning, dress uniforms for Air Force personnel, spit and polish for the Army, and clubs and parties. It seemed wrong somehow when I compared these conditions with what the grunt endured. This experience helped me remember how grateful I'd been to go to the 1st Cav in the first place.

✳

I was promoted to captain sometime in October. At the time I had completed 10 months of active commissioned service and had been in Vietnam less than two months. The new rank changed nothing so far as my duties and operations were concerned.

The evening of October 25, I flew to LZ Oasis (near the Cambodian border) and spent most of the night debating various philosophies with doctors and pilots. About noon the next day, I headed for An Khe aboard a Caribou. We stopped en route at Duc Co Special Forces Camp and then headed east over the Mang Yang Pass, flying just above the treetops because of the weather and cloud cover. A trooper said later that he kept repeating every Catholic prayer he knew and had expected that any minute we would crash into the trees. I understood, because that was the scariest fixed-wing flight I ever had.

✳

During November 1966, I continued to move almost constantly around the 1st Cav AO and conduct Sunday services for the Medical Battalion, except on the first Sunday of each month, when I had a visiting chaplain conduct a communion service, a practice I'd begun at Fort Ord, California. Overall, November was much quieter for me than October had been, though I was probably busier, knowing by then how best to use the systems.

✳

On November 7, I moved into my hooch and office, a fine building under the circumstances and one I truly hoped would soon be occupied by someone else. The hooch was ready, except for lighting, and medic Keith L. Hardy kindly donated the materials and installed it. While installing the lights, Hardy mentioned that he was LDS — he requested and got a Book of Mormon.

Chaplain Garadella visited me on November 8. He had been honor-graduate in our basic chaplain course class and had given me a free ride from New York City to Chicago. After lunch Garadella and I visited Sin City so he could see what it was like. This was my one and only trip past the MP station at the entrance.

Later in the afternoon, while Garadella and I traveled in his jeep to Qui Nhon, he confessed a wish to ride in a helicopter, an experience denied him thus far in his Vietnam tour. I, being a 1st Cav chaplain, could hardly imagine chaplains and troops in Vietnam who didn't regularly ride in choppers.

On November 9, I delivered to Chaplain McClements a collection of food for the refugee camp he supported. I appreciated McClements' work with refugees, but avoided becoming heavily involved in such projects because I believed my time and energies as a chaplain belonged to American soldiers, especially infantry.

✳

Major General John Norton, 1st Cav. Division Commander, gave me a compliment. A meeting between the chaplains and General Norton had just broken up. I stood talking with Chaplains McGraff, Webb and Browne. General Norton approached the group and said, "Excuse me, Chaplain Newby. I mean no offense, but you look more like an infantryman than a chaplain." He made my day.

✳

I was especially lonely on November 18, James' twelfth birthday. The loneliness was bearable, though, mostly because this far into my tour the mail flowed in both directions, if spastic on occasion.

Sp4 David Lillywhite visited me on November 20. His battalion sergeant major, upon learning Lillywhite was a carpenter in civilian life, had kept him in the rear on R & U Detail (repair and upkeep). In this capacity Lillywhite helped build billets in the battalion rear area (a foolish practice — rear-area accommodations for troops who seldom saw the rear area). Anyhow, Lillywhite was back in my life and about to involve me in another situation.

✳

On Thanksgiving day, I conducted a worship service at 0930 hours for the Medical Battalion. Eleven men attended. I also offered Thanksgiving blessings in both the officer and enlisted messes (dining tents) at about 1300 hours. After lunch, I visited with the sick and with several troopers in their tents and then flew to LZ Hammond on a Medevac chopper.

At Hammond I visited personnel and patients at the medical clearing company and was there when Medevac and other ships brought in the remains of two 1-9 Cav troopers. The two troopers had been killed in an action in which 20 others were wounded. All the wounded were in very bad condition. The dead troopers, crew of an H-13 scout chopper, were killed when the chopper was shot down in flames. One of the dead was almost unrecognizable as having been human; the blackened skull had exploded.

Questions haunted me as I moved among the wounded and dead: *What of the families of those killed and maimed on Thanksgiving?* Probably a family sorely missed each killed and wounded trooper. And, probably, each trooper's loved ones were readying the traditional Thanksgiving meal even as he fell in battle. Thanksgiving would come hours later in the states. Over the land families would soon be offering Thanksgiving prayers for the safety of these who had already fallen, only to have hope dashed to pieces in a few days when a messenger of death arrived at the door. What would happen to hope in days ahead, when each family received word that a loved one — a son, husband or father — fell on Thanksgiving, despite their hopes and prayers? Would these tragic sacrifices mar all future Thanksgivings, or would time dull the memories and pain and allow hope and joy to return on some future holiday?

✳

I was at Phan Thiet when November 1966 gave way to December. There in the medical clearing company mess I enjoyed the best meal I'd eaten since arriving in Vietnam. That evening, back at An Khe Base Camp, I became soaked as I hitchhiked (mostly hiked) to my hooch from a secondary airstrip, one well away from the center of the camp. By bedtime, chills and fever whacked my body. *Malaria,* I wondered.

✳

A phone call at 2334 hours interrupted a night spent alternating between chills and fever. It was about a badly wounded LDS patient at the 67th Evac Hospital in Qui Nhon. Later in the night, the sound of gunfire infringed on my suffering. The shots remained a temporary mystery because I was too sick to investigate. The shots had been fired during a drinking party in the battalion area.

At 0930 hours the next day in no-fly weather, still weak and chilled, I went by cold, open jeep to Qui Nhon, 45 miles across the mountains to the east. At the 67th Evacuation Hospital, I administered and gave spiritual counsel to John Martin, the trooper I had been called about the previous evening. Martin had sustained very serious gunshot wounds to the shoulder, chest, groin and leg. After seeing Martin, I visited other grunts from the 5-7 Cav and 1-9 Cav, each of whom had been wounded in the same fight as Martin.

✳

On December 4, while making rounds of the medical wards, I saw a dry blood-encrusted flak vest lying behind a Quonset hut. An hour earlier the vest had been on Military Policeman (Sp4) Richard Grumberg, who was guarding the commanding general's quarters. A 105mm-howitzer shell exploded near Grumberg's guard post, killing him and wounding his partner, Sp4 Robert Simon. A "friendly" unit, American or ARVN, had fired the shell from a nearby base. This was, I think, my first exposure to so-called short rounds or "friendly fire" incidents.

I found it very curious that just one artillery round hit near the commanding general's quarters, in the middle of our very large base camp — the general wasn't in at the time. This is curious because artillery was usually fired in barrages, three or more tubes in unison, all with identical aiming settings. I wondered if this so-called friendly fire was all that friendly or if perhaps the shell actually landed where someone intended it to hit.

Of course, the phrase *friendly fire* as used by soldiers in the field had everything to do with the source of the fire and nothing to do with qualities or relationships. The phrase was very utilitarian in an us-versus-them (allies or "friendlies" and enemies or "bad guys") environment where quick recognition often spelled the difference between living and dying.

About December 5, I visited David Lillywhite on a building construction site in his battalion rear area. After visiting a few minutes with Lillywhite and his companions, I went my way, unaware I had left behind a special impression on a very troubled member of the building crew, which impression would soon draw me into the aftermath of a heinous war crime.

Chapter 6

An Atrocity: "Casualties of War"*

The temptation is great to omit the events in this chapter because they shamed so many great men and mar the record of an outstanding unit. But to omit this would defeat my objective of giving an honest portrayal of those who served.

After dark on December 9, David Lillywhite and another soldier appeared at my door at 1900 hours by my journal and 2200 hours according to the soldier's later court testimony. I looked into the eyes of the man with Lillywhite and quickly dismissed my initial impression that this was a social call.

The man's countenance and demeanor broadcast a heavy weight on mind and soul, and he was nervous about being in my office.

I welcomed the two troopers into the sleeping area of my combination office and hooch. The troopers took the two available folding chairs, and I sat on my mosquito net-draped bunk. After brief pleasantries, Lillywhite explained his purpose in coming. His companion, Sven (part of his alias in a future *New Yorker* magazine piece), had requested an introduction to me.

Sven began by hinting he was aware of a horrible crime and wanted help in dealing with it. Interrupting Sven, I advised him he forfeited privileged communication by talking in front of Lillywhite. Sven insisted he wanted Lillywhite to hear what he had to tell me. This is his story as I remember him telling it, and it agrees in most details with what he later testified to in court and with what he told magazine writer and author Daniel Lang. For convenience in telling, I shall assign the key characters the aliases that author Daniel Lang gave them in his *New Yorker* magazine piece and book, both titled "Casualties of War."

＊

The previous month, about November 16 or 17, Sven's platoon leader, Lieutenant Reilly, assigned him and four others to a five-man pony team mission under the leadership of Sergeant Meserve, with Corporal Clark as second-in-command. Two cousins, Rafe and Manuel Diaz, completed the makeup of the pony team. Meserve was respected by troopers, officers and fellow sergeants for his courage and combat feats.

The 1st Cav used five-man *pony teams* for missions of several days duration, during which time the teams watched and searched a specified area, in this case in the vicinity of a hill designated as "Hill 192," to gather intelligence on the enemy. As I recall, the teams were called pony teams because they were too small and too lightly armed for serious fighting — not "stallions."

The evening of November 17, Meserve briefed Pony Team three — called "Pony 3," — which was scheduled to begin it mission about dawn the next morning. He concluded his briefing by announcing the team would leave earlier than usual to allow them time to snatch a young woman from a local village. The team would take her along on the mission to *boost morale.* Hoping Meserve was joking, but fearing he wasn't, Sven immediately reported Meserve's words to a friend in his squad. His buddy shrugged off Meserve's stated intentions as a joke. But Meserve wasn't joking.

Sven became very anxious the next morning when under cover of darkness Meserve moved the team out and headed east toward the hamlet of Cat Toung, opposite from the direction of Hill 192, their assigned surveillance area. Sven, fearing the worst, cursed himself for not reporting Meserve's mission *briefing* to an officer.

✻

In the village, after Meserve and Clark had entered and exited empty-handed from several huts, Rafe pointed out a hooch where he'd occasionally seen a pretty young woman. This time Meserve and Clark came out with a young woman in tow. Her real name was Mao. She was in her late teens and pregnant. They had snatched her from her home while her mother and younger sister, Phan Thi Loc (from court-martial records), cried and pleaded for mercy. Departing the hamlet, the team pushed hard to be clear of open and populated areas and into their jungle AO before dawn, to decrease the risks of being spotted by other Americans with the kidnapped female in their custody. Risk of discovery remained high until they reached thick jungle, especially because the 1-9 Cav routinely flew "first light" sweeps of the AO, with very impressive results.

Manuel hit on a bright idea for lightening his combat load by making their hostage, frail, pregnant Mao, carry his heavy rucksack during much of the climb up into the hills.

After a while, well out of sight of any villages and concealed from the air by heavy jungle, Pony 3 stopped and ate chow, but gave

Mao nothing to eat, though they removed her gag. Soon after the chow break, the team came upon an abandoned native hut near the center of their assigned AO. Meserve ordered the team to clean out the hut; it would be the team's base of operations and become the scene of the crimes they yet intended.

Leaving Mao inside the hut, Meserve announced it was time for fun. Perhaps because he suspected Sven's dismay at what was going on, Meserve asked Sven to take his turn first in the hut. When Sven declared he would not take part in raping the young woman, Meserve warned him that he risked becoming a *friendly casualty*, unless he took his turn with Mao. Clark enthusiastically seconded Meserve's threat.

To press their threats home, for several minutes, Meserve and Clark berated Sven's courage and manhood and accused him of being homosexual and disloyal to the team.

Torn by conflicting loyalties and uncertain what to do, Sven moved a few yards away from the others and set a watch for the VC. He said the others would not allow him to move far enough away for his weapon, an M-79 grenade launcher, to be effective against them — rounds, once fired from these weapons, must travel some twenty-five yards, as I recall, before becoming armed.

Led by Meserve, each of the other team members entered the hut, in turn. During each visit, rising and falling screams pierced Sven's soul. Between these visits, Mao's screams were interspersed with moans and sobs. Clark, the second to enter the hut, came out bragging he had raped Mao with a knife to her throat, while her hands were tied behind her back.

During the gang raping and for hours afterwards, Sven endured his teammates' boasts about "how good" Mao had been and how she compared to other women they had "had." Sickened to his heart, Sven spent these hours wrestling with himself, torn between his searing conscience and that unexplainable loyalty that develops between fellow grunts in combat.

In the quiet of the evening, Meserve announced his intentions to keep Mao alive overnight to provide more fun the next morning, Sven said. Mao, having been kidnapped, used as a beast of burden, repeatedly raped, terrorized, and growing increasing ill, was tied up and left alone, moaning and bleeding through the night.

*

The next morning, as if everything were as normal as things can be in combat, Meserve set the team to accomplishing the mission assigned to it. Shortly after dawn, Pony 3 spotted enemy troops nearby, and Meserve dutifully reported the sightings. In response to his report, higher echelons ordered an air assault into the area of additional ground troops and sent in the ever-alert 1-9 Air Cav Scouts. Apparently, a decision was also made to pull Pony 3 out before the arrival of nightfall, for at 1145 hours Meserve requested permission to remain out an additional night. Though this request was denied, Pony 3 was ordered into a blocking position on a streambed.

Concerned about increased risks of discovery by approaching reinforcements, Meserve decided it was time to kill Mao, toss her body off a cliff. "Kill her," he ordered Sven, "or we report you as KIA," he threatened.

Sven refused to kill Mao and braced himself for the violent death he expected — knowing full well by now what Meserve and the others were capable of doing. But instead of shooting Sven, Meserve ordered first one and then the other of the Diaz cousins to kill Mao — they each refused. Clark volunteered.

Dragging Mao's abused, sick body from the hut, Clark shoved her into the nearby bushes. A moment later Sven heard what sounded to him like a knife being plunged into Mao's body. Clark returned alone from the bushes, wiping blood from the ten-inch blade of his civilian hunting knife. "She's dead," he declared.

Moments later, preparations to depart the area were interrupted when the heavily bleeding Mao crawled from the bushes, staggered to her feet and across a small clearing away from Pony 3. Clark and Meserve let go a stream of obscenities, and the latter ordered, "Kill the bitch!"

Everyone opened fire, including Sven, though he aimed an M-79 grenade to the side of Mao's direction of flight. Immediately, he cursed himself for having even pretended to fire at Mao, either for his own safety or in the heat of the moment.

Mao, her body riddled with bullets, made it across the clearing and disappeared into the bush. One of the Diaz cousins pointed to where he thought he saw a bush move, and Clark approached the spot and sprayed it point-blank with automatic fire. This time he made sure Mao was dead. Half her face and head were shot away.

✻

Charlie Company received this message at 2015 hours, almost eight hours after Mao was murdered: "[Pony 3] reports that at 1230 hours killed one VC woman, fleeing from Hill 192 … shot warning shots, but she did not stop, so they shot to kill … at grid-coordinate 978736."

"Well done," radioed Lieutenant Reilly to Pony 3.

At 1440 hours, a member of Pony 3 was medevaced from the field with a possible broken shoulder, unsure which number of the team it was. While these things were going on with Pony 3, Charlie Company sustained three WIAs that day during a long day of continual contact with the enemy. The war went on, situation *normal*, except for Sven.

Sven believes he survived the day on Hill 192 only because Pony 3 expended all its ammunition against the VC in the subsequent fighting.

Thankful to be alive, Sven vowed to himself to see justice done for Mao and her family, no matter what. Hoping for advice about how to proceed, Sven told his buddy everything immediately upon arriving back in his platoon area. The buddy relayed Sven's accusations to Lieutenant Reilly.

Lieutenant Reilly discouraged Sven from making an issue of the matter with, "After all, this is war, and she was a gook." At least Reilly replaced Sven on the pony team when it returned to the jungle to continue its mission — Pony 3 had come in temporarily to repair its radio. Reilly had replaced Sven, knowing he "would not come back alive."

Assuming nothing was happening, Sven went directly to his company commander, Captain Vorst (an alias), during another operation. After talking with Captain Vorst three times, Sven concluded his accusations were being swept under the rug.

Meserve, Clark and the Diaz cousins had been split into different platoons, and each busted one grade for sleeping without mosquito net — a joke, as few nets were even carried by grunts in the field.

Manuel Diaz remained in Sven's platoon, in a different squad. Immediately, Sven became the focus of intense animosity by his fellow soldiers and former buddies. "The animosity reached its limit," Sven decided, a few days after the pony team members were dispersed.

Sven's squad came "accidentally" under friendly fire by the squad to which Manuel had been reassigned. Sven said, "Most of the incoming fire was cracking and impacting around me, while the rest of my squad gave me plenty of space."

Sven added in essence, after the shooting stopped, "I looked into Manuel's cold, hard eyes and decided I'd had enough. Upon returning from the patrol, Sven formally refused to remain any longer in the field with Charlie Company. Captain Vorst sent Sven to Division Base Camp at An Khe to await transfer to a helicopter-door gunner position.

Sven continued to wrestle with his conscience at An Khe. By

December 1, he was convinced command was not investigating his accusations. Meanwhile, he worked on the battalion Repair and Utilities (R&U) detail with David Lillywhite. While he worked on the detail, Sven witnessed a visit between David Lillywhite and me.

As he watched Lillywhite and me together, Sven suddenly "knew" a chaplain was the answer to his problem, but not just any chaplain. It had to be the one talking with Lillywhite.

For the next few days, Sven questioned others about Lillywhite's reputation, hoping to find in him someone who would not turn on him. Tentatively satisfied about Lillywhite's trustworthiness and having learned he was from Arizona (presumably a cowboy), Sven approached Lillywhite and asked him to go for a walk. After walking for a few minutes, Sven explained his reason for asking Lillywhite to walk with him, that he wanted Lillywhite to arrange a meeting for him with the chaplain who had visited him a few days before. Without hesitation, Lillywhite brought Sven directly to my hooch.

✳

With years of law enforcement experience, I tended not to accept things as they first appeared. So I listened with a policeman's ear to Sven's strange story, not doubting serious crimes had been committed, for Sven's demeanor convinced me of this from the start. Rather, I listened to detect the depth of Sven's involvement in the incident he unfolded.

Soon, though, my suspicious policeman's nature yielded to the more compassionate and trusting chaplain. In Sven, I discerned a man with a heart racked with guilt, not for crimes committed, but for having failed to prevent atrocities against Mao, or die trying.

Before me was a man immersed in remorse, self-recrimination and shame because fear had immobilized him until it was too late for Mao. Here was a man torn by conflicting loyalties to buddies in combat — one of the strongest of human bonds — and to what is right, a coward in his own eyes whose behavior dishonored his own dear wife.

✳

About midnight, I called in the Criminal Investigation Detachment, having satisfied myself Sven was for real. Within minutes, two investigators arrived. After listening with cool professionalism to Sven's brief synopsis of the crimes, the investigators explained to Sven his rights — just in case, though I think they also believed him — and took him off into the night. In parting, the investigators ordered me to talk to no one except my commander about Sven's allegations.

✳

The next morning I wrote to inform Elder Hinckley of what I was involved in. The Brethren would keep confidences, and I believed they should be alerted in case the incident became public — which seemed probable considering the growing antiwar, pro-enemy movements back in the "world."

At 0900 hours the morning following Sven's visit to my hooch, I briefed Lt. Col. Leighton about the Mao incident. Then I attended a meeting of chaplains, where I learned I was being transferred — to Sven's battalion!

✳

I saw Sven twice more. A few days later, we were both passengers on a Caribou headed to LZ Hammond, me to join his battalion and Sven to return to the scene of the crime in company with the CID. Sven thanked me for getting the investigation started and told me what had occurred after he left my hooch with the CID agents. He'd spent the first night locked in a CONEX container — metal shipping box — in "protective custody." Then he was reassigned as a military policeman. Obviously, his allegations were being taken seriously. I saw him for the last time during a court-martial in April 1967.

✳

The day following Sven's visit to my hooch, I was informed of my transfer to the 2-8 Cav (read that 2nd Battalion, 8th Cavalry), the parent unit of the company involved in the Mao incident at Hill 192.

With the infantry at last! I should have been elated, but this transfer was rife with potential complications. Chaplain McGraff was understandably perplexed by my lack of enthusiasm, after all the lobbying I'd done to get an infantry battalion.

I explained to Chaplain McGraff my part in putting the Mao incident into criminal investigative channels, how I was violating CID instructions by telling him, and that the alleged incident occurred in the unit to which I was being assigned. Yes, I still wanted an infantry unit, but wanted him to know about the potential for conflicts of interest.

Chaplain McGraff said I should take the transfer, for he knew I could do the job, despite the secret I carried. I appreciated his attitude because I wasn't about to turn down an infantry assignment — I might not get another chance at one. So I went to the 2-8 Cav and kept my secret for about three months, but it wasn't easy.

*

The chaplain of a unit is required by Army regulation to interview any soldier charged with a capital crime. But how was I, as chaplain and confidant, to counsel the four accused soldiers, about whom I knew stuff they did not know I knew? I couldn't even explain to my new commander why a month passed before I visited the prisoners in their makeshift, CONEX-container stockade. During the prisoner interviews, once I finally got around to them, I focused on spiritual aspects of the prisoners' lives. I carefully steered discussion away from their alleged crimes. One or more of the prisoners might, I feared, confess what I already knew, and that might somehow, under their right to privileged communication with a chaplain, tangle up the legal process and prevent it from taking its course, wherever it might lead.

*

Sven's company commander, Captain Vorst, was relieved of command of his infantry company in combat — presumably death to an Army officer's career — and sent to the rear to be the Battalion S-1 personnel officer — also not a great career move. I got to know Vorst and liked him. Neither of us brought up the Mao case until he learned of my involvement in bringing it to light.

Upon learning I had linked Sven with the CID, Vorst approached me, and my worst fears were not realized. Though I'd fully expected Vorst, other battalion leaders and even troopers to angrily condemn me once my part became known, no such reaction materialized.

Captain Vorst seemed open and honest as he shared with me his part in the matter. He was appalled and momentarily incredulous when Sven reported the crimes to him, he said, and couldn't believe any of his men, especially Sergeant Meserve, could commit such horrendous acts as Sven alleged. Vorst said he promised Sven immediate action and tried to keep his promise.

According to Vorst, he personally reported Sven's allegations to the battalion commander. The colonel responded, according to Vorst, "We can't have a stain like this on our unit record. ... Split the members of the team up into different units and bust (demote) Sergeant Meserve, Corporal Clark and each of the Diazes, for sleeping without mosquito nets." These demotions under Article 15 (non-judicial punishment) of the Uniform Code of Military Justice, if they were in fact administered, could have left the accused men free of criminal records and the unit record free of a horrible stain.

I never heard the battalion commander's side of the matter. He was reassigned out of the battalion before my orders of secrecy were lifted. Perhaps I could have gotten his side by attending the court-martial proceedings, but I was there only once, being unwilling to leave my troops in the field to satisfy curiosity.

*

According to the *New Yorker* magazine, Sergeant Meserve, Corporal Clark and the Diaz cousins were each convicted. All the accused were dishonorably discharged; Sergeant Meserve was found not guilty of rape, but guilty of premeditated murder and given ten years in military prison; Clark got life for rape and pre-meditated murder; Manuel Diaz got fifteen years for rape, and Rafe eight years for rape and unpremeditated murder.

Mao's mother disappeared before the original trial, presumably kidnapped by VC. Two weeks after the trial, a Vietnamese teacher told Sven Mao's sister was missing. Sven later said to Daniel Lang of *New Yorker* magazine, "Charlie kidnapped her, just as he did Mao's mother. So now it's only the father who's left — or is he? Who says we don't get along with Charlie? Between us, we've taken care of that whole family."

The Diaz cousins were retried, separately, at Fort Leavenworth. Manuel Diaz was set free because the CID had, allegedly, slipped up and not informed him he could have a civilian lawyer at *no expense* to himself. Rafe Diaz was convicted again, but his sentence was later reduced to 24 months, resulting in his immediate release from mili-tary prison. Clark drew a life sentence, later reduced to 20 and then to eight years, as was Meserve's. None of the four accused men spent a dime in his own defense.

The Mao incident appeared to hurt neither the battalion com-mander's nor Captain Vorst's careers. They each went on to achieve general officer rank.

*

My predictions about the Mao incident, officially "The Incident on Hill 192," were born out only gradually — in a magazine article, a book and two movies.

In 1969, the incident was published in the *New Yorker* magazine, under the title "Casualties of War." A major American movie company bought movie rights to the incident, as reported in the *New Yorker*. About 1970, a Berlin, Germany-based underground, counterculture group apparently plagiarized the *New Yorker* and produced the movie "Mao," which reportedly won honors at the

Cannes Film Festival. The Hollywood film company sued the producers of *Mao* for film-rights violations. The World Court ruled in
favor of *Mao's* producers, presumably because *Mao* was based on
official records, though *Mao's* producers lifted aliases for the main
characters from the *New Yorker* magazine, not official records.

In 1969 McGraw-Hill republished *Casualties of War* in a 115-page
book. About 1990, the American film company that owned the
movie rights released *Casualties of War*, starring Michael J. Fox, rated
R. This movie, while it remained true to the gist of the Mao incident,
took license with some details, misrepresenting how Sven met me
and representing me as a Methodist, though Sven in his interview
with Daniel Lang had made a great point of my being a Mormon.

*

The Mao incident was overshadowed by another war-crime incident on a much larger scale, the infamous My Lai incident, from which
the chaplaincy came away looking less than good. Chaplain involvement in My Lai was given almost three unflattering pages in the
seven-volume *History of the U.S. Army Chaplaincy.* Its authors, seeking
something to place the chaplaincy in a better light, added a paragraph
about the Mao incident — thus I attained a tiny mention in history.

Three weeks passed between the Mao incident and Sven's getting
to the CID, through me. Chaplain Carl E. Creswell passed allegations
of the My Lai incident to the Americal Division Chaplain shortly after
it occurred, but more than a year passed before it came to light.

Nearly five years after My Lai became known, Chaplain
Creswell commented:

"I felt...betrayed by the Chaplains [to] whom I had entrusted
my knowledge of the My Lai event. If a history of a fumble enables
future Chaplains to hang onto the ball, this exercise will be
worth...our troubles...God forbid that in a similar situation, any
Chaplain should ever be content with the actions I took."

This from the *New York Times:*

"Such incidents, along with general frustration about the
conduct of the war, have served to revive the old 'two masters'
problem concerning chaplains in the armed forces."

The Chaplaincy History account added:

"My Lai certainly did not enhance the image of the chaplaincy. ... At least one author strongly insinuated that the chaplains' ministry was virtually ineffectual. ... While the terrible circumstances at My Lai received more publicity, another situation of a similar, though less complex [nature] involved the kidnap, rape, and murder of a Vietnamese girl by a small group of U.S. soldiers. Though little credit was given to him for it, Chaplain Claude D. Newby, latter-day Saints, was the first to properly respond to the report when a troubled soldier related the incident as he had heard it. Newby, a former military and civilian policeman, took the report to the Army's Criminal Investigation Division (CID) and the responsible individuals were eventually arrested and tried."

One of the authors of the seven-volume history, Chaplain "Smoky" Stover, saw the book *Casualties of War*. Wondering if it reported a true incident, he checked it out. Logically, Stover first contacted Chaplain (then captain) Wayne Kuehne. Kuehne was at the time (1972) co-located with Stover at the U.S. Army Chaplain Center and School at Fort Hamilton. Stover was on the staff and faculty, and Kuehne was a student in the Chaplain Advanced Officer Course.

Besides being in the same building at the school with Stover, Kuehne fit the description of Chaplain (Captain) Gerald Kirk — my alias in *Casualties of War* — better than I did. Kuehne in real life, like Kirk in the book, is six-foot, blond, long-nosed, and a Mormon who was once a Salt Lake City police officer. (He might challenge the long-nosed part). I, on the other hand, have brown hair (now streaked with gray) and was a police officer for Ogden City, Utah.

Anyhow, Kuehne denied any knowledge of the Mao incident. Stover almost wrote the matter off as a work of fiction, until Kuehne suggested he contact me, as I had been with the 1st Cav in Vietnam about the time the Mao incident allegedly occurred. Smoky Stover wrote to me, and the rest is, as they say, history.

Well, I'm glad my actions helped place the chaplaincy in better historical light and am pleased over its inclusion in the Chaplaincy History.

I'm sorry this horrible incident happened. I'm espcially sorry for the victims and for the stain it placed on us all.

19, November 1966, 2015 Hrs: "Pony Soldier 3 reports that at 1230 hrs. killed 1 VC woman, fleeing from Hill 193. They shot warning shots, but she did not stop, so they shot to kill."

Chapter 7

Infantry Assignment at Last!

An Army unit belongs to its commander, but I quickly developed a special, possessive relationship with the 2-8 Cav, as I would with subsequent units in which I served in combat. Sunday, December 11, I conducted my last general Christian worship service for the 15th Medical Battalion. In the afternoon, I attended LDS services at the 2nd Surgical Hospital for the last time on a regular basis. I'd grown very close to the men of this little congregation, most of whom were valiant and true, a tribute to their roots. I formed lifelong friendships with some of them.

A recent letter from a member of the group touched me deeply:

Dear Brother Newby:

Your letter arrived and suddenly time seemed to stand still. Within the chambers of my mind I suddenly saw you again as the man I deeply loved and admired while in Vietnam many years ago. I can never forget the experience I had the first time I met you. Of course your unique voice had the quality to capture the attention and respect of everyone. Your stature was tall, lean, energetic and captivating. But, above all, I felt the whispering of the Spirit confirm your spiritual assignment as a servant of the Lord. On that particular day, you had a majestic spiritual glow around you. I immediately recognized it as a spiritual shield given as a gift of protection by the host of heaven. ... There was no doubt that you were truly on an errand for the Lord ... always prayed that I would someday be allowed to become a friend to you. ... It was my observation that most everyone wanted to be your friend. ... You did a phenomenal job of helping them feel better about themselves. ... You were an angel in mortal clothing.

Sincerely,
Lanny Owens
(signed and dated June 16, 1994)

I was touched by this tribute, a tribute I believe many soldiers would like to have paid to their own chaplain because of what the chaplains represented to them.

✳

Transfer orders arrived on December 14, 1966. These orders assigned me to the Headquarters, 1st Brigade for duty with the 2nd Battalion, Eighth Cavalry (2-8 Cav). The 2-8 Cav was unique among the battalions in the division in that it was first to have all its line companies use distingushing call signs for their platoons, a practice that was subsequently adopted across the whole division.

Even with the Mao incident in mind, I gladly left my self-made hooch and reported to Captain Vorst, S-1 in the 2-8 Cav. I went eagerly, but with a hint of reluctance at giving up the freedom I had to range across the division AO. I was on the way to join the grunts — *where I belonged.*

I moved my belongings into the battalion chaplain's rear-area accommodations, a leaky, dank, dark, mildew-smelling, gloomy, spider-infested small-wall tent. The tent sat off by itself on a flat spot above a road in the battalion area, in front of a vine- and vegetation-covered cliff, and beside a CONEX and a makeshift shower — a barrel on stilts. By lantern light, I explored the tent. It wouldn't do. I slept in it twice, December 14 and 15, during which time I drew gear and negotiated to get David Lillywhite as my chaplain assistant.

✳

On December 16, I flew to the battalion combat trains area on the west perimeter of LZ Hammond. There, I reintroduced myself to the same sergeant major I had called on in October, the day I attempted to visit Danny Hyde just hours before Hyde was blown up by a claymore. Already, I felt that my destiny was linked with this battalion and had been from the time that I arrived in country.

Sp4 David Lillywhite, combat infantryman-turned-unit-carpenter, gladly left the security of the rear area and joined me in the field — he arrived at LZ Hammond later in the day, having come in a ground convoy. We set up a small tent about 30 yards from and 10 feet above the west perimeter. We dug a trench around the tent — rainwater frequently poured in torrents off the steep volcano-like mount in the center of LZ Hammond. Next we filled and stacked sandbags three feet high around the tent. Finally, we dug two foxholes inside the tent, one by each stretcher — Lillywhite's idea, based on experience.

Lillywhite and I, officer and enlisted, would share a tent in the forward-rear area, just as we would share ponchos in the field. I was very glad to start with an experienced infantryman, especially with Lillywhite. I thought we needed overhead protection from incoming rockets and mortars, but such preparations were not then common on LZs, except for TOCs and commanders' accommodations.

✳

In the absence of Army doctrine for religious support in combat and having never heard of battlefield analysis, I intuitively assessed the situation during the first week of 1967 and established a general outline of how I wanted to operate — my operational concept.

METT-T is the Army principle of continuous battlefield analysis. The acronym, METT-T, stands for the Mission; Enemy force capabilities, deployment, actions and presumed intentions; friendly Troops deployment, current and anticipated operations and needs; Terrain and weather as these affect everything else; and Time and energy constraints.

Without applying my version of METT-T, I would have had to sacrifice the mission for personal safety, or wasted time, energy and perhaps life, with little affect on the soldiers and unit.

In the Battalion rear area — usually on a base camp — I kept a stretcher to sleep on and a place to store my duffel bag, dress uniforms and so forth. My base of operations was a sandbagged tent or bunker co-located with Battalion operations on its firebase — combat trains.

I operated forward of, not at, my base — my rucksack and the field were home. Occasionally I returned to the rear to change clothes, read my mail, mail letters, restock supplies, gather tactical information, obtain transportation to hospitals or another unit in the AO, and sometimes to rest overnight. By remaining flexible, carefully analyzing the key situation, and using the assets of the unit to support the unit, I usually managed to successfully rotate between the infantry companies and to also work in frequent hospital visits.

My goal was to spend two or three nights in 10 with each infantry company, during which visits I conducted worship services at every reasonable opportunity, usually at the platoon or squad level. My 10-day worship cycle occasionally caused tension between me and those chaplains whose theological focus was on the worship service as opposed to being with the troops. Some chaplains disapproved of operating forward with the grunts more than was necessary to conduct services.

For best results, I synchronized religious support with the battalion mission and operations. Thus the places and frequency of worship services were driven by situations and circumstances, rather than day of the week. Consequently, though I observed the Lord's day personally, Sunday was just another day in the hell of war, excepting the occasional holiday truces and respite at base camp.

Other considerations being equal among units — similar levels of stress and activity — I went to the company most overdue for a visit, traveling usually on resupply flights or the commander's *Charlie-Charlie* chopper. Other considerations being unequal, which was usually the case, I focused my attention where the hurting was greatest, in consequence of recent events, current action, or because imminent action had high casualty-producing potential.

In practice, only rarely did a company wait longer than two weeks for a visit. On those rare occasions, weather was usually the culprit — I wasn't about to get people killed by placing my schedule above the situation.

In the field I attempted to divide each visit between the company command group and its platoons, and to conduct worship services at platoon level, as it was seldom secure enough to bunch up for a company-size service. Usually, I spent nights with whichever platoon or element I was with at the end of the day. My three-day-visits objective meshed well with the companies' practice of "logging" — being resupplied — every three days, barring heavy casualties and contacts and so forth.

Regularly I went along on platoon and company-size operations, which I considered maneuvers, not patrols, where the chaplain belonged. Seldom did I intentionally accompany squads, in deference to unwritten, unofficial chaplaincy "doctrine," because it was usually unnecessary to do so. Unintentionally, I accompanied many a squad-size operation because I'd be accompanying a platoon when it split into smaller elements, leaving me no choice but to go with a squad on a patrol or occasional ambush.

My on-loan infantry chaplain assistant usually accompanied me in the field; not so with school-trained assistants — the former was always an asset and the latter were often a liability. The chaplain assistant's primary duty in combat is to protect the chaplain. With school-trained assistants, I usually had to protect them. For example, one school-trained assistant couldn't keep his M-16 rifle in operational condition — I unjammed it for him in the midst of two firefights. In fairness to school-trained chaplains and assistants, lacking any Army doctrine for religious support in combat, each assistant had to feel his way along as I had to, but usually without my infantry tactical training and experience to fall back on.

7, December 1966, 1st Cav Div G-1 Journal: Pfc. Jesus Salalas, gsw, D 2/8; Pfc. Gregory Collon, frag, legs, A 2-8.

8, December 1966, 1st Cav Div G-1 Journal: Sp4 Robert T. Daugherty, swept away to sea, HHC 2-8.

Chapter 8

Holidays of Horror

In anticipation of lonely troopers at Christmas time, Helga sent to me some songs she got primary children to record on reel-to-reel tapes. There wasn't much else for me to prepare for Christmas celebrations in the field.

＊

On December 17, I helped at the medical clearing company on LZ Hammond because 36 (my journal says 40) dead American grunts were hauled from the battlefield. A chinook helicopter brought in the dead, which were slung beneath it in a cargo net.

These troopers gave their lives in the 506 Valley (though my journal says Happy Valley, I remember it, and have confirmed it was the 506 Valley). Charlie Company, 1-12 Cav had been decimated, according to Shelby L. Stanton (Anatomy of a Division). In fact, the casualties were in A, B, C and D companies of 1-12 Cav and in the 1-8 and 1-9 Cav, with the largest number being 1-9 Cav, according to the G-1 casualty list.

At Hammond, Graves Registration personnel had laid each of these 36 bodies — America's sons, dads, husbands and sweethearts — on his back with his head to the west. Seventy-two eyes, less the occasional empty socket or missing face, stared vacantly into the rain-laden heavens.

I moved among the bodies and looked deeply into those staring, glazed-over eyes, letting the strange images burn indelibly into my mind. Every body was contorted. Many rigor mortis-stiffened arms reached upward to ward off some horrible evil, as it were, while other arms stretched heavenward as if to grasp solace or rescue from some source visible only to the spirit, which had so recently departed the body.

I prayed for the souls of these men who gave their all in terrible, mortal combat, and for their loved ones. I prayed for each soldier as he stood about the dead in solemn contemplation of his own mortality. I even prayed for the news photographer, who in my mind greatly offended the memory of the dead and the senses of the living. And I prayed for the politicians and leaders who rightly or wrongly had placed these men here to die so horribly at Christmastime.

During these moments with the dead at LZ Hammond, I became convinced that a just and merciful God will requite these soldiers for their sacrifice in the 506 Valley. I was convinced this was so, even though many of them may have ended their short lives with profanity on their lips, as was so often the case during heavy fighting in Vietnam. I would soon discover in battle after battle that obscene and profane babbling frequently punctuated the horrible sounds, sights and smells of close combat. Sadly, profanity against deity and obscenities involving motherhood were the most frequently heard expletives during times of such extreme stresses. These foul utterances were commonly used to emphasize urgency, orders and to express the terrors the men endured.

Even so, as I walked slowly among the massed dead, all laid out in military formation, I kept remembering Christ's declaration: "Greater love hath no man than this, that a man lay down his life for his friends" (John 15:13). These men had lain down their lives, reluctantly in most cases, but they'd done it. They'd chosen the risks of service to country, squad, and buddy over the personal security offered by fleeing to Sweden, Canada or onto the college campus. These grunts "fought the good fight" (1 Timothy 6:12).

Those minutes there with the dead uniquely prepared me, I believe, to bring some hope to the hopeless in the months and battles ahead.

After attending to the dead, Lillywhite and I went forward for the first time together. We joined Bravo Company 2-8, which was securing LZ Strip somewhere east of LZ Hammond, named Strip because it was in the sand dunes by the seashore.

That evening we began our field ministry. In the darkness we crept from position to position and visited and played Christmas music on very low volume. The next morning I held a worship service with 17 attending — puny numbers for a unit in the field. Later I met Sergeant Wade, a black NCO who loved his men. His platoon had no lieutenant, so Sergeant Wade was also the platoon leader.

When I first saw Wade he was running his platoon through training maneuvers to improve their fire and maneuver tactical skills. Rarely did I witness such training drills in Vietnam because mostly there was no time, and when time and security were adequate the grunts were usually too exhausted.

Wade told me proudly and gratefully, "Chaplain, I've been with this platoon for eight months and never lost a man KIA." With Charlie 1-12 fresh in my mind, I prayed for Wade's success in sending all his men home alive. His noble, great hope would be dashed before Christmas.

❋

Back at LZ Hammond at 1100 hours, I held a worship service for the 2-13 Artillery Battery. Fifty-seven troopers attended, about 50 percent of the unit — a small percentage compared to future service for infantry elements. From this day forward, every day was a day for worship and every bomb crater a potential worship site — I held services whenever and wherever I could for squads, platoons, companies, firebases, even two-man foxholes if necessary. For example, this same afternoon I held a second service at LZ Strip, just before the battalion moved to a new firebase farther inland, LZ Santa.

❋

December 20, was a rare sunny day during the rainy season on LZ Santa. Around the perimeter, grunts struggled and sweated to sink foxholes into very rocky soil.

A trooper with his back to me as I approached cursed the rocks, the sun, his entrenching tool, sergeants and so forth with generous use of God's title. Upon looking up and recognizing me as a chaplain, though he didn't know I was his new chaplain, he mumbled a weak apology for his language.

Seriously, but with a touch of tactful humor, I said, "You've got to quit talking like that, else you may die and go to hell."

Said he, "Promises, promises. I never get promoted." He left no doubt about his opinion of what and where he was.

One might feel to censure me for allowing any degree of humor in the face of profanity. But without being told, I knew appropriate humor, in combat, would reinforce parental training and past and subsequent teachings and admonitions — provided my actions supported my words, humorous or solemn.

❋

For the most part, I dealt not with spiritually motivated Mormons and Baptists nor with devout Catholics, but with soldiers of multiple faiths, men who frequently lacked any significant spiritual and religious foundation. To support these men of such diverse backgrounds, I prayed hard for discernment to match each situation, person and moment.

For example, while on a patrol soon after our first meeting, I watched Sergeant Wade become irate at some troopers who bunched up (got too close to one another), making themselves inviting targets of opportunity to a VC or NVA sniper. Later, in a more secure area, Wade gathered the careless troopers around him and tore into them, using God's name liberally. Slowly, Sergeant Wade realized his troops were looking at something behind him. Turning, Wade saw me and dropped his eyes ashamedly. "Sorry Chaplain Newby, but you know what I mean."

"Yes, I know what you mean, Sergeant Wade. You love your men and want to keep them alive. But God knows what you said. Remember, God will not hold him guiltless who takes His name in vain."

Nothing else needed to be said. Sergeant Wade accepted my gentle admonishment, and he and his troopers were impressed with both the brevity and content of my sermonette, some said.

✳

Later in the day, after the above conversation with the trooper at his foxhole, Lillywhite and I took a little patrol of our own. Our destination was a stream that flowed west to east about 200 meters north of the LZ Santa perimeter. Our objective was cleanliness.

The fresh, clear water in the little stream invited us in, never mind that it was less than three feet wide and no more than three inches deep. Soon we found a small, secluded, sunlit clearing. After checking for booby traps and making sure we were not being observed, we went into action.

While I guarded against marauding VC, Lillywhite stripped down and washed out his undergarments. Then he dammed up the stream by lying on his back in it, head upstream. Soon the water backed up enough to flow soothingly over his shoulders and chest. We switched roles after he had enough of the deliciously cold water. What a break this was!

Under Lillywhite's mentor-ship, I quickly picked up several tricks for taking advantage of the environment and enhancing my chances of survival. The new assignment was going well, except for one tiny problem — I felt vaguely unfaithful to Helga and the children because I was so pleased to be with the infantry. These mixed emotions made little sense; I can't describe or explain them now. Well, Helga and I had both wanted the chaplaincy, and I had a mission there — here. It helped to believe deeply that I was finally at the core of our mission.

❋

About this time, in response to receiving word of the wounding of a lieutenant and a sergeant in Alpha Company, I visited them at the Medical Clearing Company on LZ Hammond. The pair had gotten themselves ambushed while attempting to travel by jeep to LZ Hammond from the Alpha Company AO. I should have learned from their mistake.

❋

In another incident that occurred just before I joined the battalion — I don't recall which company — a platoon came upon a booby-trapped butterfly bomb. These were anti-personnel devices dropped by the American Air Force to saturate enemy-held areas. Well, the platoon leader gathered his men about him and showed them how to disarm the bomb. His lesson completed, so he thought, the lieutenant stood and said something like, "There, it is harmless now," and tossed the device over his shoulder. He awakened a few days later in a hospital in Japan and moaned, "I killed my platoon." A slight exaggeration — he only decimated his platoon.

This lieutenant's tragic mistake helps to emphasize the fallacy of the Army policy in Vietnam of replacing experienced leaders after six months. Extrapolating from my experiences, I'm convinced that thousands of U.S. deaths and untold maiming of our men can be chalked up to this policy.

From the start of my tour in Vietnam, I considered the six-month rotation policy almost as criminal as our civilian leaders' policies of "business as usual" for American society, limited war objectives and the strategy of gradual escalation against an oriental foe. Consequently, like generals-in-the-making Colin Powell and H. Norman Schwarzkopf, I promised myself to remember the errors of Vietnam and, if ever I got the chance, do something for grunts in future wars.

On the other side of the six-month command issue, the fighting is almost always done by soldiers and leaders who possess excellent, adrenaline-reinforced reflexes, but whose bodies and mental faculties are exhausted almost beyond imagination by the demands for constant vigilance and existence on the battlefield. This combination, given the frequent need in combat for instantaneous decisions and actions, makes for mistakes, deadly mistakes. For this reason, perhaps six-month commands could have been partially justified at the company and platoon level in Vietnam.

❋

At the end of the day, December 20, on LZ Santa, Lillywhite and I dug a foxhole and set up a one-poncho shelter for the night. The next day, I returned to Qui Nhon via LZ Hammond. At Qui Nhon I visited wounded troopers in the 67th and 85th Evacuation Hospitals, ate a hamburger at the PX and spent the night with a Dust Off unit.

✳

December 22 began in gloom and ended in blood. About 0730 hours, Bravo Company air assaulted into a small clearing in the thickly jungle-covered foothills to the west-northwest of LZ Hammond. I saw the company off. Had this combat assault happened a week or two later, I would have gone with them. But at this point I questioned if I'd be welcome and not in the way.

Bravo Company, commanded by Captain Charles R. Getz, landed without taking fire, and everything appeared quiet for a few minutes. At about 0800 hours, heavy automatic and assault weapon fire shattered the quiet of the jungle, as Bravo Company moved into it and away from insertion LZ. An estimated platoon of NVA forces, dressed in khaki, had opened fire on the advancing troopers from well-dug-in and concealed fighting positions. During the next two hours Bravo Company suffered five soldiers killed and three wounded — most of the casualties were from Sergeant Wade's platoon.

Finally, a heroic or angry corporal broke the attack almost single-handedly — I can't remember his name. He, upon finding himself surrounded by dead and wounded buddies, leaped to his feet and charged the enemy positions, yelling and shooting from the hip. Apparently, he so unnerved the NVA that they fled their well-prepared fighting positions to escape his wrath. The corporal killed several of the fleeing enemies before breaking off the chase some 50 yards beyond their original fighting positions. The enemy sustained eleven KIA. Blood trails leading away from their positions suggested at least five more NVA were seriously wounded.

Meanwhile, from the air in the commander's Charlie-Charlie chopper, I could hardly tell a battle was raging and men were dying — the only evidence I had was the muffled explosions of artillery shells and wisps of smoke trickling up through the trees.

A few days later, that same courageous corporal learned how it felt to be chased by armed, angry foes. He and his pony team were chased for about two kilometers — a downhill race, fortunately.

Bravo Company, by the way, was the first unit in the division to earn a Valorous Unit Citation in Vietnam. The citation was for its performance on May 16, 1966 in an action that kicked off Operation Crazy Horse.

*

On December 23, I flew via a Caribou through very bad weather from Qui Nhon to LZ Hammond, then to An Khe. I reached LZ Hammond on Christmas Eve, having been weathered in at An Khe the day before. That was just as well because my tent at LZ Hammond washed away during the night. Lillywhite and I spent the rest of the morning clearing the area and putting up a new tent.

At 1300 hours, Christmas Eve, I reported to Chaplain (Major) Dowd for special duty as escort officer for evangelist Billy Graham. The famed evangelist was appearing at LZ Hammond, as was Bob Hope. I've no idea why I was selected for this duty; it surely seemed odd to pick me, a Mormon, what with all the Baptist and other chaplains who were available.

Platoons of infantry were flown in from the jungles and rice paddies to attend, as a group, either Billy Graham's Christmas service or the Bob Hope Show. By this arrangement a trooper got to attend one of the events only if his platoon was chosen, and the choice of which event he attended was decided by whomever selected his platoon in the first place. Of course, things got mixed up on occasion. For example, a platoon of Alpha Company came for the Bob Hope Show, but got deposited at Billy Graham's service, instead.

My escort duties amounted to nothing. At the appointed time a CV-2 dropped from the overcast skies and deposited Billy Graham and an entourage of chaplains and media people, with a sprinkling of commanders and division staffers. Billy Graham moved from the aircraft into a press of chaplains. This group engulfed him and stuck so close on the way to the site selected for his service that I couldn't get near enough to him to introduce myself as his escort, much less to actually escort him.

Despite doctrinal differences between Billy Graham and me, I taped his sermon and subsequently shared it with all my grunts over the next month. I did this because Graham's visit and words meant a lot to many of them.

*

On Christmas day, after conducting a service for the 2-13 Artillery Battalion, I joined Bravo Company at the site of its tragic battle three days earlier. There I found Sergeant Wade understandably downcast over the dead and wounded members of his platoon. Wade was a very caring, even spiritual man, despite his occasional bout of foul language.

For a few hours, I mingled with the troops and leaders, offering what support I could. Sixty-two men attended the Christmas service that followed.

After leaving Bravo Company, I held two services at LZ Santa, two more for Alpha Company in the hamlet of Nha Tuo, and finished the day with two services at LZ Hammond, my sixth and seventh on Christmas day. Merry Christmas!

*

Following the heavy casualties it had sustained on December 17, Charlie Company 1-12 had been lifted to LZ Bird, an isolated firebase near an area known as the Crow's Foot, to rebuild as a fighting unit and to, incidentally, spend Christmas. The company was hardly combat-ready when the NVA overran LZ Bird the night of December 26.

An urgent call brought me to the medical clearing company on LZ Hammond early on December 27, my 30th birthday. There I witnessed a horrible replay of December 17 as casualties poured in from LZ Bird, most of them from Charlie 1-12 Cav, part of the same unit that had been mauled in the 506 Valley fight 10 days earlier.

And from LZ Bird came another Chinook, this time with the bodies of 27 troopers swung underneath it, piled atop each other in a cargo net. Again, the troopers' bodies were laid out in formation, each with its glassed-over, terror-filled eyes staring blankly at the sky, each face frozen in the terror it endured at the moment of a horrible death, and every body mangled.

Following half an hour with the dead, I ministered to the 65 wounded troopers inside and around the medical tents. The wounded, too, were mostly from Charlie 1-12 Cav. Back at LZ Bird, about 50 uninjured American soldiers moved about in shock among the 49 NVA bodies scattered in and around the perimeter.

At the aid station, a wounded sergeant told me of lying in the dark during the attack, while within arm's reach two enemy soldiers whispered and gestured in the manner American commanders might in the midst of a fight. The sergeant, out of ammo except for a hand grenade, let these enemies move on without attacking them because the grenade would probably have killed him too at such close range.

A lieutenant related how a trooper, on his first night in the field, died behind a machine gun after stacking up a dozen NVA bodies in front of his position. Military historian S. L. A. Marshall wrote extensively about the December 27 attack on LZ Bird.

*

After attending to my duties among the dead and wounded, I returned to our newly erected tent and packed much of our gear and equipment for Lillywhite to take back to An Khe. After a week in the field and once having my tent washed away, I had a better idea of just what I needed to operate, which wasn't much. I came to Vietnam with but little luggage and to LZ Hammond with little more than personal clothing, essential field gear and some office stuff. I'd found that most of the office stuff and some of the personal clothing was in excess of my needs.

Our lightened load included a tent, two medical litters to occasionally sleep on, a field desk, a chaplain's combat kit, a lantern and a few office supplies. This stuff remained at my base of operations. For operations forward, I wore jungle fatigues, jungle boots, socks and undergarments. I also wore a steel helmet with camouflage cover and band and a bottle of insect repellant in the band at the back, web gear (load-bearing equipment — pistol belt and suspenders). On the belt and suspenders hung a first aid kit, two one-quart canteens, two ammo pouches, a much-too-small rump pack, a flashlight and a hunting knife. A gas mask was ever present on my left hip beneath a canteen. In my left front pocket I carried what I dubbed my *.45-caliber camera* for close-up shots. On my left arm I wore a wrist compass, and tied to the rump pack — until Helga sent me a rucksack — was a poncho, poncho liner (a wonderful item in the jungle) and air mattress. Inside the pack were the real essentials: a can opener with handles, Tabasco sauce and my scriptures. For the first few months I humped a chaplain kit, in which I had replaced liturgical items I didn't use with field hymnals and a battery-powered reel-to-reel tape player/recorder.

During my early days in the field, besides the canteens on my belt, one over each hip, I carried two canteens attached to the rump pack. Later, I got a civilian rucksack from home and hung two half-gallon canteens on it, one on each side. Oh yes, I eventually replaced the 32 field hymnals with selected hymns, which I had printed out and laminated to protect them from the weather — these I rotated biweekly.

When I first arrived in-country, I was outraged to discover grunts in the field sometimes had to wait for items of clothing and equipment that were found in abundance in the rear, items designed for waging combat in the jungle — jungle boots and fatigues, poncho liners and air mattresses.

On good authority, I heard that during 1965 and early 1966, grunts in the field wore water-retaining fatigues and combat boots until these rotted off their rash-covered bodies, while many rear-area troops and commanders sported spit-shined jungle boots while working and living on dry wooden floors. All U.S. Army personnel in Vietnam wore jungle fatigues and boots when I arrived in country.

Still, disregard for the grunt was evident. For example, in the 2-8 Cav, our grunts were issued little, almost useless rump packs, while the U.S. Army supplied fine American rucksacks to ARVN soldiers. The ARVN soldier, in turn, sold his rucksack to an American grunt, reported it lost in combat and got issued a new one, no questions asked. Thus, American grunts helped finance their participation in the war by buying American rucksacks (or "rucks") from ARVN soldiers with their own money. Adding insult to injury, many ARVN units in our AO could easily have gotten by with the little rump packs for the short forays they made into the field.

Rear-area soldiers reflected disdain for the grunts by how they treated the personal possessions the grunts left in the rear. Each trooper arrived in country with a full duffel bag and usually some sort of suitcase and an AWOL bag. These contained the soldiers' issue of dress uniforms, and personal items such as tape players, radios, wedding albums, saved love letters, and so forth. The grunts' excess luggage was stored in unguarded tents. Grunts, upon returning to the rear, found duffel bags cut open; locks broken; suitcases, radios and cameras gone; and love letters and photo albums strewn about and tramped into the mud. Still, these long-suffering troopers returned to the jungle and fought to protect the rear. Surely, these grunts were America's best and brightest sons in the ways that count most.

＊

Not wanting to be foolish, I reasoned that in the field it was prudent to not be easily recognized as an officer — a prime target. Consequently, I took pains to enhance survival by looking at myself from the perspective of an enemy sniper: I'd expect an officer to be empty-handed if anyone was, to have distinctive uniform markings, to always have someone nearby with a radio antenna sticking up. Within the bounds of regulations, I did what I could to lower my profile.

Chaplaincy policy required the chaplain insignia to be worn on the helmet — for easy identification by the troops. I reasoned my troops would recognize me after a few days, else I wasn't doing my job. To comply with the insignia-on-helmet policy, I drew a green cross on my green helmet camouflage cover — invisible in good light beyond 10 feet.

The brownish-green Army towel served three important survival functions: It padded pained shoulders under rucksack straps; it sopped sweat from my brow so I could distinguish between friend and enemy, and it hid my officer insignia from hostile eyes.

As added camouflage, I usually carried a pick or shovel, later, when many platoons began humping (carrying) these tools to augment individual entrenching tools. This practice relieved a grunt of the extra weight, while it allowed me to avoid standing out as the only man in a column with empty hands.

Initially I questioned whether these self-defense methods increased the odds of someone else catching a bullet meant for me. *No*, I reasoned, *an experienced sniper will allow any number of soldiers to pass while he waits for a leader or someone with an antenna sprouting from his back. An inexperienced sniper will probably fire on point elements, before I even come into sight.*

In combat I was relieved, temporarily, of a problem that plagued me since the age of 12 — a tendency to gain weight. Here in combat, for the first time in my youth and adult life, I lost weight without dieting, heavy exercise or a combination of the two, and I did this while subsisting mostly on high-calorie Army C-rations. This serendipitous blessing I attributed to heightened body metabolism that was brought on by living continually on the thin edge between life and death, in a sphere of existence found only in close, personal combat. It certainly was not due to running, which activity would have gotten me shot by one side or the other. Now, back to the action.

✳

On December 29, Lillywhite and I flew to the village of Nha Tuo near the coast east of LZ Hammond. Alpha Company, commanded by Captain Yon, had remained behind after the Battalion Combat Trains moved northwest of LZ Hammond to LZ Santa. Alpha Company continued daytime patrols and night ambushes, with almost no contact during the days leading up to and right after Christmas. Conditions were about to change.

It was another welcome sunny day when I landed and introduced myself to Captain Yon. Yon, a Catholic, was in his late twenties or early thirties, old for a company commander in Vietnam. His background was in Special Forces and Military Intelligence — he was getting his chance at a combat command, and he was very good at his profession. I'd hardly finished introducing myself when a patrol came up on the horn — called in on the radio. The patrol had just been fired on by an unknown size force and suffered three friendly casualties. Pfc. Robert Petrimoulx died of gunshot wound

(GSW) to the chest, and Sp4 Joseph Terrel and Pfc. Terrence Bishop were shot in the left arm and right hand, respectively. The enemy had immediately broken contact and headed into the nearby hills.

Captain Yon, obviously affected and frustrated, ordered most of the company to "saddle up" and moved out to try to overtake or block the enemy element. This time, I decided to go along and not ask. Still uncertain of the kind of reception my presence would receive, I took a position toward the rear of the two-column reaction force.

Frank Yon led the reaction force almost at a run to the north for about a mile. Then, while Yon coordinated with the patrol, I visited troopers as I moved forward in the column and met Sp4 Kenneth Steel. Steel carried an M-14 rifle, though most of the men carried the lighter M-16 assault rifle because of its advantages in close-up fire-fights. Steel and a few others carried the M-14 because with its greater effective killing range and heavier punch, it filled a gap between the M-16 assault rifle and M-60 machine gun. Of course, a few men carried Light Anti-tank Weapons (LAW) for "busting" bunkers or shotguns loaded with buckshot or slugs. Steel was a very likable, open young man who seemed mismatched with his weapon. He and I became close during the last months of his short life.

After the delay, during which I'd worked my way to the forward half of the column, we moved into the hills in pursuit of the elusive VC. Chasing the VC like this was futile, but I understood why Captain Yon had to try.

Pretty soon I knew Yon had spotted me and half-expected him to accuse me of burdening his troops with the extra risk of protecting me. However, Yon surprised me by assuring me that the troops were grateful for my company and that I would always be welcome. "Your voluntary presence works wonders for morale and morals," he said.

*

On December 30, Helga's birthday, Lillywhite and I met Sergeant Ralph Jensen, a grunt from Idaho, one of two LDS men in the 3rd Platoon of Alpha Company. Jensen's humorous grin and down-to-earth attention to his duties made it hard to tell at first glance just how serious he was about his faith. He was the only grunt I knew who refused to use an air mattress, no matter how muddy, rocky, cold or wet he became. He could sleep anywhere, not that he was inclined to do so at inappropriate moments.

*

Lillywhite and I spent most of December 30 with the 3rd Platoon of Alpha Company. There we remained on full alert throughout the night because 200 VC were reported to be within two klicks of the platoon in ambush position.

We were told a temporary truce was in effect for New Year's Eve, and didn't care for the idea. Troops in the field commonly believed these frequent cease-fires gave the enemy opportunities to get in better position and condition to do them harm. According to reports we received in the battalion, an NVA regiment had used the Christmas truce to move into position to Attack LZ Bird, which it did the following night and cost us dearly in life and blood. It was understood at battalion and below that we would engage the enemy if the enemy acted in any way hostile toward us, truce or no truce. Thus, in practice, if the VC bumped into our security patrols and ambushes, the fight was on.

Back at LZ Hammond, on New Year's Eve, we happily found our tent and laundry dry. Unhappily, there was no mail from Helga. I spent a lot of the past two days yearning to be with and hold Helga in my arms. Already, I was nearing the mid-point in my tour, the preferred time for a six-day R and R with Helga in Hawaii.

*

To begin the New Year, the year I would go home, I had my most discouraging experience. At 0930 hours I conducted a worship service for an Artillery battery. Just two men attended, which wasn't the discouraging part. To that point, I assumed music was essential in every service. Trouble was, I neither sang, played a musical instrument nor even hummed in tune. Well, for the first time, no one present could help me with the music, and my efforts to lead in singing were a total failure. I left the service after it was finished convinced I could never go through such an experience again, and very much doubted I had what it took to be a chaplain.

For the rest of the day I wrestled with discouragement and prayed for strength. By day's end I understood I could have services and influence men toward God without music. I felt spiritually assured I would never again feel so discouraged, provided I remained adaptable, ever ready to take advantage of available talent and willing to dispense with music, if necessary. The next day I remounted the *bucking horse,* so to speak, by conducting a worship service, a very successful one, and I resolved to obtain taped music from home to augment my services. My worship services went much better from then on.

*

Around New Years several grunts developed a very painful condition simular to immersion foot, in consequence of being constantly wet. The troopers with bad feet were evacuated to the battalion field trains area at LZ Hammond for treatment and recuperation. Soon afterward, the battalion AO shifted to the Crow's Foot region — so named because of the pattern of a network of rivers and valleys — in the rugged mountains west of LZ Bird and the 506 Valley.

Our mission was to search out and engage the NVA regiment that had overrun LZ Bird on my birthday. I first learned of the operation from several barefoot grunts that waited at LZ Hammond for flights to the field. The Battalion Commander was committing them to provide perimeter security on one of three LZs we would open in the Crows Foot area — LZs Ho, Chi and Minh. The battalion TOC and attached artillery battery would be on LZ Minh.

✳

About 0929 hours January 4, I combat assaulted from LZ Hammond with A Company, the lead assault element. A few minutes later, we leaped from the choppers onto a ridgeline to open LZ Minh. My helicopter, about the fifth one in the combat assault gaggle, hovered in above tall elephant grass. The prop wash from the chopper flattened the grass in waving patterns outward in all directions from beneath it.

Standing on the landing skid of the hovering chopper, I hesitated a moment, estimated the distance to the ground, picked what I thought was a soft landing spot, and jumped, expecting to drop three to five feet onto a soft mattress of grass. To my surprise, I fell about 10 feet and impacted with my right hip on a protruding rock. Naturally, I came to a sudden stop, but inertia, my body and 40 pounds of gear tried to drive my right hip into the stone.

A sharp pain shot down my leg and spread throughout the hip area. I struggled to my feet and went limping about the business of helping check out and clear the area for the battalion main party. Over the next few hours the pain subsided into heavy numbness and I shrugged the incident off. After all, I was young and used to bruising. The pain gave way to soreness, then to tenderness and finally faded away as my tour drew to an end, leaving only a lingering numbness, in my big toe — which numbness hampered my gait for about two years. I wouldn't suspect my injury was more serious until I returned to the states and started running again, and even then I never immediately connected my problem to this injury — more on that later.

The rain was falling hard when we jumped onto the hilltop, as it had for days and would continue to do all day. A barrage of mixed artillery shells — high explosive and white phosphorus — had burst all about the hill just before we arrived. Immediately, my senses were assaulted by the nauseating, distinct, unpleasant stench of mingled white phosphorus and traumatized vegetation. Of all the remembered smells of war, the aroma of white phosphorus and vegetation mixed with human blood and flesh is the most vivid.

Enemy action against LZ Minh during the short time it was open consisted of just three incoming mortar rounds, all of which exploded outside the perimeter. Exposed as Minh was, it would have been much easier for the NVA to attack than LZ Bird had been and harder to support with artillery from other bases and LZs. However, the enemy forces were inconvenienced because they were deprived of a holiday cease-fire during which they could move up attack forces around LZ Minh.

✳

Late on an overcast, wet afternoon I stood by the battalion TOC on LZ Minh in company with a visiting general and several officers. The commander of the artillery battery on the LZ, to show his stuff for the general, called a fire mission — two HE shells from LZ Bird — onto some vacant huts in the valley below us. The huts were on a direct line between LZ Bird and us.

Moments later we heard the radioed message from LZ Bird. "On the way, wait," meaning the two artillery rounds were in the air. Seconds later a single shell exploded in a bright flash, exactly on target. But before the sound of the explosion reached us, the second shell screeched past some 30 to 50 meters above our heads and exploded some 300 meters behind us — a very close call. The general wasn't impressed. Short rounds kill people.

✳

On January 7, 1967, Lillywhite and I visited several wounded troopers in Qui Nhon. Lillywhite became ill while we were there and was admitted to the hospital. He rejoined me two days later, just in time to share a memorable, quite unusual small-unit action, and to become infected with malaria.

Chapter Notes:

17, December (Military Index) KIAs, 506 Valley Battle: Sgt. Cesar Bryant, Deland, A/1-9 Cav [unit, when shown, comes from G-1 Journal]: Pfc. Richard Lee Carothers, Franklin, TN; Sp4 Howard Chisholm, A/1-12; Sgt. William Donald Cook Jr., San Jose, CA; 1LT Chester Garvis Cox, Lawrenceburg, KY; Cpl. Jack Joe Deaton, Indianapolis, IN; Pfc. Michael Earl Dent, C/1-12, Evansville, IN; PSgt. Willie Lee Earnest, Sunflower, Miss; Sp4 Dennis Keith, Erdos, Athens, OH; Sfc. Ellis Casiano Espinosa, A/1-12, Chicago, IL; Pfc. Timothy David Ewing [Dwing in G-1 Journal], D/1-12, Exeter, CA; Sgt. Antonio Garcia, Chicago, IL; Sgt. Jesse Yutze Gomez, C/1-8, Tempe, AZ; SSGT Julius Greathouse Jr., Corpus Christi, TX; Pfc. Eddie Dean Hollandsworth, Big Spring, TX; Pfc. John Elia Horn, A/1-9, Honolulu, HI; Pfc. Arnold Melvin, Hull, Oak Hill, NY; Sp4 Ronald Joe Johnson [Donald in G-1 Journal], A/1-9, Santa Cruz, CA; Cpl. Alton Ray Kennedy, Norfolk, VA; PSgt. Donald J. Leemhuis, Clinton, OK; Sp4 Joe Lee Lemon, Guy, Aakansas; Pfc. Angel Rafael, Luna, D/1-12, New York, NY; Pfc. Charles Henr McClennahan, New York, NY; Sp4 Henry J. Nelson, New Haven, CN; Pfc. Raymond Dennis Olzak [Obyak in G-1 Journal, where listed as MIA], Pittsburg, PA; PSgt. Roque Perpetua Jr., A/1-12, Kauia, HI; Pfc. Harry Turner Poland, Tompkinsville, KY; Pfc. Kennedy Eugene Schultz, D/1-9, Creve Doeur, IL; Sgt. Stephen Joseph Szijjarto, Wamego, KS; Pfc. Reginald Michael Thomas, Chicago, IL; Pfc. Raymond Delano Torry Jr., New York, NY; Pfc. Jimmy Vasquez [Vasquig in G-1 Journal], D/1-9, Pico Rivera, CA; Sp4 Jack LeRoy Wilbur, D/1-12, Dayton, OH.

Note: Only 11 of the above KIAs and the MIA are listed in the G-1 Journal for 18 Dec. 66, plus Sp4 Mark L. English, US 55838617, B/1-8. Another 56 soldiers from all units are listed as WIA in the same fight.

22 December 1966, Bravo Company casualties, — KIA's: Pfc. Gerald F. Gooden, home town unknown, gunshot wounds (GSW), chest and right arm; Pfc. James S. Hollis of Sacramento, California, GSW head; Pfc. George W. Jones of Los Angeles, GSW head; Pfc. Renold W. Peterson of Minneapolis, GSW neck and right arm and burns; and Sp4 John L. Schmecker of Shelton, Connecticut, GSW chest. WIA's Sp4 Thomas L. Thompson, GSW right thigh; Pfc. Dennis P. O'Brady, GSW chest; and Sp4 Israel V. Martinez, GSW thigh, broken. In addition, three medevac crew members were wounded while attempting to pick up Bravo Company casualties: 1LT Robert Richards, frags in neck; SSG Jack Craichen, frag in arm; and Pfc. James Clifford, frags both arms

27 December (Military Index) KIAs, LZ Bird: Pfc. Samuel Quenton Asher, Milford, OH; Sp4 Freddie Lee Burnette, Durham, NC; Pfc. Anthony

Charles Coffaro, New Brunswick, NJ; Pfc. Alfred Lee Davis, Long Beach, CA; Sp4 Gregory James Fischer, San Bernardino, CA; Pfc. Herbert Aaron Erwin, Jonesville, LA; Pfc. Howard Stanley Goldberg, Saddle Brook, NJ; Pfc. Armand Roy Graham, Long Beach, NY; Sp4 Robert Joe Hardesty, Lafayette, IN; Pfc. Randall Lee Hixson, Chattanooga, TN; SFC Paul Gray Jackson, Fayetteville, NC; Pfc. Richard A. Knaus, Cheektowaga, NY; Cpl. Robert Dennis Lajko, New Boston, MI; Pfc. Donald Herman Lederhaus, Milwaukee, WI; Sgt. Daniel L. Miracle, Williamstown, WV; Pfc. Ronnie Eugene Norris, Greer, SC; Sp4 James E. Nunley, Gary, IN; Pfc. Jerry E. Schmeltz, Chicago, IL; Sp4 Ronald J. Sheehy, Derby, CN; Sgt. Hugh G. Skipper, Paramount, CA; SSgt. Rodney Dale Staton, Guyan, WV; 1LT Jerald D. Wallace, Cisco, TX; Pfc. Roger Duwaine White, Battle Creek, MI; Sp4 Larry Joe Willis, White Heath, IL; Cpl. Roscoe Wright Jr., Wynnewood, OK; Pfc. Ronald Jerome Zitiello, Cleveland, OH.

Note: One source said that some 90 of the 140 soldiers on LZ Bird were killed or wounded. However, Stanton, give the figure as 58 KIAs and 77 WIAs as against 266 NVA KIAs (Anatomy of A Division, p. 89).

29 December 1966, 1540 Hrs: A 2-8 casualties, KIA, Pfc. Robert Petrimoulx; WIA's, Pfc. Terrence Bishop and Sp4 Joseph Terrel — all gunshot wounds.

Chapter 9

Lost Patrol

Early on January 9, Lillywhite returned from the hospital, alleging that he felt fine again, and we flew to Alpha Company, which was operating near the head of a southern valley in the Crow's foot, near a north-running river. We landed in hip-deep water about 300 meters from the company position. We came upon three grunts as we waded toward the CP. One of the grunts, with his back to us, was cursing the situation, generously using divine titles. A grunt whispered, "Watch it, the chaplain." The offending grunt, Pfc. Theodore Lysak, pleaded, "Forgive me, Father."

Recognizing Lysak as a practicing Catholic, I said, without pre-meditation, "My son, do three rosaries, two Hails Mary and stop using God's name in vain."

Though I then confessed I was not a Catholic priest, Lysak assured me it made no difference, and he would obey my instructions. I never heard Lysak curse again, and henceforth he couldn't do enough for me — always trying to carry items for me, besides his gear and heavy M-60 machine gun, to dig my foxhole and so forth.

✳

Minutes later in the CP area, 1st Sergeant James S. Catron invited me along on a patrol. The makeup of the nine-man patrol included Catron, Sergeant Theberge, the Mortar Sergeant and his radioman, Sp4 Kenneth Steel, three other grunts, Lillywhite and me. At 1100 hours, we moved out. Our objective was to reconnoiter — recon — a valley 300 meters to the west, beyond the flooding river, for a better location for a forward operating base (FOB) for the company.

We fell in with Catron's provisional — nonstandard — squad, and headed for the river. Everyone except Catron kept his feet while fording the swift current. About halfway across, Catron lost his footing and the current carried him away. Quickly, I ran down the bank, and leaping into the river below Catron and catching him as he passed, I pulled him to the west shore. Then I retrieved a tactical map — it had floated from Catron's pocket. We continued the mission as if nothing unusual had happened. Nothing had, really, as emergencies are the norm in combat.

A brief recon convinced the sergeants the FOB should stay where it was. But instead of turning back, Catron led us up a mountainside — perhaps to delay re-crossing the frightening river — to search for sign of enemy movement and activity.

Leaving the valley floor, we started up the mountain at the point of its nearest approach to the river, 50 meters southwest of where we'd crossed the river. I wondered, *Is this trip necessary or wise? Why hasn't the mountainside already been reconnoitered? Is this patrol just to test my willingness to share the grunts' life?*

The weather continued rainy, overcast and cold most of the day, which kept us soaked, cold and miserable and hampered recon and navigation. We crossed a well-used north-to-south running trail about two-thirds of the way up the mountain. Because of the heavy rains, any sign of recent usage was washed away, if it were there in the first place. Catron called in a Situation Report — Sitrep — and we moved to the top of the mountain.

There, Catron decided to follow a different route back to the company FOB, and we moved out in single file along a well-used, distinct foot path. Several minutes later the clouds broke momentarily and gave us a distant glimpse of a valley and river. Taking advantage of the increased visibility, Catron and Theberge oriented a map with the mountain sides and peaks and the river and valley below — or so they thought. Seeing the scene differently, I opined we were not where Catron and Theberge thought we were, that the valley visible below was not our valley. "You can tell by the pattern of the white water; the river is flowing from our left to right. Our river should flow from our right to our left," I pointed out.

After a moment of hesitation, Catron and Theberge rejected my opinion. "The course of the river is deceptive because it twists and turns so much," said one of them.

"A river has to be mighty crooked to flow upstream," I said, then held my peace.

We continued down the leech-infested trail in the direction the sergeants said we should go, naturally. Soon the clouds closed in again. And leeches attacked us, tiny leeches two or three inches long and only a little thicker than a coarse human hair — until they dined on our blood and swelled to the size of a man's finger. Not only did the leeches come out of the ground whenever we stopped, they even dropped on us from the trees. Frequently we paused and plucked leeches from one another's body and uniform — except that none were picked off me. While everyone else attracted several leeches, I found but one on me and pulled it off my neck before it attached itself to dine. This leech had the dubious distinction of being the only leech I found on my person during two years in Vietnam. According to my theory, leeches, like mosquitoes, prefer warm blood, so the bloodsuckers naturally gravitate toward other bodies, given an option, as my body temperature averages two degrees below normal.

*

Sp4 Kenneth Steel took the point moving down the trail, with his M-14 set on full automatic. As I recollect, the overcast lifted again at about 1400 hours, as we moved northerly past a clearing on the downhill side of the trail. My suspicions were confirmed. We weren't where the sergeants thought we were, for 50 meters below us, two flooding rivers converged, but only one river flowed in the Alpha Company area. I knew for sure that we were near a different valley, one I'd seen before from a different angle. A hill some 600 meters across the valley seemed vaguely familiar. I was on my way forward to discuss our position with Catron, and halfway past the clearing when Steel's M-14 shattered the quiet.

Steel, at the point, had let loose a 20-rounds magazine with one pull of the trigger. Returning bursts of AK-47 fire echoed his fire.

I dashed off the path and stopped in the tree line on the downhill side of the clearing. My reactions were intended to get me out of the open area and to a point where I could provide a lookout on our right flank. Meanwhile, several M-16 rifles joined Steel's M-14, and the AK-47 bursts ceased almost as soon as they began.

Fortunately for us, the enemy ambush was focused downhill — I suppose the NVA squad figured everything up the hill belonged to them, which would account for their having no security to their rear. A fatal mistake.

Steel said he came up on seven NVA soldiers near the trail, all facing downhill, and opened fire the instant one of them spotted him and started swinging a weapon around. He insisted his initial M-14 burst downed two NVA. The evidence supported Steel's word. Several fresh blood trails led from the ambush site, in the direction we needed to go. Days later, a captured, wounded NVA soldier said that two of his comrades were killed and the others all wounded — by Steel's assault.

The sergeants checked their maps, agreed between themselves about where we were, and called in artillery, first round smoke, to clear the area ahead.

"On the way, wait." came over the horn (radio). And we waited. Nothing. Not even the distant sound of a bursting smoke round.

The battalion sent a chopper to search for us near the grid coordinates Theberge provided. Meanwhile, recognition flashed on when a chopper arose from the hill to the northwest, across the valley — LZ Minh, the battalion firebase. After grunts secured my side of the clearing, I went to Catron and Theberge and told them where we were. Again the sergeants rejected my opinion, until events confirmed it, which confirmation we received when we glimpsed the search helicopter above the mountain. It was searching for us on the other side of the mountain and had flicked into sight during a turn.

"We spotted you for a moment above the mountain. Fly north and I'll guide you in by sight," Theberge radioed to the search chopper. Soon help arrived and aerial rockets were clearing our route into the valley.

In defense of Catron and Theberge, I had the navigational advantage on them because their perspective was limited to a ground level, jungle-limited view of the Alpha Company AO, while I frequently saw the bigger AO from the air. Perhaps Catron and Theberge were also handicapped by a stereotype of chaplains, that none could read a tactical map.

We moved out into the valley carrying three AK-47s, two Chinese Communist — chicom — rifles and lots of enemy gear that the NVA had left behind in their hurry to escape Steel's deadly fire. In the valley we followed the river to its juncture with the river we'd crossed that morning. There we turned south toward the Alpha Company FOB.

Just before dark, an Alpha Company platoon got into a firefight and killed two or three NVA right along the route we'd have to pass. That platoon was pulled back to the company ahead of us to preclude our accidentally shooting each other in the darkness. In consequence of the possibilities, I carried a captured weapon the rest of the way, loaded. We waded the last kilometer without further incident and arrived at the FOB well after dark having humped, fought, swam and waded about 15 grueling kilometers since morning.

Arriving at the Alpha Company FOB well after dark, Lillywhite and I found our packs and opted to forgo setting up a rain shelter because we didn't want to violate noise discipline. Instead we each blew an air mattress part way up, folded about a foot of it under so it wouldn't stick out from under the poncho, drove an entrenching tool into the ground between the mattresses, and spread a poncho over both bags. Then we wrapped up in poncho liners and settled down under the driving rain to try to sleep. To capture an illusion of warmth, we placed a single lit candle on the ground between our faces. Lillywhite, showing his toughness and infantryman skills, went promptly to sleep on his left side, his face toward me.

Moments later in the dim light from the candle, I watched a red leech rise out of the ground between our two faces and raise up on its tail like a cobra. After quivering its head toward the candle and me, the leech headed for Lillywhite's nose. For my last heroic act of the day, I killed the leech with a burst of insect repellent, just in time.

The relative importance of our incident in the events of the day was reflected in a battalion journal entry: "Item 27, 1505, A/2-8: Patrol made contact w/ 7 VC, VC BE 735758. VC fled, leaving behind 3 wpns (2 AK-47, 1 Mauser)." Command was more interested in Lillywhite later, after the medics estimated he caught malaria sometime during this eventful day.

*

On Wednesday, January 11, I returned to An Khe to draw pay and attend to personal matters and found I'd been charged for $500 pay I had not received. The error corrected, I drew $450 dollars and returned to LZ Hammond, where a tape from Helga awaited me. After listening to the tape, I recorded my answer and sent it off along with a money order for $398.

*

In early January, the remainder of the First Brigade returned to operate near the relative comfort and light-combat area around the 1st Cav base camp at An Khe. However, the 2-8 Cav stayed in place under the operational control (OPCON) of another brigade. According to unconfirmed rumor, our battalion commander volunteered his battalion to remain in the field so he could acquire more glory for himself. Mysteriously, our malaria infection rate shot upward.

One cold, dismal morning, the battalion commander asked me, in effect, "Why do the men let themselves catch malaria? Don't they realize malaria can lead to blackwater fever and permanent brain damage?"

"Yes, sir," I responded. "The troops know that, but they know permanent brain damage from an AK-47 round is much more likely." Tactfully I told the battalion commander some of the men believed he had let them down by volunteering them for another month in a very hostile AO.

Actually, the increase in malaria cases in the battalion — a real threat to a commander's tenure — came too soon after the brigade left us behind for the cause of the malaria to have been the result of lessened loyalty to the commander.

✳

We spent January 12 and 13 with Bravo Company. On Friday the 13th we joined Bravo on an air assault into a blocking position on a hill to the northeast of LZ Minh. The blocking action resulted in nothing, so we swept down a rock- and jungle-choked canyon to the valley floor. Our point element killed two VC during the descent. Back in the valley, we had a worship service and spent the night without foxholes in an abandoned hamlet among dead palm trees. The area had been defoliated to deny concealment to the enemy.

✳

On January 14, I learned a school-trained chaplain assistant was being assigned to me. This was sad news for me but good for David Lillywhite; he would return to the relative safety of the R&U detail at An Khe. After receiving this message, I escorted Lillywhite to An Khe, where I stayed to attend church meetings with him the next day. At the airfield Sunday afternoon I cooled my heels for four wet, cold hours awaiting a flight to LZ Hammond. This allowed me plenty of time to consider how I would miss Lillywhite's spiritual strength, courage, savvy of the field, and comradeship.

✳

Meanwhile, Alpha Company continued to operate in high mountains among rain-laden clouds and skilled enemy snipers. The company AO was somewhere east of LZ Hammond between the Crow's Foot to the north and Happy Valley to the south. Happy Valley had seen many recent battles and heavy 1st Cav casualties.

I finally got a flight to LZ Hammond, and from there I hopped a ride on the resupply chopper to Alpha Company. Upon reaching our destination, the chopper landed in a clearing on a rugged hillside where a platoon of infantry secured the LZ.

A high-powered rifle shot rang out as I leaped from the chopper. A grunt fell wounded about 30 feet from me. Ignoring the threat, we hurriedly loaded the WIA on the chopper, leaving his wound for the chopper crew to treat en route to the 15th Med.

At the FOB, Captain Frank Yon requested an immediate worship service. The men were very edgy and frustrated because of the snipers. They were eager to worship, to seek spiritual refuge. To deprive the snipers of a large target, I conducted three small services. Almost every man who could attend did attend a service, without regard to his religious preference. During singing in one of the services, done at a whisper, I noted a beautiful voice. It was

Lieutenant Miller, the artillery forward observer. Miller willingly sang a solo during the three services that day and during many services to come.

I was talking with Captain Yon after the services when a burst of M-16 shots shattered the quiet. Yon and I dashed off toward the sound of the shooting and found Sergeant Reese, 1st Platoon. He stood over the bullet-riddled body of a VC. There was no doubt he was VC, for no farmers inhabited these high mountains. Up here it was just them and us. Apparently, the VC snipers were having it rough too, for this one was killed during broad daylight while he rummaged through our garbage.

To clear the trail, Reese and a trooper dragged the body 20 feet from the trail and dumped it. Feeling compassion for the VC and wondering if his loved ones would ever know how he died, I prayed for him and for the troopers. But there was no sympathy in the troopers' eyes, just relief — one less sniper to worry about.

On January 17, I conducted another worship service for Alpha Company, and then left it to deal with the snipers without me. Later at Qui Nhon I purchased a Canon half-frame camera, which I selected for its size and economy. It fit well into an ammo pouch and gave me twice as many shots for each roll of film. Subsequently, I carried the camera encased in one of those plastic bags that PRC-25 radio batteries came in.

Oh yes, Battalion Operations called while I was on the mountain with Alpha Company to remind me I had four prisoners to visit at An Khe — the Mao case. I couldn't put it off any longer.

On January 18, I flew to An Khe via Qui Nhon, but I arrived too late to visit with the prisoners in their CONEX prison. The delay came as a relief because I still had no idea how to go about counseling the prisoners. How could I counsel them and at the same time keep silent about what I knew and avoid legal pitfalls?

*

The visits with the prisoners the next day were as bad as I anticipated, not between the prisoners and me, but within myself. In an attempt to minister to them, I approached each one with the attitude that he was my man and a son of God. I tried to blank from my mind the gruesome details of the crimes they were accused of committing against the young, pregnant Vietnamese woman, Mao. But foreknowledge was a difficult barrier to overcome, made more difficult because the prisoners were upset at chaplains. They'd been informed that the actions of a chaplain had led to their arrests.

Perhaps they assumed their chaplain at the time of the crime, Charles Lockie, had caused them to be arrested and charged. I couldn't tell them otherwise.

All along I had believed another chaplain should counsel these men. Following the visit, I was more convinced than ever that it was a mistake for me to counsel them. But I had no choice, I thought, as I was their unit chaplain.

To rectify my predicament, I convinced the CID agents of the negative aspects of my position and got their permission to break my silence. Immediately I told Captain Vorst everything. He seemed surprised and relieved, not resentful or vindictive. With my part out in the open Vorst confided in me that, upon learning of Sven's allegations he had gone straight to his superior, the same who had since been reassigned to Division Headquarters. This individual had offered to take Vorst with him, but Vorst thought it in his best interest to decline the offer.

Over the next three days I divided my time between visits and services in the field and on LZ Minh. During a field service for Bravo Company, I took pictures of grunts gathered to worship in "Death Valley," the name I gave the place because of the spooky feel of a hamlet of vacant huts and the dead palm trees. I especially remember the night in Death Valley because of a whispered discussion with the company medic, a Seventh-Day Adventist, about the "proper" day for the Sabbath.

*

Word came on January 24 that Dave Lillywhite was in the hospital with malaria. That same day the battalion was ordered to An Khe for green line duty. The next day I returned to An Khe and worked on my office and living area. I wanted to be ready to meet the troops the next day when they arrived from the jungle. My efforts were premature.

The next day the brigade commander ordered my battalion to continue operations where it was. Realizing how down most of the grunts would be feeling, I returned to the field taking with me a new Army hammock. It had an A-frame-shaped rain cover and all-around mosquito netting. I'd never slept in a hammock and would field test it. I hadn't yet gained the respect I would eventually have for bursting mortar shells, how their deadly shrapnel sliced across the ground at just the right height to maim anyone just above the ground — in a hammock, for instance.

Well, with the hammock in my pack, I collected Sp4 Allen

Kirkpatrick, my new school-trained and airborne-qualified chaplain assistant, and rejoined the demoralized troopers of Alpha Company in a valley near LZ Minh. Having run out of food and being unable to receive supplies by air, the company had humped off the mountain for extraction to An Khe and a month of base security. Instead, the company was ordered back up the mountain on foot, a real letdown. Orders to return to the sniper-infested mountain angered the troops, but they grumbled and did their duty.

At 1200 hours, before moving out, we had a company-size worship service (Kirkpatrick's first in the field) with 52 troopers attending. Being concerned that in their discouragement the troops and leaders might become careless, Kirkpatrick and I climbed the mountain with Alpha Company for whatever morale and spiritual support our presence might give. All afternoon we struggled upward through the dripping jungle. We climbed grades so steep we could reach straight out in front and touch the ground. It was so muddy and slick, we made progress only by grabbing onto whatever was available, as we slipped back a foot for every two we advanced. Kirkpatrick became ill from the exertion. He was not in true airborne condition and not acclimated. Fortunately for him, the normally hot weather was cold and damp for his first in-country hump.

Finally at the top of whatever hill we had been ordered to climb, we found punji stakes everywhere — sharpened slithers of bamboo that had been hardened in fire, smeared with human feces and placed in the ground and in pits to impale unwary grunts. A well-used trail came up the hill opposite of where we climbed. Well-concealed enemy fighting positions were placed strategically along the trail. There had been a lot of recent movement through the area.

While the men dug in and Kirkpatrick recuperated, I made the rounds and met Lieutenant Michael E. Berdy for the first time. Berdy, was just beginning his tour in Vietnam. He was about six feet tall with the build of a weight lifter. He had light blond hair and was Jewish. When I first saw Berdy, a West Point graduate, he was engaged in the foolish, all too common error of new lieutenants — trying to set up night positions and ambushes in disregard of the advice of his more experienced platoon sergeant.

I introduced myself to Lieutenant Berdy and asked him to come with me and examine some enemy fighting positions on the trail. Out of earshot of his men, I shared with Berdy some lore about sergeants and lieutenants and suggested he have more respect for his platoon sergeant's experience. I never saw Berdy make the same type of mistake again. Unlike some officers and sergeants, Berdy considered my advice and acted on it without discounting it because it came from a chaplain. This marked him in my eyes as an officer destined for greatness in the Army.

Meanwhile, back on the mountain with Alpha Company on January 25, I cleared away the punji stakes between two trees and set up my new hammock. What a disappointment. First of all, I could lie only on my back in the hammock. Second, I could hardly wiggle. Third, after about half an hour, my knees were locked and on fire from the unusual stress generated by the curvature of an occupied hammock. After an hour, fed up with hammocks, I dropped to the ground, wrapped my poncho liner tight about me and slept the sleep of the restless. I returned the hammock to the supply sergeant the first chance I got. None in the field wanted it.

The morning following my one and only attempt at hammock sleeping, Alpha Company was ordered back to the sniper-infested area it had vacated two days before. All day we humped up and down ridgelines along rain-slicked hillsides, and by evening we came within smelling distance of the decaying VC Sergeant Reese had killed on January 16. There was no sign that other VC had attempted to recover the body, though the snipers took little time making their presence known. The weather broke before dark, allowing choppers to bring in supplies, at which time the snipers recommenced their deadly, demoralizing work. Kirkpatrick missed the excitement, having departed with me on a log bird.

We left Alpha Company intent on visiting troops in the hospitals at Qui Nhon. However, we got stranded at LZ Minh for a cold, clear night, the first moonlit night in months. Perhaps the rainy season was about to let up, I hoped. It was.

On January 27, I flew to An Khe via LZ Hammond, having been unable to catch a flight to Qui Nhon. After showering and changing clothes, I flew on to Qui Nhon to visit Lillywhite, but he'd already been evacuated to Cam Ranh Bay, farther south on the coast.

*

Tragedy struck Brigade Headquarters on January 28. Grunts had killed an NVA officer who had in his possession an ammo box full of official-looking documents. The ammo box eventually arrived at the Brigade TOC at LZ Uplift. There several people gathered around the S-2 (Intelligence) officer as he separated the documents, which were booby trapped. The exploding booby trap killed two people, one of which was probably Vincent J. Weedo Jr. of Hackensack, New Jersey. Chaplain Dowd conducted a memorial service for the booby trap victims, at which I offered a prayer. Following the memorial service, I flew around the AO for four hours with the battalion commander, then to An Khe for the night. The next day I reunited with the LDS troopers and attended meetings. That same day Corporals Donald Yates and Peter Keller were killed in some engagement that Delta Company was involved in.

✳

I learned something about dealing with the news media on January 30. The chaplains had been called to LZ Hammond to meet with General Norton. Also in attendance was a correspondent who allegedly worked for a major American magazine. During the meeting we received encouragement to talk candidly with the reporter because he promised to write about the fine work of the chaplains in combat.

Several chaplains thronged around the reporter and eagerly expounded about their individual duties and philosophies. With two other chaplains, I held back from talking with the reporter. I'd become suspicious because of some of his subtle questions. Events confirmed my suspicions, as it turned out.

The reporter's true intentions would become clear when his piece was published. It focused on perceived conflicts of interest between a chaplain's avocation to God and his serving under a mortal commander — the old "two masters" straw man. The article was but one of a growing number of media attacks on the Army, the fighting soldier and the chaplains who served him. The article quoted, not too accurately, several chaplains who'd eagerly shared their views and philosophies. None of the quotes, misquotes or twists favored chaplains, nor were they complimentary of the service we provided the soldier.

✳

During the meeting with the general and reporter, I arranged for Chaplain Marvin Wasink to provide a communion service for my headquarters element on LZ Hammond. From the meeting I headed for Alpha Company back up into the mountains because snipers were again giving the grunts a hard time. Troopers were being hit daily. One died to snipers on January 27, Pfc. Jose T. Boyless of Taylor, Michigan, I believe.

The chopper dropped from the clouds toward a steep mountainside, flared briefly and came to a hover in a small clearing. The terrain was so steep that with the right landing skid about two feet off the ground, the main rotor blade skimmed within inches of the ground on the uphill side. We made a perfect target for the snipers in the area. Appreciating that fact, the crew chief began pushing supplies out the open door even before the chopper had leveled out and hovered.

Taking the actions of the crew chief as my signal to dismount, I jumped to the ground from the left skid. This caused a sudden shift of balance on the chopper that caught the pilot by surprise. Barely, he avoided overcorrecting, which would have driven the rotor blades into the hillside and into many of the grunts in the clearing. Had the pilot been less skilled, the carnage would have been beyond description. Naturally, I was very grateful for the pilot's skills and because no one was hurt or killed by my tactical error. I was also relieved that no one ever mentioned my mistake, though the look the co-pilot gave me spoke volumes.

*

We loaded the one dead and four wounded (grim testimonials to the effectiveness of disciplined snipers) troopers onto the chopper. A moment later the chopper disappeared into the relative safety of the lowering clouds. Disappearing from the snipers seemed like a good idea, so we hoisted the supplies and moved quickly into heavy foliage in a draw about 40 yards downhill. Under the relative cover of the jungle, we redistributed the C-rations, ammunition and such. Moved up the other side of the draw toward the Alpha Company FOB, some 150 meters east of and higher than the LZ. I was fourth in line as we cautiously moved up a well-defined path. Ahead of me were 1st LT William H. Thompson, his RTO and the point man.

A single high-powered rifle round cracked past our heads when we were about 50 meters from the company position. I saw the muzzle flash of the sniper's weapon and glimpsed the sniper for an instant as he disappeared behind a tree by the path directly ahead of us. Reflexively, our point man sprayed the area with M-16 fire. Thompson joined in with a magazine of his own a split-second later. But it was too late. The sniper had withdrawn, leaving not even a blood drop for our satisfaction.

This gave me but a small sample of what the men of Alpha Company had endured from the moment they returned to this hill. Under constant harassment from snipers, they saw a steadily growing list of friendly casualties and were frustrated over their seeming ineffectual efforts to hurt the enemy in return. Each trooper was vividly aware that at any moment he might feel, rather than hear, a sniper's bullet. Captain Yon had his emotions in tight control, despite his frustrations over a search-and-engage mission that had degenerated into one of trying to find individual snipers before they hurt any more of his men. Understandably, the men were jumpy, and none smiled in greeting.

Throughout my military career, I had heard that the sniper is the most effective weapon on the battlefield and the most destructive of troop morale. The situation seemed to confirm the sniper's effectiveness against morale. The snipers were Montagnard VC, I suspected, because of their American Indian-like stealth and effectiveness. This effectiveness was matched, in my experience, only by sappers.

*

On January 31, following a very wet, cold night, Alpha Company continued defensive operations. This included perimeter defense, small patrols and *counter-sniper* ambushes (I coined the phrase; at least I'd never heard it before). The sniper or snipers kept shooting, but with less success than the day before.

Three different times during the day a sniper round cracked near me — cracked past, not whined like in the movies. Many more shots were fired at other targets.

*

Good and bad news came early on January 31. The good news: Alpha Company was alerted to prepare for pickup and movement to An Khe! The bad news: first Alpha Company had to hump off the mountain because its LZ was too rough for a pickup. Then the bad bad news: higher headquarters cancelled the move of the battalion to An Khe.

Intending to fly out, at about 1800 hours I joined the patrol to secure the LZ so a chopper could bring in hot chow and a scout dog with its handler. We moved onto the hillside LZ, where I'd arrived the day before, as the chopper made its final approach.

The chopper dropped fast and steeply through the overcast sky and came to a hover. We'd barely begun off-loading supplies when a shot rang out. A grunt on security fell wounded, a little below and in front of the chopper. The helicopter took off posthaste without the wounded trooper or passengers and with part of the supplies Alpha Company desperately needed.

We stayed near the LZ until full darkness in case the chopper — any chopper — came for the wounded trooper. Finally, well after dark, a very brave medevac crew snatched out our WIA, despite the darkness, low clouds, worsening weather, and snipers. The medevac chopper dived through the clouds, flared, and hovered. Almost instantly the chopper departed with our wounded. I'd decided to stay with Alpha Company. The night was wet and cold, but quiet.

On May 8, Berdy earned his first purple heart when he and six other Alpha Company troopers were wounded in a firefight. Berdy sustained "frag" wounds to the right eye and both legs. Several months later, almost at the end of his one-year tour, Berdy — a new captain — would take command of one of the companies. Then on 26 December 1967 — still Christmas in the states — he would die while returning with his men from a Bob Hope Show in Qui Nhon. The rotor blades on the Chinook that was transporting them malfunctioned and slashed through the fuselage. Berdy and 11 others were slashed to death by the rotor blades or die in the subsequent crash. Berdy would be one of four 2-8 Cav commanders to die during a two month period in late 1967 and early 1968 — a 100 percent "Killed" ratio for line company commanders in the battalion. Among the troopers killed with Captain Michael E. Berdy of New York City following the 1967 Bob Hope show were Sp4 William H. Campbell III of Burlington, Massachusetts; Sp4 Ronald D. Evans of Cincinnati, Ohio; SSG Allen D. Ford of Pueblo, Colorado; Sp4 Barry S. Kyle of Bradford, Massachusetts; Corporal Bernard F. Poblock of Detroit; Cpl. James L. Russ, Jr. of Youngstown, Ohio; 1LT Thomas M. Van Zandt, hometown unknown; and Sgt. Stephen M. Vuga of Pittsburgh, Pennsylvania.

Jan. 28 1967, D/2-8 Honor Roll, Internet: KIA. Cpl. Donald Francis Yates, Round Lake, New York; Cpl. Peter Joseph Keller Jr. Detroit, MI.

Chapter 10

Close Contact

On February 1, Alpha Company was ordered off the mountain to replace Delta Company in the valley; Delta Company was heading to An Khe. With the scout dog team — the handler and his beautiful German shepherd — in the lead, we moved out at 1015 hours. I joined the lead platoon and took position in the middle of the point squad.

We'd moved no more than 25 meters beyond the FOB perimeter — most of the company was still inside it — when the scout dog alerted the first time. Squads fanned out downhill on both sides of the trail and swept forward. Nothing. We moved another few yards and the dog alerted again. Another sweep with the same negative results.

After we maneuvered through several dog alerts, Captain Yon, under orders to reach the valley during daylight, told the point platoon to disregard further alerting by the dog and keep moving, carefully. So we moved on with the dog's behavior working on our nerves.

"Take 10," we were told, about an hour after we first started moving. We were still within 200 meters of our starting point. About a minute into the break, the platoon leader radioed the point to move out. Captain Yon had countermanded the break order.

Just as I started forward, I saw the dog handler jerk his M-16 45 degrees left and let loose a 20-round magazine. Then, still standing, he grabbed into a pouch for another magazine. Pfc. Martinez, the handler's backup, made a flying tackle and took him to the ground under a hail of AK-47 fire. The beautiful point dog was hit in the left rear hip, but Martinez and the handler were unhurt. Next, the lead squad (sweeping me along with it) dispersed to both sides of the path and swept forward.

A dead VC or NVA officer lay in his own blood, just around the bend from where the handler had opened fire, about 40 feet from the spot where I'd sat for the aborted break. Upon reaching the dead officer, the troopers in the lead squad sprayed the surrounding jungle with M-16 and M-60 machine gun fire. Captain Yon and Lieutenant Miller rushed forward. We in the point element pushed on some 20 meters, past the excellent, wounded scout dog; then we held up for artillery support.

*

We were ordered to hug the ground. Lieutenant Miller had called in a barrage of 8-inch artillery 200 meters to our front. (We were almost out of range of our usual 105mm artillery support.) The 8-inch artillery had longer range and legendary accuracy, not to mention a heavier punch.

Well, this time the artillery was off about 150 meters, due either to the 8-inch tubes' inaccuracy (which I doubt), to the cannoneers' aim, or to Lieutenant Miller's fire control coordinates (which I also doubt). In any event, the incoming artillery exploded in the triple canopy jungle 40 or 50 meters to our front, beyond the crest of our hill. Protected by the little crest, we were shaken and shocked, but otherwise unhurt by the blasts and shrapnel. Fortunately, Lieutenant Miller's frantic call stopped the incoming after the first volley.

Looking back on the scene, I imagined lying there with the earth pounding me in the chest and trying to crawl under my brass belt buckle for overhead protection.

*

Between the brief firefight and the artillery barrage, the dog handler explained what had happened. When the anticipated 10-minute break was interrupted, the dog handler arose with his dog and took about three steps forward into the curve in the trail. There sat five enemy soldiers about 20 feet beyond the curve, also taking a break. The enemy and handler saw each other at the same instant, but the handler reacted a fraction faster and killed the NVA officer. Then as he scrambled for a full magazine, four weapons tracked toward him. *"I'm a dead man!"* the handler thought. And he would have been dead but for Pfc. Martinez's quick thinking. The handler heaped praise on Martinez for his better combat skills and reflexes.

On reflection, I believe the enemy squad had been intentionally "stalking" us from the front, perhaps to delay our movement or withdrawal from the area. I think the VC accurately interpreted our obvious preparations for a break and decided to have one of their own — a fatal error on their part. Before we moved out, I noticed the dead officer's right ear was missing. I was saddened for the dead and for whoever had desecrated his remains.

*

We continued humping and sliding down the mountain without further enemy interference. We were leaving the snipers behind, the anticipation of which was dampened by neither the rain and mud, nor our aching and chafed shoulders and backs; I carried more than 40 pounds, about half of what most grunts carried.

By 1830 hours we were in place to relieve Delta Company. Our first order of business was to fill our canteens from a stream that flowed through the valley from the north. The floodwaters had receded and the water was crystal clear. Of course, we added water purification tablets to our canteens. Despite being constantly soaked, we'd been hard pressed for drinking water. Most of us waited the required 15 minutes before sating thirsts and soothing parched mouths and throats.

I spent the night at LZ Hammond and got to An Khe the next morning, ready for operations in a quieter AO, I hoped. Alpha Company joined the battalion at base camp a day or so later.

∗

During the move from the jungle to the base-camp perimeter, one of my companies was hit by yet another of the all-to-common tragedies of war. Still in the jungle, a platoon leader, upon receiving word we were going to An Khe, foolishly formed his platoon into formation to inspect the grunts' appearance. The matter would have ended there, but just then a machine gunner in another platoon, hidden from the formation by light ground vegetation, succeeded in clearing a jammed machine gun. Several of the grunts in the formation fell wounded, friendly "casualties of war."

∗

Beginning February 2, I entered what was probably the quietest 20 days of this tour in Vietnam, excepting the first 83 days. Best of all, battalion casualties were low for the whole period.

I enjoyed attending LDS services at Camp Radcliff two weeks in a row and had fun some days patrolling the vast base-camp perimeter on an unreliable two-wheel scooter or tote goat. Another time I visited Lillywhite in the hospital at Cam Ranh Bay. He was better and in high spirits.

∗

During a lighter moment the afternoon of February 17, Lieutenant Frazer of Delta Company challenged me to show my skills with my "camera." This occurred at one of the bridges being defended by Delta Company along Highway 19 between An Khe and the Mang Yang Pass to the west.

"What shall I use for a target?" I asked.

"I'll walk down the road 10 feet, and you use me for a target, ha-ha. Nobody can hit anything with that damn thing," answered Frazer.

"Okay, but let me zero in on something else first."

So a sergeant paced off 50 meters and placed an empty 90-recoil-less casing on the stump of a burned-out tree.

Casually, I raised the .45, left-handed, pointed and fired, all in a single, seeming nonstop movement. Frazer and the troopers were impressed. Calmly, I said to Frazer, "I'm ready. Pace off 10." Frazer declined to pace, and I declined to repeat the performance. I, too, had been impressed by my *lucky* shot.

At evening chow, the adjutant informed me I had been put in for a Bronze Star for Valor for an action in January — the recommendation would get lost. Oh well, my actions hadn't rated a hero's medal, anyhow.

*

At base camp the grunts, after five uninterrupted months in jungle and paddies, spent each day filling sandbags and patrolling beyond the perimeter. They spent each night guarding the perimeter or on ambush beyond it. Base security, though it was generally safer, offered little rest for the grunts.

During this period I attended an LDS Conference at Nha Trang, along with 15 troopers from the 1st Cav. I spoke during the conference, as did Sp4 Paul Moody, a grunt from a 7th Cav battalion. We received inspiring talks and counsel by Keith Garner, head of the Southern Far East Mission, and Colonel Rojsa, the leader of LDS personnel in the III Corps area of Vietnam. Master Sergeant Fanoimoana, with whom I had served briefly at Fort Ord, California, led the music.

My pleasure in the conference was lessened when Fanoimoana informed me Captain Stephen A. Childers of Alton, Illinois, a friend from the recent Fort Ord days, had been killed when he hesitated to fire on a VC who shielded himself behind a child. More sad news awaited me the next day back at Camp Radcliff. Pfc. Gerald W. Gannon of Poughkeepsie, New York, had been killed during my absence.

*

An old Army saying goes like this, referring to breaks: Take 10. Expect five. Get two and a half. Well, the saying applied to our promised one-month break.

On February 21 we headed back to the field, this time a few klicks (kilometers) farther north to the Bong Son Plain and surrounding mountains and coastal areas. LZ Hammond was closing down. The new battalion forward base would be on LZ English, a klick or two north of the town of Bong Son.

*

At LZ English, I set up a tent for temporary accommodations and sandbagged around it. Then I put Kirkpatrick to work constructing a more weather- and shrapnel-proof hooch of sand-filled ammo boxes — good thing for him, too, as events would prove.

On February 23 I linked with Bravo Company in our new AO on the Bong Son Plain where we would operate for most of the remaining six-plus months of my tour. The company AO was generally flat with palm tree-shaded hamlets dispersed on raised plats of ground among underwater rice paddies. Late in the day, the company split its AO into sectors for platoon-size operations. I joined the platoon. The first night we patrolled. Night patrol was a rare tactic for American infantry units.

Moving in three columns through a rice paddy, we spotted, fired at and chased two shadowy figures. The enemy had been moving casually along a rice paddy dike, mistakenly confident the night belonged to them.

While some troops chased the two VC, the platoon leader, medic, RTOs and I dropped behind the rice-paddy dike we had been moving on, and just in time. We were barely behind the dike when enemy machine-gun fire commenced raking it. Simultaneously or perhaps a moment after, nine dark forms rose from a position about 30 meters to our south and fled to the northwest, straight into a Bravo Company OP. The troopers on the OP killed one VC and wounded at least one other. We made it through the night without friendly casualties. *Welcome back to the war.*

Sometime after midnight, we moved into a hamlet and set up a platoon-size ambush. I waited in the predawn behind the stump of a long-dead giant tree, cold and clammy in the morning dew and air.

At 0530 hours, February 24, we moved out toward the Company CP. Minutes later, as we started around the outskirts of a hamlet along our route, I spotted and called attention to three dark figures fleeing across our front from the hamlet. The grunts opened fire, but the shadows escaped, possibly unhurt.

About noon, in company with the second platoon, I rejoined the rest of Bravo Company. From there I flew to An Khe, met with attorneys concerning the Mao case and drew some pay.

*

On February 25 Delta Company troopers, while securing LZ Santana, cornered four VC in a cave that was snuggled so close to the LZ that artillery could not reach it. Two VC were captured immediately and one was killed as he tried to flee. A fourth VC, deeper in the cave, refused to come out. A trooper crawled in as far as he could and "was able to reach him only by knife. Knew Cong wasn't dead as he kept emitting cries ... Several .45 cal. rounds finally killed him," wrote 1st Lieutenant Nathaniel Ward in his personal journal.

To get the dead VC out, Ward wrote, the men tied a rope to his feet, threaded it over a tree limb, hoisted the body up, and left it hanging until a 1-9 Cav scout spotted it from the air. Lt. Col. John C. Dashiell chewed out the platoon leader, and a squad was sent back to take down the hanging remains, said Ward.

Meanwhile, that day or the next I arranged a six-day (only five nights) Hawaiian relaxation and recuperation (R&R) leave for Helga and me. The Armed Services were committed to giving an R&R to every American military member in Vietnam during each one-year tour. Many married soldiers opted for R&R with their wives in Hawaii, as opposed to exotic places of easy access to prostitutes like Bangkok, Kuala Lampur, Hong Kong, Japan and even Brisbane, Australia.

On February 27 I visited hospitals in Qui Nhon, where I purchased an airplane ticket for Helga to come to Hawaii. I arrived back at LZ English at 2200 hours. Back in the battalion AO, things heated up while I was in Qui Nhon.

*

Upon arriving at the battalion late in the day, I learned it was engaged in heavy combat. A platoon of Delta Company had met heavy resistance as it attempted to enter a village. The situation had developed rapidly and the whole battalion was involved. Bravo Company had already sustained one killed and several wounded, and Charlie Company three or four friendly KIA and 9 WIA.

Upon learning of the battle, I immediately visited our wounded grunts at the 15th Medical Clearing Company, and the dead at the Graves Registration point, next door. Following these ministrations, I tried until just before dawn the next day to catch a flight to Bravo or Charlie Company, which supposedly had an NVA force of about 300 surrounded in a hamlet. Lt. Ward wrote in his journal that during the wee hours of the morning one of his squads reported seeing a small element of NVA sneaking from the village. Thinking smartly, the squad leader let the NVA pass, assuming it to be an enemy recon team seeking an exfiltration route for a larger body of NVA. "Squad leader allowed recon team to pass [back in]. … When the VC started back out, it was merely a matter of killing them as they filed past. Excellent thinking. … I probably would have fired on the first figure I saw," wrote Ward.

Lt. Ward wrote of his troops during this engagement: "My soldiers have more guts and strength than I could ever conceive. They are unhesitant and brave beyond belief. Some of our U.S. 'citizens' should actually witness them work."

*

Just after dawn February 28, I reached Charlie Company on the cordon line, at the south side of the village. Shortly after that we entered An Do. Though fighting had ended in the hamlet, the scars of battle were all about. An elderly man poked through the ashes of a hut, probably for personal valuables or the remains of family members — which, I wondered. Meanwhile, the artillery continued to pound a larger village about 200 meters north of us.

At 0745 hours Charlie Company was ordered to back off into the open rice paddies so more artillery could be placed on the village north of An Do — An Noy, I think it was. Moments later, a combination of naval gun and 8-inch field artillery shells nearly drowned out the 105mm and 155mm explosions, which had been continual for several hours. I took advantage of the wait to move along the line of troops and visit some very weary grunts and leaders.

The artillery stopped at exactly 0900 hours and Bravo Company assaulted, sweeping on line from the west across a large rice paddy. From my vantage point in the Charlie Company blocking position, I saw the muzzle flashes from the Bravo Company grunts' weapons as they advanced into enemy fire amid geysers of water being kicked up around them by return fire. No trooper faltered or lagged behind his place in the assault line — each marched ahead as if he were unaware of the enemy small-arms fire cracking about him. Bravo Company would take heavy casualties during the assault, I feared — it didn't.

Coming into the village behind Bravo Company I saw five dead NVA, each missing a right ear. I also saw a dead man and woman, whom I assumed were husband and wife. The body parts of several children were strewn about, none large enough to tell which body it belonged to.

We searched the village through the early afternoon for intelligence, enemy equipment and bodies. At 1330 hours my troops cornered a small element of VC and killed one. They captured two wounded and promptly killed them.

Officially Companies B and C sustained seven friendlies killed and 10 wounded. Alpha Company sustained two KIAs after it arrived to search and secure the larger village (actually two villages divided by a deep, heavily vegetated streambed).

*

The Alpha Company CP settled along the south bank of the riverbed, between the two villages. A few minutes later, an NVA sniper round fired from the south riverbank caught Kenneth Steel under the chin, killing him instantly. The shot came from below, from the riverbank he had been standing on. Steel fell back and a medic, probably Sp4 Peter P. Malacznik of Los Angeles, scrambled to his aid — too late. A moment later, two chicom grenades sailed upward from below and landed by Steel. One of them hit the foot of the medic who was trying to treat him. Both grenades were duds.

Lieutenant Thompson (the same who had escorted me among the snipers back in January) went after the sniper, backed by Sp4 Herbert A. Fralix. The two sneaked down into the riverbed at a point several meters to the east and worked their way toward the sniper's hiding place on the bank. A single shot rang out, followed almost instantly by a burst of M-16 fire. Thompson lay dead, shot through the head from above. The NVA also lay dead, his body mangled by fire from Fralix's weapon.

Pfc. Kenneth L. Steel of Fremont, Nebraska, was the first trooper I got to know in Alpha Company. It was he who thwarted the NVA ambush back on January 9.

Before leaving the village, I stood where Steel fell, and there I grieved and prayed for Steel, for 1st LT William H. Thompson of Belleville, Illinois, and for all who fell that day, on both sides.

*

Someone awakened me with a low whisper at 0200 hours on March 1. A Delta Company squad on ambush had sustained five friendly wounded and two killed — seven out of eight men — when it was counter-ambushed.

A few minutes later at the 15th Med I saw to the dead, Sgt. William Hopkins and Cpl. Robert Johnson, and to the wounded, one whose large left thigh muscle was torn loose above the knee and peeled back over his abdomen, looking just like a good-sized prime roast awaiting the pot.

I accompanied the wounded to Qui Nhon. There I also visited troopers who had been wounded during the previous two nights and the day before.

Writing of the counter-ambush action the next day, Lt. Ward described what happened this way: "Engineers had scooped out positions for the perimeter guard. ... About midnight I awoke to...tracers pouring into the engineer command post. ... I crawled to the CP when I heard the cries from the wounded out beyond the perimeter — one of our ambushes had been hit. ... The patrol [ambush] leader panicked...ran back through our positions. ... It's amazing that he wasn't killed trying to cross back in. ... He suffered a head wound. ... We had communication with someone in the ambush — he was afraid to use his radio for fear of being overheard by the Cong. I could hear the cries over the phone. ... It was imperative to send out a recovery team, and I had an idea the VC were waiting for such foolishness. But there were wounded. ... Thank God my platoon sergeant volunteered — it is difficult to write of the fear one has when men have been killed, and suddenly it's one man's responsibility to direct others — or go himself — out into the unknown darkness to confront a killing opposition. Sergeant Wilson and five others made contact with the ambushed and fortunately encountered no fire. Impossible to move wounded so we secured a landing zone. ... Those eight men hit were torn all up from grenades and rifle fire...tore open heads, back, blew web gear right off of the bodies, ripped off arms and legs. Sickening — one man begged to be killed, and he probably would have been better off ... a buck sergeant due to leave the field in a few days. Yesterday he threatened a suspect with a .45 pistol — I remember thinking how one bad turn someday might deserve another.

"I knelt down by one of the wounded — his knee bent as if resting. The wind blew sand across his face and into his eyes — I brushed away the silent cover and attempted to elicit a response from him. I put my hand behind his head to hold him up...then I realized he was quite dead, for the entire back of his skull had been blown away. Even my shock couldn't prevent the wind from slowly, methodically, drawing cover over his face.

"1 March. This morning we returned to look back over the ambush site. The men had set up in a small patch of sugarcane about 100 meters from the engineer perimeter — not in the area that had been designated. ... Don't know why the patrol leader selected this area — cane provides good concealment but no protection while every movement can be heard. They fell asleep about 2200 hours when the VC began moving in on them ... from three directions ... the men must really have been asleep for enemy didn't crawl along the rows but across them ... exposing themselves over each mound. But knowing how well the Cong can infiltrate undetected. ...

"They had moved to within five meters of the machine-gun position ... only one of the ambushed returned fire. ... Obviously the Cong wasn't aware of the severity of their damage ... three Americans killed and five wounded ... in the background the Buddhist temple. ... Recommend my platoon sergeant be considered for a decoration" (From Lt. Ward's personal journal. pp. 24-26).

Lieutenant Nathaniel Ward's personal journal, which he kept during his almost four months in Delta and Charlie Companies, 2-8 Cav. I quote from it often because his entries often correspond with my own.

March 1, 1967, D/2-8 Honor Roll, Internet: KIAs Sgt. William Burton Jr., Hopkins, SC and Cpl. Robert Edward Johnson, Highland, NY.

Chapter 11

Left Behind in "Indian Country"

At 0900 hours, March 1, back at LZ English, Kirkpatrick and I joined Chaplain (Catholic) Phil Lucid — the same who had pressed 40 dollars into my hand a year before upon graduating from the chaplain basic officer course — for his first trip to the field. Lucid had recently joined the 1st Cav. He was going with us to provide Catholic services to my units.

Before boarding the chopper to fly to the field, I briefed Lucid on a few points of survival and conducting austere religious support operations. Then we flew to Bravo Company, near the scene of the previous two days of fighting.

Instead of getting off at the Bravo Company *location*, my destination, I asked the pilot to fly us to the other company, stand by while I introduced Lucid, and then return Kirkpatrick and me to Bravo Company. He agreed. In 10 minutes or less we were back, feeling confident all was in order, as an infantry company usually took at least 30 minutes to break down supplies and move out.

Upon arriving at the Bravo Company location, Kirkpatrick and I jumped off the chopper into the cloud of dust cast up by the down wash of the chopper rotors. The chopper took off the moment we hit the ground, and the dust quickly settled. That's when we knew we might be in trouble!

This was no longer the Bravo Company location. No friendly, familiar faces greeted us. We'd been dropped in enemy territory — just two of us, in a clearing surrounded by battle-scarred huts and palm trees, where two days of battle had probably left the locals feeling extremely hostile. The clearing we were in joined two others, one which stretched to the southeast and one that angled westward toward the jungle.

"Naked and exposed" hardly describes how I felt. For a moment, amazement distracted me from the immediate danger. How could the chopper pilot have dropped us off without first assuring American forces were still present? But he had, and here we were. It took little imagination to appreciate the dangers we faced.

Between us, we had but two weapons, and one of them usually jammed — a chaplain and his assistant smack in the middle of NVA and VC-infested territory. To make matters worse, we had neither radio nor other means to call for help, nor could we expect to be missed for several days; the commanders and staff didn't keep track of my movements. Several kilometers lay between us and LZ Santana and there was little chance we could evade all the enemy and enemy sympathizer eyes between us and there. There were too many open areas on the plain, and most of what wasn't open was heavily booby-trapped. *We have little chance of avoiding capture or death by any number of means* was my assessment of our situation.

Reflexively, I headed us out of the open toward one of the lines of palm trees leading westward toward the jungle. The jungle, I figured, would be less heavily booby-trapped, and it offered us the best chance of concealing ourselves. In the jungle I could keep us alive, I believed. We could overcome the obstacles and drawbacks, despite the odds against us, ... unless the enemy had us spotted already, or unless an enemy patrol literally stepped on us in our hiding place, unless random friendly harassment and interdiction (H&I) artillery got us, unless a strategic bomb strike blew us up, or unless one of a thousand other vagaries of war worked against us.

Our most urgent need was to avoid immediate death or capture, for the VC and NVA habitually searched American logging sites after the companies vacated them. In this manner, the enemy took advantage of the grunt's tendency to lighten his load by tossing aside an occasional stick of C-4 explosives and the less tasty C-ration items.

Barring the vagaries of war, we would hide in the jungle, I figured, and pray a 1-9 Cav aerial scout patrol spotted us first or that another American unit entered the area. But even these possibilities were fraught with risks. Likely, aerial scouts would appear first. However, being prime targets themselves, feared and hated by the enemy, these aerial scouts tended to shoot first and count bodies when they spotted soldiers in places "friendlies" weren't supposed to be.

And should another ground unit be sent into the area, the area might be prepped first with tube and aerial artillery — which would also be very bad for us. Still, we much preferred these and other risks to being discovered by the enemy. Yes, the situation looked bad, despite the confidence I had in my escape and evasion (E & E) capabilities, untested under fire though they were.

*

While I assessed our situation and moved us toward the jungle, the Bravo Company Commander, Captain Getz, wondered why the supply chopper had returned only to depart the area without making radio contact with him. To be on the safe side, Getz ordered the rear platoon to send a patrol back and investigate, which was very fortunate for us. Also fortunate for us, we were still in the open when the point man of the patrol reached the edge of the clearing. This gave him plenty of time to positively identify us from within the shadows of the jungle.

I've little doubt, based on experience, that the point man would have blown us away had we reached the jungle before he saw us. His natural, proper reaction would have been to blast away at any noise or movement on the company's back trail.

In hindsight, which the Army calls an After Action Review or AAR, several factors combined to almost kill us or see us captured. The Army had no effective doctrine for religious support operations in combat, nothing for the chaplain and assistant to train to. No standard procedures or checks existed to trigger prompt concern for the chaplain and his assistant's whereabouts. Nor did the chaplains have radios or other means of independent communication. Besides these drawbacks, I made matters worse by assuming the pilot would communicate our intentions to Bravo Company and that Bravo Company would remain at the logging site longer than it did. I assumed too much.

✳

After a quiet night in the jungle with Bravo Company, I held a worship service at 0830 hours, March 2; then I humped with the company back to the villages where the fighting had raged February 27 and 28.

Back in the village we received orders to destroy all structures still standing, the coconut log bunkers beside the ashes of former native hooches. A bulldozer was being sling-loaded to us beneath an Army flying crane — the biggest chopper on the battlefield.

While we waited for the dozer, I conducted another worship service for those who couldn't attend the earlier one. Later, during the bunker-razing operation there occurred a touching scene that revealed the complex makeup of the American soldier.

✳

Pfc. Harry E. Kerrpash arrived with his bulldozer and began knocking over bunkers, working northward from the south side of the village. These bunkers were above ground and consisted of an A-frame of coconut logs covered with halved coconut shells, with two or more feet of hard-packed soil over those. The bunkers typi-

103

cally were closed all around except for a crawl-through opening on one end. The almost enclosed bunkers provided adequate protection from all but direct hits by heavy artillery, by bursts directly in front of the tiny entrance, or by near-misses by air-dropped bombs.

Considering the strong enemy resistance we'd met here, destruction of the bunkers seemed a reasonable precaution. The Vietnamese, though, had a different perspective — the bunkers were all they had left.

The demolition operation went smoothly until we came upon two Vietnamese women and several children, lined up in front of a bunker. One of the women cried hysterically as the dozer approached. Our Kit Carson Scout — a former VC — said the woman pleaded for us to spare the bunker because it was all the home the two families had. I suspected the bunker concealed her VC husband or one or more NVA soldiers. The second woman, with a child on her hip, stood stone-faced, as we'd come to expect of the Vietnamese, especially the VC.

Well, Kerrpash, intent on doing his duty, revved his engine threateningly and moved resolutely forward, only to hesitate 20 feet in front of the women and children. After hesitating, Kerrpash inched the dozer blade closer to the civilians, only to stop again. Turning off the dozer engine, Kerrpash dismounted and told the platoon sergeant, "I can't do it. I have children that age."

The platoon sergeant turned the matter over to the lieutenant. The lieutenant called the company commander. Breathing fire, Captain Getz rushed to the scene, but once there, he hesitated to stare at the women and children and declared, "That bunker is one foot outside my company AO. Let it stand."

Next, a grunt approached the bunker with a grenade in hand. The crying woman became hysterical, and "stone-face" even showed alarm, thus convincing me one or more husbands hid in the bunker. The grunt never threw the hand grenade, despite his suspicion that the bunker concealed one or more NVA, foes who had so recently tried to kill him and had killed his buddies, probably with the help of these women.

I held my peace, amazed at the compassion of troops who had lost buddies in the last days and (some of whom) had in the heat of battle probably killed wounded NVA or removed ears from the dead. Now, these same hardened grunts couldn't ignore the crying families, perhaps part of the enemy. Every trooper on the scene admitted, after the fact, that he was convinced an NVA hid inside the bunker. I understood the dozer driver, the captain, and the troops and was relieved at the outcome, but haunted by recollection of Childers' recent death when he hesitated in the face of a VC behind a human shield. I'd see the dozer operator again, in a hospital in Japan.

The two Vietnamese families lined up for pictures. (I'd already taken several of them.) The bulldozer moved on, and the grunts and I took a break in the shade of a palm tree. A few minutes later the stone-faced woman delivered to us two green coconuts (the natives favored green coconuts), opened and ready to eat, a thanks offering, I thought.

*

I spent the night of March 2 with Delta Company, which had sustained two KIAs and five WIAs at 0151 hours. The next morning, after conducting worship services, I returned to LZ English and to the first day in the last 10 without combat — for me, but not my unit.

On March 3, I covered the 15th Medical Clearing Company at LZ English. The day was quiet, so I played chess and discussed matters spiritual with Kirkpatrick and Paul Moody.

*

On March 4 I received orders to testify March 11 in general courts martial in connection with the Mao incident — smack in the middle of my scheduled R&R with Helga. I hurried to An Khe in the highest state of anxiety I'd experienced in a long time. But good things happened there the next day. First, I was excused from appearing in court so I could go on R&R. And second, I took part in the baptism of Sp4 Deloyd (Dee) Bailey.

*

With Boring and Bailey dressed in white cook's clothing, we gathered on the south bank of the cool, deep Song Be River that ran through Camp Radcliff. Lieutenant Scott B. Thereur conducted the service, and Boring baptized Bailey.

After the war, Bailey became a very successful Texas lawyer, published a book on the scriptures, and retired quite wealthy before age 50. In 1994, Helga and I would ride to Arizona with Bailey to attend a funeral for Wayne Boring's son, Wayne.

Chapter 12

Illusion: R&R vs. Reality of War

After a few days of low-intensity combat, I returned to An Khe on March 8 to prepare for R&R. Preparing for R&R brought me in conflict with some despicable rear-area policies.

At Camp Radcliff, I accompanied two grunts to a small Post Exchange (PX). They were also going on R&R. The PX was situated on the inner side of the belt road that circled Division Headquarters and the Golf Course or airfield. We were shopping for ribbons and other items we needed for our uniforms.

An overweight sergeant in clean, pressed jungle fatigues blocked our entrance to the PX. The dialogue went like this, in essence: "What's your unit?" asked the sergeant.

"Second of the Eight," I answered for the group.

"Well, you can't shop here."

"Why not? This is an Army PX, isn't it?"

"You can't shop here because your battalion doesn't help with police call," the sergeant stated, with finality.

I controlled my rising ire and quietly said, "Army PXs are open to ALL soldiers. Our battalion doesn't help with police call because it is out in the jungle fighting. We are coming in, and we shall take what we need. Whether you accept our money is up to you, but it will require at least a general officer to stop us."

Having had my say, we pushed past the sergeant and did our shopping. Meanwhile, the sergeant ran to the rear and cranked up his field telephone to call for reinforcements.

After a few minutes, we went to pay for our selections. The sergeant rang up our purchases and took our military script in scowling silence. I reported this matter to Major Harold E. Iverson, battalion executive officer, but heard no more about it.

Meanwhile, our shopping complications were not over. The PX had few of the items we needed. Perhaps we could do better in town.

*

Accompanied by the same two grunts and Wayne Boring, I headed for the main gate and An Khe. The military policeman at the gate had his own ideas and orders though. He demanded we each show him a condom. I said I didn't have a condom and didn't intend to have one. "Then, by the commanding general's orders, you can't go into town," the MP insisted.

This was too much, coming on top of the incident at the PX. In the same careful voice I'd used on the PX sergeant, I addressed the MP. "Neither Specialist Boring nor I will show a condom. We are not about to have such an item in our personal effects should we be killed. And we are going through the gate. You'll have to shoot us to stop us, either that or get a colonel or general here to order us not to pass."

We passed. I protested the condom policy through command channels, probably to no effect.

❋

I departed An Khe for Cam Ranh Bay on March 9, headed for Hawaii. At 0400 hours, March 10, after 15 hours and a fuel stop on Guam, I was hugging Helga at the Honolulu Airport.

Our five nights and six days in Hawaii were wonderful. After resting and becoming reacquainted for a day and a night at the Fort DeRussy Hotel, we rented a Honda motorbike and toured the Waikiki area. The first evening, we attended an luau at the invitation of the wife of Sergeant Fanoimoana. After the luau we moved into a cabin in Haaula for our remaining four nights.

Our extracurricular activities included attending the temple and church meetings, snorkel fishing at night with a couple we met at the luau, visiting the Polynesian Cultural Center, and shopping. I think we also ate a few meals and took in the movie, *Doctor Zhivago*. Our R&R was marred in only two ways — Helga became ill and required treatment at the Tripler Army Hospital, and time flew as if it were on wings of lightning. Leaving Helga at the airport was harder even than it had been to leave her at home. Parting was such sorrow — nothing sweet about it.

❋

I was dreadfully torn during the return flights to my unit. Part of me flew eastward with my darling Helga while part of me reached anxiously ahead to my grunts in the field. *Which of them died while I was away? How many?*

Of course, given any choice in the matter, I wouldn't have missed R&R with Helga — none in the field would have wanted me to. But the guilt, unreasonable though it was, was very real. One trooper died in my absence — Pfc. Robert L. Van Gieson of Van

108

Nuys, California, gave his life on March 12.

*

I landed at Cam Ranh Bay at 1545 hours on March 17, my mind already adjusted to returning and intent on reaching the field as quickly as possible. But it took until afternoon the next day to reach An Khe via Qui Nhon and Pleiku — each about 45 miles from An Khe, one to the east and the other to the west.

That night, while I worked my way "home," Lt. Ward took his platoon into an ambush position not far from the Buddhist Temple on the Bong Son Plain. "In the distance we saw a group of men collected ... so deployed in pursuit until I realized the threat — they wore the khaki uniforms of the North Vietnamese Regulars. They were ... obviously drawing us into something. ... Decided the wisest course was to move into a defensive perimeter until nightfall. ... After SSgt. Wilson reconned our ambush position, we ... moved into the site by pairs. Set up around an isolated house that was bordered by a natural tree-line defense. Did not dig in for fear of disclosing our location. ... At five minutes after midnight they hit us on four sides. ... Threw it [assault] back and my machine guns finally neutralized their fire after 20 minutes — could have been much longer. ... From time to time we could see the khaki uniforms as they took up new positions. I was sure we would be overrun as the rest of the company was too far away. ... NVA hugged out perimeter knowing they would be safer from artillery. I decided that if it came to being overrun I would bring the HE ... on our position — Wilson agreed ... changed the gun's [M-60's] positions. Moments later they attempted to storm the southern end, only to run directly into a repositioned machine gun. I felt great.

"An artillery round struck dangerously close, showering us with fragments ... scared the hell out of us but the NVA also backed off. Guess they believed we would sacrifice our position for them. ... I had two dead and five wounded. One of the men, Pfc. Michael Neal Johnson, lay there snoring through the entire fight — we kept kicking him trying to wake him up. Later we realized his head wound ... Johnson just kept snoring and never regained consciousness. ... "I called for "dust off" in the midst of the battle because of the seriousness of the wounds ... warned pilot it would be a hot pickup — then it becomes his discretion as whether to go in or not. He sounded so cool and merely requested suppressive fires ... enemy ceased firing until wounded had been evacuated — then resumed firing. Could it have been a gesture of honorable warfare? I feel sick — why must our people die like this? How many more fights can we emerge from? ... As I look back on last night, I see my mistake was ..."

The light NVA company that attacked Ward's platoon sustained six killed and 11 wounded. It had "repeatedly attempted to overrun the position, but heavy fire had forced them back," according to Ward's journal for March 26.

"The enemy backed off in several directions. ... SSgt Bohannen took off with two squads in chase ... I heard a heavy firefight ensue, but sergeant indicated over the radio that he needed no help ... returning several hours later with six VC hamlet guards. ... Sergeant claimed he had dropped approximately 20 suspects fleeing towards Tam Quan. ... Battalion commander wanted accurate body count ... he personally flew over ... no evidence — bodies or footprints — was visible. Either suspect had played dead, carrying off those who were hit, or my sergeant manufactured the kill ... several men said they had personally killed and physically checked the dead. Battalion commander wasn't satisfied ... by now was more than displeased with me. Platoon sergeant gave ... call sign of an observation chopper that had assisted during the chase by scouting overhead ... pilot not only confirmed a count of 18 bodies but indicated that the troops on the ground had employed outstanding tactics.

One of Ward's men had fallen into a punji pit a week earlier but had not been hurt because he fell just right. Moments later a grunt was severely wounded about the face and chest when he tried to pull one of the punji stakes from the pit — booby trapped.

❋

It being Saturday when I reached An Khe, I delayed going forward so I could attend LDS services the next morning, after which I went to LZ English, arriving there at 1520 hours. The good news when I arrived was that none of my companies was engaged in battle. That changed, though, before twilight, and the frequency and intensity of combat and our casualty rates heated way up.

❋

Alpha Company got into a fierce battle minutes after I reached LZ English. During the fight, which continued through the night, the company sustained two friendlies killed and 14 wounded. Delta Company sustained three seriously wounded in a separate action.

At 0230 hours, March 20, I visited the three wounded Delta Company troopers at the 15th Med — they'd been ambushed. At 0730 hours, I returned to the 15th Med and visited three wounded troopers from Alpha Company and one from Bravo Company. I don't recall anything about the Bravo Company action but assume the company was engaged beside Alpha Company.

Finally, at 0830 hours, I got a flight to Alpha Company, which was engaged in an ongoing fight with a strong, tough combined VC and NVA force. A grunt killed a VC just as I joined the CP group. The company was spread out along a steep, muddy bank between two terraced levels of rice paddies. The CP group hunkered behind a berm (mound of protective earth) on the east side of a village.

Captain Yon updated me: his company had been ambushed the evening before as its lead element crossed the berm at the point where we now crouched. Under intense enemy fire, Alpha Company withdrew behind the berm and spread out. Pfc. Donald E. Jones of Kewanee, Illinois, had been left behind, presumed dead.

After the company had pulled back, another trooper was shot in the forehead when he raised his helmet-covered head above the berm, probably in an attempt to see Jones. As Yon briefed me, the dead trooper's bloody helmet lay at my side, a bullet hole centered about an inch above the front brim. I believe but haven't proven that the trooper shot through the helmet was Pfc. James Curran.

At 0930 hours, we assaulted across the berm and into the trees and village on the other side. Light, sporadic, ineffective small-arms fire greeted us from deeper in the village — the NVA and VC had exfiltrated the scene, leaving some of their buried dead and a few well-concealed snipers to delay us. They left Jones, too.

Pfc. Jones was dead. He had been disemboweled, mutilated and killed within 30 feet of the berm, a little to the left from Captain Yon's position. Thousand-meter stares and taut faces bore solemn witness to Yon and Jones's buddies' haunted, grieving souls.

At 1400 hours, an M-79 grenade wounded Pfc. Jonnie Nickerson in the leg. The grenade was one of our duds. Nickerson was treated at the 15th Med and returned to duty.

Meanwhile, after Alpha Company searched the area where it had fought all night, we patrolled westward to a hill about two klicks distance. On the hillside, with security measures attended to, I conducted a worship service. The troopers were very attentive and quiet, more in-drawn than usual. It would require time for them to shake off the memory of Jones' treatment at the hand of the enemy. *Heavenly Father, please use my words of worship to comfort these men,* I prayed silently.

*

The morning of March 22 found me still trying to reach either Bravo or Delta Company. Having no success out of LZ English, I flew to LZ Santana, and there I languished the rest of the morning. About noon I got a lift and joined the men of Delta Company, which had spent the morning doing a battle-damage assessment of the village where a fight had occurred the day before. I joined in the search that continued most of the afternoon and included damming a stream so we could search along the banks for normally sub-merged cave and tunnel entrances. The afternoon action included several grunts shooting at and missing an armed VC as he fled from us across a rice paddy.

During the search, I shot the head off a King Cobra with a .45-caliber pistol; the snake had threatened (at least it was a threat) us from the side of the trail. We had a very subdued worship service at twilight.

*

A burst of small-arms fire shocked me into instant wakefulness at 0610 hours the morning of March 23. Two VC or NVA soldiers had stumbled into the Bravo Company perimeter, which was fairly near to Delta company, and paid for it with their lives. The NVA, one of whom had been humping a mortar base plate, came from the direction of nearby LZ Santana, which had been mortared a few hours earlier.

At 1050 hours, still on the 23rd, I held another worship service. Troops came to attend from all over the village. We were very spread out because of the size of the village. A grenade exploded about 10 minutes after the service ended, followed almost immediately by a radioed call for medics.

The company medic and I dashed some 200 yards to the scene of the explosion. Six grunts lay scattered about a 30-foot-diameter clearing — all wounded. Five of the six wounded had been with me in a worship service just minutes before. Moments before, while the troops searched the area, one of them saw a dud 40-mm grenade. It lay near the edge of an approaching grass fire. Reflexively, the trooper kicked the grenade away from the grass fire. The resulting explosion took off half his foot and took out five buddies. One grunt had been searching a depression, bent over with his back to the blast. One of his wounds came close to castrating him.

Lieutenant Ward recorded this incident as follows: "23 March. During the search operation, I ... recalled platoon back to original starting point adjacent to a bridge. Men began collecting, when someone saw a dud grenade round lying in a smoldering fire — remnant of a burned hooch. Fearing the heat would detonate the explosive, he attempted to kick it into the water — the result was six wounded. ... One boy had his toes blown off. ... Another soldier took multiple fragments in the face, chest, and groin."

Though the details differ somewhat, I'm pretty sure Ward and I wrote of the same incident, from our separate perspectives. "Captain McGowen, despite his 13 years of prior enlisted experience and being a great commander, found upon returning from R&R that he had been relieved of command for having too many accidental casualties — the dud incident and others," said Nathaniel Ward.

The crunch of time was hard to fathom. A week before I had been with my sweet wife in Hawaii. This week, while other troopers took my place in Hawaii and pretended Vietnam wasn't real, I sat among my grunts and agonized about Jones' cries of terror, now silent. After three days back in combat, Hawaii seemed the distant, unbelievable fantasy.

*

I accompanied the wounded on the Medevac chopper and did what I could for the Delta Company wounded while we were en route to the 15th Med. The next day I continued to Qui Nhon and visited our men in the hospitals. From there, I went to Nha Trang and met with Major Lord, U.S. Air Force and LDS. He called me to be a member of the LDS leadership for the Central District of Vietnam. Though the call seemed impractical, considering my assignment, I accepted on condition the call wouldn't detract from my battalion duties — in accord with guidance to all LDS chaplains.

*

I rejoined Alpha Company in the early evening because it was again engaged in a prolonged battle and had sustained casualties. My journal is blank for this evening and the next day, but I remember this fight in particular because it occurred on Good Friday, and because of what happened to the mortar sergeant.

Sergeant Theberge had been wounded earlier in the day and evacuated. A sniper had shot him in the back of the head, the shot passing through a light-colored bottle of insect repellant on the back of his helmet. Theberge returned to duty a few days later with his head swathed in white gauze — even better markings for an enemy sharpshooter.

*

That morning, moving from the helicopter after it dropped me off, I headed to the company CP. In passing, I asked Pfc. Smith, Smitty, a slender black soldier from St. Louis, to sing a solo in the worship service I intended to conduct as soon as conditions allowed, likely after nightfall.

Later, right after dark, those who wanted to and could do so gathered to worship near the center of the FOB. I commenced the service, held at a whisper, and at the appropriate moment I announced Smitty's solo. Strained silence met this announcement, and then from the dark came, "Chaplain, Smitty was Medevaced, shot in the stomach."

Smitty had grasped a buddy's M-16 to help the buddy up a muddy bank, and the weapon discharged accidentally. Smitty's former girlfriend wrote me sometime later. She said Smitty collapsed and fell dead while he danced with her, a month after he was released from the hospital.

Easter morning I joined with Chaplain Dowd, to provide concurrent Catholic and general worship services to all elements of my battalion. An ABC television crew accompanied us to film Chaplain Dowd in action for a television special, *The Combat Chaplain*. A helicopter was at our disposal for the whole day, as we were supposed to be in an Easter cease-fire.

Beginning at LZ Santana and going from company to company, we celebrated Easter, conducting services concurrently, usually within 50 feet of each other. The services were strikingly dissimilar.

Chaplain Dowd's masses, even in the field, were formal and traditional, with bright-colored alb and other priestly garments. My services, on the other hand, were informal and included more singing.

Before our third set of services, the television crew prepared to film my congregation. "We'll shoot your congregation singing and splice it into a mass to improve the show," the camera operator explained — a little journalistic license there.

This is a good point at which to insert a special note about my congregations' singing during Easter services. In each service we sang *The Battle Hymn of the Republic,* which in those days contained the phrase "as He died to make men holy, let us die to make men free." We changed this to "let us live to make men free," which set well with young men in the jaws of death. More recent LDS hymnbooks also read "live to make men free." Did we start something?

＊

Our final joint Easter services occurred almost astride of Highway 1, the main north-south thoroughfare in Vietnam — a pitted asphalt road hardly wide enough for the jeeps to pass each other. After those final services, the reporter prevailed on the company commander to send out a mock patrol so he could film it *coming in,* for inclusion in the television special. A platoon leader drafted me to lead the patrol. "So they can see a real combat chaplain," he said. I accepted the honor, but took care to conceal my chaplain insignia from the camera. Chaplain Dowd went along with the ruse.

Lt. Ward's journal, diagram, 18 Mar. 1967: "2 KIAs, Woodall; 2 WIAs, Johnson and Schmidt, (Ward's RTO).

D/2-8 "Honor Roll," Internet: 18 Mar. 1967: KIA Pfc. Ralph Traylor Woodall Jr., Jesup, Georgia; Pfc. Michael Neal Johnson, Breutwood, MD.

Note: Lt. Ward says five of his men were killed in the action, and three others besides Woodall and Johnson are listed in the U.S. Army Casualty Information System as having died: Pfc. Michael E. McNeal, Sp4 Clayton Middleton and John H. Willis. Only Johnson and Woodall's name appear on a page in Ward's Platoon leader memo book, and both names are scratched out.

Chapter 13

Hard Core VC

On March 27 or 28, I was with Charlie Company two klicks from the sea and three klicks from a small peninsula that jutted out into the sea. From our hilltop we saw that the peninsula was about 25 meters wide where it connected with the mainland, 100 meters long and the same distance wide. It rose from sea level at the beach to about 20 to 25 meters high near its point. The jut of land ended in a cliff. The cliff extended half the length of the peninsula on each side.

About midafternoon a platoon chased and cornered a squad of armed VC on the peninsula. The platoon leader quickly deployed a squad to block off escape from the peninsula, and with the other squads he searched the peninsula. Nothing. The VC had disappeared, as it were, into thin air.

I accompanied another platoon to the peninsula and helped search for the VC. After an afternoon of turning over rocks, probing crevices, poking in every bit of vegetation, we concluded there must be a hidden cave entrance below the water line. Sure enough, near dark the lowering tide revealed a cave entrance on the southeast side, under a high cliff.

To reach the suspicious opening, we shimmied 12 feet down a crevice in the rock. Yes, it was a cave, with two side-by-side entrances, both partially concealed by an almost flat, slanted, 10-foot-wide rock.

Probing the darkness of the opening, we saw two areas of sandy bottom, above which were small ledges that slanted upwards and out of sight. Turning off the flashlights, we settled to wait. I spent part of the evening hours visiting in whispers with troopers in blocking positions. Just before midnight I descended quietly down the crevice and joined the lieutenant and men on watch before the openings.

Exactly at midnight, responding to some instinct or skill I could not detect, two troopers turned on their flashlights and focused their beams into two parts of the cave. Each beam illuminated a right foot. The feet were simultaneously, tentatively descending into the water from some place above and 10 feet in from the entrances.

Instantly, two right feet and ankles were shattered by bursts from four or five M-16 rifles. The two shattered appendages froze in place, dangling in the seawater. Neither wounded leg was withdrawn from exposure to more shots. For 45 minutes the mangled feet were immobile; then a foot descended beside the foot on our left, and a woman of about 30 years dropped slowly into the beam of the flashlights.

We quickly bandaged her mangled foot and ankle, and she joined the Kit Carson Scout in another 45 minutes of pleading for the other wounded VC (her husband) to surrender and receive medical attention. Then the VC couple and scout took another half hour to coax four more VC from the cave.

With six enemy prisoners in hand, we began moving them to the beach for evacuation to the rear, wounded first. I climbed up the crevice and, reaching down, helped hoist up the wounded VC male, whom I passed off to two troopers who were designated to carry him across the face of the cliff to the beach. As I turned back to the crevice to help with the female, I heard a whispered "We'll slip and drop him halfway across." Swinging around, I ordered the troopers to surrender the VC to me (I don't think the two had realized who I was in the darkness) and to keep the female safe until I returned for her.

Fortunately, the cliff face slanted away from the abyss just enough to allow me to cross the ledge upright, with one hand against the cliff for balance. So with my left arm under the VC's legs and his left arm around my right shoulder, I crept across the cliff and placed him in the care of the troopers on the beach. Then I carried the female across. By then emotions seemed to have yielded to compassion.

On the beach I went to my knees, still holding the female VC in my arms. So far, she had remained stone faced and stiff as wood, cooperating only enough to allow me to carry her across the cliff.

To ease the wounded POWs' pain, the medic injected the male with morphine, but he seemed flustered about where to inject the female — not wishing to expose her body, perhaps because I was there. I helped the medic over his problem by pulling her black "pajamas" uniform top down over her right shoulder. The medic administered morphine to the woman just as the helicopter made its final approach to pick up the prisoners of war. The chopper swept in and hovered to a landing about 20 feet behind us, with its whirling rotor blades driving beach sand at us like a million stinging needles.

To protect the woman and her wounds from the blasting sand, I shielded her with my own body. Her hard core demeanor melted. The tension slipped from her body, and she cuddled her head willingly against my chest. I felt a momentary connection with the VC woman, a moment when kindness overcame her fears and hard core antagonism toward American soldiers, her deadly enemies.

*

Easier or not, April came, as all things do, given enough time. The first two weeks of April were very busy, though my unit engaged in fewer firefights and battles than in the previous month. On April 3, I worked with tanks for the first time and was not impressed.

At some level of command, it was decided we needed armor on the Bong Son Plain, so a battalion of tanks and armored personnel carriers of the 4th Infantry Division joined us. On April 3, accompanied by Chaplain Lucid, I joined Alpha Company for its first combat operation with tanks, a flop. Someone failed to give weather and terrain enough consideration. The rainy monsoon had recently ended, and the paddies and lowlands were still soft.

Alpha Company was operating about three klicks northwest of LZ English, just off the Bong Son Plain, behind a mountain ridge that jutted into the plains from the southwest. The lead tank approached our position from the east, crossed a dike into a solid-appearing paddy, and bogged down halfway across.

With the infantry providing a defensive perimeter, we spent the afternoon watching tank after tank bog down as they tried to extract the lead tank and then one another. Last of all, a tank retriever arrived; it got stuck, too. The tanks and retriever were still bogged down when I flew away the next morning.

*

Two days later I was again in the field with Alpha Company, this time with Lieutenant Berdy's 2nd Platoon. We were patrolling somewhere on the plains. Kirkpatrick was with me. To cover more ground, we dropped our rucksacks (I had a civilian one from home) in the company FOB. The action of the day was light — occasional sniper shots and light resistance as we entered a hamlet, with no casualties on either side. At one point we came upon a pagoda (a Buddhist religious structure) that had been riddled with gunfire and shrapnel, in front of which I took pictures of Kirkpatrick, grunts, and Lieutenant Berdy (my last picture of him).

Moving on, we came upon an armed VC who fired on us and fled toward the heavy foliage along a riverbank to the northeast. The crew of an Aerial Rocket Artillery (ARA) helicopter came on our frequency and volunteered to help. Hoping to avoid friendly casualties when we searched for the VC, we marked our position with smoke and Berdy directed the proffered ARA support into the foliage along the riverbank to our east. Already in a picture-taking mood, I squatted by a palm tree ready to snap shots of the rockets as they left the tubes and of the explosions when they hit 200 yards from our position. Not too smart.

The ARA ship attacked from south to north, diving from about 2000-foot altitude. Timing my shots carefully, I snapped a picture as the rockets left their tubes on each side of the chopper. The shot snapped, I swung left while I advanced the film and snapped the rockets the instant they exploded. The last shot, though, was by reflex, not good timing; the rockets exploded 70 meters from us, not the 200-meter distance we expected. We escaped injury from the shrapnel that screeched by and rained down among us.

*

Night was almost upon us when Berdy's platoon finished its futile search for the VC along the riverbank. The decision was made for the platoon to stay the night in the area where we were, rather than shoulder the risks involved in moving through VC-infested country in the night to rejoin the company. So we settled in until full darkness; then, discretion being the better part, we moved to a new position, where we shivered away the night without poncho liners.

*

On April 6 at An Khe, I suffered temporary shock at the "blatant" behavior of a fellow chaplain and friend, Jack Keene. Keene was assigned to the 1-12 Cav, the battalion that took such heavy casualties before and after Christmas.

Keene's office was on the north end of a long building that had been intended for troop billets originally, though troops seldom saw the place. His office faced east, and an inside door led to his sleeping area. A curtain of macaroni-like beads screened his cot from the office.

Smiling, I dropped in on Keene and stopped dead in my tracks. A pair of dainty feet, obviously female, protruded beneath the beaded curtain. Now, such behavior as I suspected I would expect from many soldiers and officers, but not from Jack — a married man and chaplain.

After having his fun at my expense, Keene called the woman out and introduced me to his wife. Mrs. Keene, who had taken U.S. government employment in Thailand during Jack's tour, had wrangled permission to visit her husband in the combat zone, forward-rear area, of course. Jack was quite pleased with himself for the joke he'd played on me and for the surprise visit — hers, not mine.

*

On April 10, accompanied by Catholic chaplains Dowd and Lucid, I for the second time held services for all my companies in one day. Then I made my first visit to the Marine AO in southern I Corps. The 2nd Brigade of the 1st Cav was operating there, with Marines out of LZ Montezuma.

In late March or early April, LDS chaplains, leaders and members in Vietnam were invited to attend a conference in Japan. Hugh B. Brown, a member of the leading council of the LDS Church, and Elder Gordon B. Hinckley would be there.

Undaunted by tradition or policy and with command approval and the Division Chaplain's blessing, I went about getting LDS troopers to the conference. For my part, I had misgivings and mixed emotions about going to Japan. On the one hand I hungered for the spiritual opportunity, but on the other hand I begrudged every moment I was away from my grunts and battalion. Meanwhile, life, death and the war continued.

----

2 Apr. 1967 Honor Roll. D/2-8, Internet: KIA Pfc. Vance George Williams, Dallas,TX.

Chapter 14

Blessed by a Dying Grunt

Sp4 Naylor returned to the field from R&R with his wife in Hawaii. While on patrol, mere hours later, he hit the ground when the point man for his squad tripped a wire and yelled "booby trap!"

"Dud," said the squad leader, rising to his feet after what seemed a safe interval.

Naylor climbed to his feet and, for some reason, turned to face the rear. At that instant, the booby trap — a butterfly bomb — exploded. Naylor fell mortally wounded by a BB-size shrapnel, which entered the nape of his neck.

Rushing to the 15th Medical Battalion Clearing Company at LZ English, I stood by Naylor's head while the medical team fought to save his life. Working without administering anesthetics to Naylor, the medics cut into Naylor's arms inside at the elbows, severed each main artery and inserted IVs. I thought Naylor flinched when the medics cut into his arms.

A few minutes later, with life signs restored and stabilized, the doctors turned to the tiny wound in Naylor's neck, by which time Naylor was paralyzed, his spinal cord severed by shrapnel. Whether paralysis occurred in the field, I don't know.

A day or so later in the hospital I found Naylor suspended, as it were, on a rack, one end of his body connected to the foot of the apparatus and his head, with clamps in his skull, to the other end. This contraption allowed the medics to turn Naylor as if he were on a spit. He was facedown, staring at the floor, when I arrived.

Lying on my back on the floor, I scooted under Naylor. Looking up into his eyes, we visited. With eye movements and labored speech, Naylor struggled to acknowledge my efforts to comfort and reassure him. Soon, I prepared to leave because talking was too difficult for Naylor, and because it hurt so to see him as he was.

"Wait," Naylor gasped out, his eyes wide and beseeching.

I waited. "God ... bless ... you, ... Chaplain ... Newby," Naylor whispered.

I had been blessed before and I've been blessed since, but never did I feel more blessed than when Naylor — the grunt — blessed me.

Word came that Naylor — perhaps Eugene Naylor of Lancaster, Kentucky, though the date of death is wrong — died soon after my visit. His benediction upon me may have been his last words in mortality.

*

Following the visit with Naylor, I hitched flights to English. There, Kirkpatrick joined me and we flew to Bravo Company. Some background is necessary here.

The battalion leaders, with two exceptions, had received me well when I joined them in December 1966. The first sergeant of Headquarters Company was one of the exceptions. He was displeased at having a leg (non-paratrooper) chaplain in his battalion and, worse still, a leg chaplain who couldn't be buffaloed into a whitewall haircut — lots of skin over the ears, in the airborne tradition. Captain David Root was the other exception. Somehow, I thought for years that this individual was Jim Bell, until his XO gave me the correct name; then I remembered.

Captain Root resented my presence because he, an avowed atheist, considered chaplains to be bad for the troops. The first sergeant I could generally ignore and did, as he stayed on LZ Hammond or English, out of my way. Captain Root, I couldn't ignore. Root was the battalion S-3 Air Officer (scheduler of helicopter support), whose cooperation and support were essential to my mission.

Root didn't cooperate. During my first months in the battalion, he frequently, intentionally gave me false information about flight schedules. At first I chalked it up to the vagaries of combat, to hectic support operations, and to variables not in Root's control. My attitude changed the day Root attempted to bump me from a flight so doughnut dollies, Red Cross ladies, could fly someplace. I refused to be bumped, and confronted Captain Root the next time I was at LZ Hammond.

Root responded, "Chaplain Newby, I've been an atheist all my life. As far as I am concerned, you are a bad influence on the troops, and I'm duty-bound to protect them from you. I'll do everything I can to make you miss flights and otherwise hamper your activities."

After thanking Root for being candid, I responded in kind. "I will not be bumped. And if you give me false information about flights or interfere in any other way with religious support, you and I will be standing before the battalion commander." *Is Root a living contradiction of the maxim that there are no atheists in Foxholes?* I wondered. Time would tell.

Chapter 15

A Long, Rough Day

Dave Root had become commander of Bravo Company early in April, I think. Surprisingly, I detected no hint of resentment during my visits to his company. *Perhaps he tolerates me because his men accept me.* The change in Root's attitude, obvious as it was, was nothing compared to what lay ahead.

When Kirkpatrick and I joined Bravo Company on April 14, it was operating with a company of armor that included several M-60 main battle tanks and some thin-skinned Sheridans. That morning the company had sustained two WIAs from sniper fire. This was a long, hard day and prelude to a longer one to follow.

April 15 dawned bright and hot. The first significant event occurred at 0630 hours. "Chieu Hoi," cried a black pajama-clad male as he stepped carefully into the open from a line of palm trees, his hands in the air.

He was Bau, a VC soldier, age sixteen years. After a quick search for weapons, Bau led us into the trees to an American M-16 rifle (we paid any VC who brought a weapon along when he *chieu hoi'd)*, two magazines of ammo and two hand grenades. He said the weapon, ammo and grenades had been there for a month, which I doubted.

Bau, as further proof of his intentions to desert the VC, said he escaped during the previous night by killing 15 VC — eight in My Trung hamlet and seven in My Huong. He would guide us to the dead VC.

At 0940 hours, I arrived with a patrol to the hamlet Bau led us to, about two kilometers northwest of the Bravo Company FOB. There we found five black pajama-clad casualties, mostly women, victims of hand grenade blasts and multiple shrapnel wounds. Bau identified one of the women as the leader of the group and VC political officer. Another was a teacher and another the chief of local rice carriers. I took pictures of the wounded VC. Four of the VC were alive, but in very bad condition.

Naturally, the intelligence people at division were excited about Bau and wanted to visit the scene. So the patrol and I attended Bau's VC casualties while we waited for helicopters to deliver intelligence officers and evacuate them. Soon, most of Bravo Company joined us. After we evacuated the wounded VC, we took blocking positions 200 meters to the west, across draws that ascended westward from the plain and upward on the mountain. Division Intelligence believed a large NVA element was using the draws to withdraw from a just-ended battle.

By then, Bau had been extracted to the rear for more intense interrogation. Apparently he satisfied the intelligence officers at division, for soon he was made a Kit Carson Scout and assigned to Delta Company 2-8. Obviously, the VC knew Bau's deeds and movements. Almost immediately, Bau's name started appearing in captured documents. The VC, it seemed, were tracking Bau's every move, which continued until they got Bau months later.

Back in the field, a few minutes after we took a blocking position near the draw, we saw a pair of hands extend into the air from a clump of bushes 50 meters south of our position. A squad leader approached the bushes and challenged, "Chieu hoi." An NVA sergeant arose and moved slowly into the open, an NVA sergeant who had endured enough.

This enemy prisoner of war was the only result of our blocking operation. After an hour or so, we rejoined the tanks for a sweep to the north. Moving on foot with armor was hot, exhausting and nerve wracking. It required increased, constant vigilance for booby traps and punji pits, combined with the struggle to keep up with tanks. Tank commanders tended to show little appreciation for the grunts' limitations and concerns. During this recon-in-force with the tanks, an incident occurred that lowered my already low esteem for the print media.

*

As we passed through a sandy area dotted here and there by Vietnamese graves, a news photographer asked a tank commander to provide him a photo opportunity by running a tank tread over some graves. The tanker told the reporter what he could do with his camera. He wasn't about to provide a staged demonstration of callous disregard for sacred Vietnamese things.

*

At about noon, after parting ways with the tanks, we patrolled to the south. On the way, as I moved along a trail east of a village, I spied a Vietnamese female who seemed out of place among several civilians who worked in a rice paddy on our right. The lieutenant with whose platoon I moved shrugged off my suspicion.

An hour or so later and farther south, we came under sniper fire from a village on our right. In response, Captain Root positioned a reinforced machine-gun team in a hedgerow just north of the village and then maneuvered the rest of the company around the village and swept it south to north.

At 1605 hours, after we'd swept about halfway through the village, two military-age men dashed from a hooch and fled northward with troopers in hot pursuit. One of the fleeing men ran straight into one of our machine-gun positions. He died in a hail of M-60 machine gun bullets. The other man escaped.

A few minutes later, while Bravo Company waited to move on, I saw the suspicious female I'd seen earlier. This time she was hurrying east along a dike toward a village — very unusual activity for a civilian under these circumstances. I suspected her of tailing us and being a spotter for VC snipers and mortar teams. This time, Captain Root, taking my suspicions seriously, sent a platoon to capture the woman. She escaped.

Next Bravo Company regained the trail, and we moved south another kilometer. There we set up a company FOB and sent out patrols. Sporadic sniper fire continued, but so far no American had been hit. At 1650 hours, 1st Platoon captured a VC suspect. Fifteen minutes later, 2nd Platoon discovered fresh bunkers and foxholes, well concealed and laid out for aggressive action. A green lieutenant who had joined the company that morning found a punji pit the hard way, by falling into it. Amazingly, the lieutenant fell between the stakes without receiving a scratch.

While the lieutenant was *discovering* his first punji pit, 3rd Platoon was attempting to capture a uniformed VC, which the troopers accomplished by shooting and wounding him.

Five minutes later, one of the sergeants in the 3rd Platoon tripped a booby-trap wire as he passed through a hedgerow. The booby trap, a nasty butterfly bomb, was a dud.

After a day like this, Root was certain the enemy knew exactly where we were. Root expected us to be attacked during the night, with good reason. During the last minutes of daylight, he had us going through the motions of preparing an FOB. Then, after full dark, we moved quietly to a vacant hamlet 300 meters south. There we set up for the night, for real.

The hamlet was laid out in an oval pattern, north to south, and surrounded by white sand. Fifty feet north of the hamlet, a heavily vegetated streambed angled past from east-northeast to west-southwest.

In the dark, two light-infantry platoons established the defensive perimeter around the hamlet and the night defensive position (NDP). The platoons also put two-man listening posts out about 50 meters in front of the perimeter, one of them being to the west about 20 feet from the vegetation along the streambed. Meanwhile the last light-infantry platoon prepared to go on ambush, and the mortar platoon planned defensive and offensive fires for the night. What happened next never made it into the battalion journal.

The plan called for the platoon going on ambush to exit the perimeter near the north side, through an element of the platoon guarding the northwest part of the perimeter. After leaving the perimeter, the platoon was to enter the streambed, follow it a kilometer to the west-southwest, and there set an ambush.

As sometimes happens, plans went awry. The lieutenant led his platoon from the perimeter through an element of the wrong platoon, on the northeast. Consequently, those who needed to know never got the word.

Meanwhile, I was recovering from mild shock. Captain Root, the atheist, had asked me to join him on an inspection of the perimeter fighting positions. Root and I had worked along the west perimeter to the southernmost point, when out beyond the northwest perimeter four grenades exploded in rapid succession. The grenade blasts were followed immediately by withering M-16 and machine-gun fire, outgoing from the northwest perimeter. Simultaneously, heavy fire poured into the perimeter from the northwest. Naturally, the troopers on the east side of the perimeter opened fire too — better safe than sorry.

Root and I rushed back to his CP group and radios through the hail of incoming fire, with flying bullets cracking around us as only near misses can, interspersed with bursting grenades.

We reached the CP group unscratched, where within the meager protection offered by a hooch on one side and a bunker on the other, Root quickly sorted the situation out. This was easy to do because all the gunfire sounded distinctly American. "Cease firing!" Root radioed.

Gradually at first and then quickly, the gunfire slackened and ceased, like applause ending in a theater.

"Give me an up on casualties," Root radioed, meaning each element was to report the number and nature of friendly casualties so he could request adequate Medevac support.

By the light of the moon, I watched Root's face as, one by one, the platoons radioed in. "Negative on casualties."

*

Piecing together the chain of events, this is what happened:

"We have heavy movement in the streambed; sounds like a company-size element," came in a whisper over the radio from the two-man listening post. "They're coming right at us! We're throwing grenades and coming in. Give us cover!" The squad nearest the LP, knowing the ambush platoon had not departed the perimeter where it was supposed to, confirmed the frantic message and got ready.

Meanwhile, in the streambed, the members of the ambush platoon were moving quietly westward along the riverbed, past the LP. Suddenly the grunts hit the ground, their hearts in their throats, when the LP's four hand grenades began bouncing off trees.

From the perspective of the men in the streambed, three things happened simultaneously. While the troopers cringed in the midst of bouncing and exploding hand grenades, some saw two shadowy figures rise from the sand and flee eastward, from which direction a withering hail of bullets from automatic weapons suddenly erupted. "VC!" the grunts yelled and opened fire at the fleeing LP. Reflexively, the rest of the platoon opened fire with machine guns, M-16s and M-79 grenade launchers. It had been amid this barrage of cracking bullets and exploding M-79 grenades that Root and I dashed to the CP radios.

The shooting over and no one hurt, Root dropped the radio handset and walked to the other side of a bunker, out of sight of his RTOs. There he dropped to his knees with his forehead on the barrel of his weapon, as though he were about to pray or blow his brains out. Coming around the bunker, this scene greeted me — I'd followed Root out of concern for how he might react.

I kept an eye on Root's trigger finger, which wasn't inside the trigger guard, and waited. While I waited, I wondered which was greater, Root's relief because no one was hurt or killed or his chagrin because with all the shooting, the troops hit nothing.

After what seemed like five minutes, I tentatively placed my right hand on Root's left shoulder and said, "Don't feel too bad, Dave. It's over. Be thankful no one was hurt."

It was a different Dave Root who responded. "Oh, I'm not feeling bad. You know, Chaplain, I've been an atheist all my life, but now I'm beginning to doubt." Root added, "It is your presence which accounts for Bravo Company going through all we did today without sustaining a single friendly casualty." Thus ended April 15, 1967, a long, rough day punctuated by the old question: Are there atheists in foxholes?

Out of the infamous Bataan Death March in World War II came the saying "There are no atheists in foxholes." Well, Root had declared himself an atheist previously. Was he? Are there atheists in foxholes? I suppose so, but it's surely harder to be one there. I never met another soldier who professed to be an atheist in the midst of combat.

That Dave Root's atheism had been shaken, that he believed what he said to me the night of April 15 became evident in the days ahead. From then on, Root was on the horn requesting a visit by One-Niner, my call sign, if more than five days elapsed since my last visit to Bravo Company. And Captain Root started attending worship services when his duties allowed.

✳

The rest of the battalion was busy that long day, too. At 0300 hours, April 15, the troops in Delta Company, which was set up in a grove of palm trees, had gone to full alert upon hearing a series of piercing screams come from a village nearby. While the screaming slowly died away and for the rest of the night, the Delta Company perimeter was probed from all directions. With the dawn, Delta Company moved into the village and found two small children. Someone had cut off their legs and arms and left them to scream away the last pitiful minutes of their short lives (Ward, p. 66).

2-8 Battalion Journal, 15 April 1969, Item 34, 1805: "1755, B 2-8 ... found punji stake pit, well concealed, approx. 2'x2'x2', destroyed."

Chapter 16

Hero Declines a Medal of Honor

In 1967, Air Force Chaplain (Major) Jim Palmer organized an LDS Servicemen conference at Fujiyama, Japan, near Mount Fuji. He invited the LDS soldiers who were in Vietnam to attend.

I left for the conference on April 18, accompanied by seven LDS troopers and my chaplain assistant, Allen Kirkpatrick. At Cam Ranh Bay, Wayne Boring and Kirkpatrick surrendered their R&R seats to troopers who were bumped from the flight to make room for senior officers. We really appreciated them for giving up their seats so others would have this opportunity.

Leaving Boring and Kirkpatrick behind, we departed Cam Ranh Bay at 1730 hours, April 21, and arrived at Camp Zama R&R Center, near Tokyo, Japan, at 2200 hours. By 0200 hours the next morning, I had arranged a bus to take us to Fujiyama. I'd also borrowed civilian pants, a shirt and, most importantly, a sweater — April in Japan was frigid after Vietnam.

We arrived at the Fujiyama Hotel conference site at 0900 hours, where I was assigned a room with Chaplain Arnold T. Ellsworth, my former seminary supervisor.

The conference began at 1000 hours with an invitation to anyone in attendance to speak. Lieutenant Scott B. Thereur, one of those who spoke and the then current An Khe LDS Group Leader, related stories about me and the VC, stories he had heard from men of Charlie Company 2-8, stories I hardly recognized.

I shared the pulpit Sunday morning with one of our two visiting general authorities. Earlier in the day, during a picture-taking opportunity session with majestic Mount Fuji in the background, Elder Hinckley had whispered, "What are you speaking about this morning?"

"Don't know, yet," I replied.

"Share with the conference the story you shared with us in the Brinks Hotel in Saigon," he instructed.

"Yes sir," I answered.

I spoke next to last in the morning session, followed by Elder Hinckley. He took the occasion to again publicly apologize to me for having "doubted" the validity of the military orders calling me into the Army Chaplaincy. Again, he related how the Lord had revealed to him that I was in the chaplaincy, though it was impossible for me to be, because it's what the Lord wanted. Again he concluded with, "which goes to show, what the Lord wants to happen will happen, military regulations notwithstanding."

Hugh B. Brown spoke in the afternoon, and I thrilled at his first-person recounting of the "currant bush" story, a very effective, instructive saga that affected his career in the British military during World War I and changed his life forever.

*

During one session, a Naval officer told of a sailor who tried but failed to attend the conference. The sailor, part of the crew of a river-patrol boat, was coming into base, intent on attending the conference, when a grenade came hurtling into the boat. "Grenade!" someone yelled.

The sailor threw himself onto the grenade. He awakened much later in the hospital to the praise of an Admiral who informed him he was being recommended for the Medal of Honor because he had selflessly thrown himself on the grenade to save his buddies. "But you can't do that, sir. Someone yelled grenade and I hit the deck, in the wrong place," exclaimed the wounded sailor. I salute that unnamed sailor for his courage and honesty. I also salute those parents and leaders who trained him so well in his youth that highly developed moral reflexes overrode false glory.

After lunch I attended the baptism of a Japanese lady. The ordinance took place in the icy waters of the hotel swimming pool. Following her baptism, still dripping water and shivering, the lady asked me through an interpreter to confirm her. This honor I gladly accepted.

Between the conference's conclusion and the flight to Vietnam on April 28, I wandered around Tokyo with Cav troopers, spending one pleasant night with Air Force Chaplain Jim Palmer and his family and another with a Price family. In company with the Prices, I visited with Elder Hinckley in Tokyo for a few more pleasant hours.

On the Ginza I attended a Japanese stage show with an all-male cast, including the female roles. The colors were fantastic. This experience saddened me because I couldn't share it with Helga or the children. Another time troopers Griffin and Clement and I attended the movie *What's Up, Tiger Lilly?* We walked out because of off-color content.

23 April, Ward's journal, with Charlie Company: "set up defenses around a large beautiful home. In one room was a magnificent four poster bed, which I promptly took over. At 2300 hours, an early warning post was grenaded as the enemy took the entire company under fire. ... I smacked the hell out of my eye getting out of bed, got entangled in my mosquito net and couldn't find my boots. ... Should have known they would choose to hit us about the time I got settled in a real four poster."

◗ Bau. Sixteen year-old Bau, a Vietcong soldier, surrendered early in the morning to the troopers of B Company, 2nd Battalion, 8th Cavalry, 1st Cavalry Division. Bau brought in an M-16 weapon and as further proof of his intentions to desert and change sides in the war, he claimed to have killed 15 of his former comrades during the previous night — eight in My Trung hamlet and seven in My Huong. He led us to a village where we found five black pajamas-clad casualties, mostly women, victims of hand grenade blasts and multiple shrapnel wounds. April 15, 1967 on the Bong Son Plain.

▶ Chaplain Newby pauses while on an operation in the jungles of Vietnam with one of his infantry companies.

◀ Chaplain Newby on a firebase beside the bunkered area where he occasionally sleeps and returns to for resupply and to change clothes.

▶ On the occasion when this picture was taken, these troopers of D Company, 2-8 Cav, one of whom is the legendary Sgt. Roy Baumgarner, presented Chaplain Newby with the "Aussie" hat he is wearing. Greenline, An Khe base camp, Central Highlands, Vietnam.

☛ A D/2-8 RTO (radio operator) rests at the base of a hill where a grunt just gave his life and where the next day Sp4 Richard O'Brien of Elmhurst, Illinois would give his foot, east of Bong Son Plain, June 12, 1967.

◀ Unidentified D 2-8 trooper takes a break during search operation among the cliffs along the seashore, east of Bong Son Plain, June 15, 1967.

◀ Sp4 Robiston (Preacher) and Chaplain Newby back in the security of base camp after being ambushed and pinned down along Highway 19 between An Khe and the infamous Mang Yang Pass, Central Highlands, Vietnam, June 23, 1967.

◀ Pfc. Theodore Lysak and grunts of A/2-8 as they wait to air assault into the Song Re Valley area in I Corps, where the company will take heavy casualties, including Lysak. Lysak, a Catholic, tried to be Chaplain Newby's self-appointed protector and servant from the moment they first met in January, 1967. By alternate airstrip at An Khe base camp, August 3, 1967.

▶ Bravo 2-8 troopers departing on combat assualt from which five grunts would not return, near LZ Santa, Dec. 22, 1966.

◀ Chaplain Newby celebrates "Pioneer Day" with fellow LDS soldiers and Preacher at Camp Radcliff, July 24, 1967. Newby is aboard a "bucking bronco" with Sp5 Wayne Boring (of Taylor, Arizona) and Preacher ready to yank on the ropes that will buck him off.

◆ Chaplain Newby receives Air Medal and first Purple Heart in front of his hooch in the 2-8 Cav area at base camp, June 1967.

◆ Sp4 Sonny Youngblood, A/2-8. He escaped the carnage on the Fourth of July only to take a spear or crossbow arrow through the thigh a few days later, which accounts for his happy disposition at a hospital in Qui Nhon, July 1967.

▶ 1st Lt. Thomas Mancini (helmet), A/2-8 with troopers on the Bong Son Plain, about April 1967.

◀ Chaplain Newby following a worship service for part of C/2-8 Cav and minutes before he departed with a platoon to reinforce another platoon that had VC cornered on the seacoast hill in the background, east of Bong Son Plain, March 1967.

▲ Bravo troopers with snake skin, Bong Son Plain.

▶ Lt. Alfred E. Lehman, B/2-8 cooking snake steaks on a makeshift grill before the beginnings of a two-man poncho shelter. The steaks came from a serpent he and his men killed, Bong Son Plain, about May 1967.

◀ Pfc. Michael Daugherty, D/2-8 nurses the ankle he sprained the previous evening while heroically retrieving the body of Pfc. George A. Sutt. After playing dead for an hour or so, he and another grunt moved forward in the twilight to their fallen comrade's body. Then through a hail of bullets they dragged Sutt's body across the open rice paddy from the village in the upper right of the picture, while the NVA soldiers did their very best to kill him. The soldier about to light a cigarette looks like Sp4 Robert Syzmanski who died about ten years later, according to the Veteran's Administration. Chaplain Newby took cover most of the previous night from enemy fire and friendly shrapnel at the base of the tree and bush behind Daugherty. A claymore mine prepared for detonation by the enemy was found in the bush moments after this picture was snapped. May 31, 1967 on the San Bong Plain.

▶ Short-timer Sp4 Boswell (or Breland), A/2-8 being hoisted from an almost dry streambed after accidentally shooting himself in the face and barely missing shooting Newby in the head, in the jungle north-northwest of 1st Cav base camp, Central Highlands, Vietnam, July 4, 1967.

◀ ARVN interpreter with back to camera had just shot a conical hat off the head of the child to make her talk. A few minutes earlier we captured the child's mother, a confirmed VC, but her father escaped. This picture was taken in case the interpreter disregarded dire warnings.

Chaplain Newby before a 1-poncho rain shelter which he shared for the night with Sp4 David Lillywhite of Snowflake, Arizona in the jungle near LZ Santa, northwest of LZ Hammond, December 22, 1966.

The young A/2-8 lieutenant is wearing the helmet that saved his life the previous night when a chicom grenade landed near him. Note the dent in the top of the helmet. The original of this picture is captioned Lt. Mandalak, A/28, but this may be 1st Lt. Richard A. Hostikka; and if it is, then another steel pot saved his life on LZ Pat when an enemy bullet circled his head between helmet and helmet liner. Cav AO, about February 1967.

Lt. Miller, Artillery Forward Observer (center) attached to A/2-8 Cav in sniper-infested mountains, Central Highlands, Vietnam, January 1967. Lt. Miller enriched many of our worship services with a singing voice that was magnificent at any volume.

◀ NVA sergeant moments after he surrendered to 2-8 troopers. Bong Son Plain, April 15, 1967.

◀ B/2-8 troopers gathered for a general Christian worship service in the company night defensive position, Crow's Foot area, Jan. 1967.

◀ Sp4 Robiston (Preacher) kneeling at spot where Boswell shot himself in the head a few minutes earlier. Picture taken from the spot where Chaplain Newby had a near miss from some bullet. Central Highlands, July 4, 1967.

◀ Sp4 Allen Kirkpatrick packed to depart LZ English and the Cav to replace shortage in an airborne unit. LZ English, June 1967.

▲ Aftermath. Elderly native digs through the ashes for belongings or loved ones even as troopers of B/2-8 sweep the village of An Do following a firefight. February 1967.

◀ Montagnard family pauses for pictures as it moves along Hwy 19, Central Highlands, Feb. 1967.

◆ Captain Frank Yon turns over command at A/2-8 to Captain Raymond Bluhm. Atop mountain west of Bong Son Plain, 1967.

◆ Sp4 David Lillywhite, LZ Sands, Dec. 1966.

◀ Lt. Scott Thereur, Sp5 Wayne Boring, Pfc. Deloyd Bailey and Chaplain Newby pose for picture prior to "Dee" Bailey being baptized by Boring. Riverbank at Camp Radcliff, February 1967.

➡ Alpha 2-8 troopers wait for darkness and the arrival of a chinook to evacuate their one dead and 19 wounded who were hit a half hour earlier. Also wounded were Chaplain Newby and a tracker dog. North-northwest of the 1st Cav base camp at An Khe. July 4, 1967.

◀ Deadly waters. Light spots on side of well bear witness to the booby-trapped bucket that killed Pfc. Daniel Nelson an hour earlier. Unidentified grunt is member of D/2-8, Bong Son Plain, May 30, 1967.

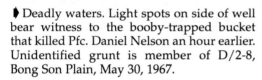

◀ Infantryman at careful rest. The author snapped this picture of an unnamed trooper of C Company, 1st Battalion, 12th Cavalry, 1st Cavalry Division. The trooper naps "at the ready," having air assaulted into the vicinity in the predawn hours to reinforce the unit Chaplain Newby was with. After the picture was snapped, the trooper and his company ground assaulted against the NVA. Six grunts in his company gave their lives in the assault and 16 others fell wounded. Did this trooper's readiness beat the vagaries of war that day? May 31, 1967 on the Bong Son Plain.

Chapter 17

False Promises and Hopes

During a staff meeting sometime near early May, Lt. Col. Dashiell announced, "Because of the 1st Cav's effectiveness, we can expect lighter action and fewer casualties in the Bong Son Plain area. Military intelligence predicts we will see fewer set-place battles, but more enemy antiaircraft fire, and more frequent and fiercer rocket and mortar attacks on our bases." However, contrary to military intelligence expectations, the NVA seemed more determined than ever to maintain their influence on and around the Bong Son Plain.

Soon after the announcement, a company in a sister battalion hit an NVA unit that was holed up in a village on the plain. The American battalion sustained about 28 killed in action. For two days, the NVA held out against continual field and navel artillery and returned fire at whatever came within range of their weapons. NVA resistance ceased only after air strikes turned the village into a maze of shattered trees and overlapping bomb craters. NVA casualties could only be estimated — the bombs rendered an accurate count impossible.

❋

On May 2, I joined Alpha Company atop the first mountain range west of the plains. This would be my next-to-last visit while Frank Yon was in command. Conditions were nicer here than on a different mountain back in January. Here, elephant grass covered large sections of the mountaintop, and punji stakes and snipers were not in evidence.

Under a double-poncho shelter, I spent the night with Sp4 (medic) Peter P. Malacznik and two other members of the company CP group. "Chaplain, I'm uptight with God," declared Malacznik during a spiritual discussion. This slang being new to me, I thought Doc was declaring closeness with God, not anger, which was what he really meant.

❋

Early May 3, a patrol bumped into an NVA unit, but the enemy retreated after a short firefight, with the Americans in pursuit attempting to maintain contact. Meanwhile, the rest of Alpha Company air assaulted beyond the contact area to entrap — fix —

the NVA and force a battle. But the NVA, choosing not to be fixed and fought, disappeared down-slope into the jungle. Later, back at the FOB, I conducted two worship services.

∗

At 1130 hours, May 4, a booby trap wounded Pfc. Buddy Smith of Charlie Company. The VC had rigged a booby trap using a C-ration can, fishing line and a cartridge. The device, when Smith triggered it, sent a bullet through both his legs and blasted fragments into his face.

On May 8, I was back with Alpha Company. In the afternoon we air assaulted from the mountain into a rice paddy on the plains, at which point I left to visit hospitals in Qui Nhon. After I departed, Yon moved his CP into a nearby village, intent on taking advantage of the shade. At about 1800 hours, a booby trap wounded Malacznik and five others. Someone told me Malacznik lost a foot — goodbye Los Angeles police career. The other wounded were 1st Lt Michael Berdy, right eye and both legs; SSG Tony McCray, right leg; Pfc. James Loftis, chest and abdomen; Sp4 Ronald Guy, chest and right leg; and Sp4 Harry K. Stackhouse Jr., right hand. Among the wounded were the other two grunts with which Malacznik and I shared shelter the night of May 3.

Minutes later, a second booby trap took off the foot of a lieutenant. Yon, fearing more booby-trap casualties, moved the company FOB into the rice paddy for the night. About twilight the troopers, having dug in, began knocking down shocks of rice straw to clear their fields of fire. A trooper in the CP knocked over a shock of straw located in the center of the perimeter and out slithered several very upset king cobras. Though the troopers killed eight of the deadly serpents in the fading daylight, they feared some had escaped. The men were especially restless that night. Sp4 Fralix said his squad killed two of the cobras. A trooper told me he was so scared that he stood all night on one foot atop his helmet (an exaggeration, of course).

∗

Meanwhile, Kirkpatrick and I were with Charlie Company on a bare plateau of red clay a few meters southwest of the paddies and villages on the plains. We had received sniper fire as we moved into our night position. At 2030 hours, I saw a flash of light on the mountain, about 300 meters to our southwest. Seconds later an M-79 grenade exploded on the mound of dirt before a machine-gun position, also on the southeast side. No one was hurt. I thought the M-79 round had come from where I saw the light on the hillside, but the troopers returned fire in a different direction — shooting probably at the sound of the firing launcher, which sound I missed.

*

The VC and ARVN forces, according to common belief, kept hostilities out of the port city of Qui Nhon because both Vietnamese forces used the city for R&R. Whether the *common knowledge* was true, I knew not. However, to my knowledge, Qui Nhon was attacked only once during my tour of duty, and I just happened to be in town for the occasion.

The attack on May 9 wasn't much as attacks go, but I'd never have guessed it by how those rear-echelon folks responded. At the 85th Evacuation Hospital, sirens were blasting, lights were turned off, and people were running excitedly in all directions, like in the movies. I chuckled at the sight of a sergeant (I learned his rank later) running about, clad only in boxer shorts, pistol belt and helmet, waving a .45-caliber pistol and shouting orders at no one in particular.

*

On May 10 I tried to call Helga via the MARS system. No luck. I spent the night of May 12 on ambush with Alpha Company. For the next few days I visited troopers, held services, accompanied large patrols, and hopped from company to company. Come to think of it, hostilities did taper off some in May. Even so, besides those mentioned elsewhere, Alpha, Bravo and Charlie Companies each sustained at least one friendly KIA and several WIAs. Delta Company amassed several casualties too, in addition to those at the end of the month.

*

On May 16 Charlie Company began taking serious sniper fire from a ridge simultaneously with a number of grenades incoming from close up. Battalion ordered the company extracted — it was working near the coast in support of American Marines and an ARVN unit. Ward's platoon secured a PZ.

While artillery suppressed sniper fire from the high ground, aerial rockets and machine-gun fire were called in to suppress the enemy, which was near enough to toss grenades. 1st Lt Ward, who had transferred from Delta Company, described what happened next: "The gunships flying escort raced over first with the outside door gunners firing wide open. The fools skillfully managed to strafe the entire length of two sides of the LZ ... don't know how many men they wounded. ... Fire [enemy] became more accurate as Cong must have been firing from maximum range and began moving closer. Directed two ARA ships in. ... Company commander took his CP out in the initial lift — such a brave leader. Second lift made their approach from the east as others had taken hits from the north ... supporting gunships got excited again ... ship on southern flank came in low and fast. His first rocket went over our position and low into the village we had departed. There was a pause, the ship's nose dipped and I saw the second round strike directly on line but short of our perimeter. Something reacted within telling me to run away (perpendicular to his sheath.) ... The concussion from the third rocket lifted me off the ground throwing me forward into a hole. The blast kept me down until the second lift had passed on ... dirt and dust filled the air with the sickening smell of the explosion. My radioman was lying on the ground where I had been standing. Blood was gushing from his nose and mouth. The rest of the men hit must have lain down but the rocket came in right on top of them — they had no cover. Tried to see if my RTO was alive as Sgt. Draper helped drag him to the waiting helicopter as the third lift came in for my platoon. I tried to keep his head from hitting a rock — all the while dragging his radio. The metal [shrapnel] had severed his handset, blowing away his ear and the side of his head. I ran back to police up what weapons I could. By now intense fire was coming in ... only hope the other dead and wounded were loaded ... in the air I suddenly realized my RTO might be alive as his mouth was moving — he was choking on his blood. Hung his head across me so as to drain the blood away and stuffed the hole in his head with a large compress. ... Final count was four killed and eight wounded. ... Sickening feeling as I remember the flash, heat and blast. ... All I could do was keep running away — impossible to warn anyone else. ... The RTO who was killed by the friendly rocket fire, was a nice, clean Christian kid who said his prayers every day. That death I will never understand. ... That's three RTOs in three months ... just learned my RTO died on the operating table — what else can I write to his parents?" (Ward's journal, pp. 84-86).

*

I returned to An Khe on May 20 to prepare for a conference in Nha Trang the next day. There I met eight replacements, all going to my battalion. We nine discussed religion and spiritual matters until 0300 hours the next morning.

With 31 men I departed An Khe on a CV-2 Caribou at 0730 hours. Two men had stayed behind because there was no more space on the plane. Had I not been in charge of the group, I would have given up my seat on the airplane.

*

At 0900 hours I sat in a leadership meeting with Elder Marion D. Hanks. I spoke in the conference, as did Sp4 Paul Moody, Keith Garner (an ecclesiastical leader stationed in Hong Kong) and Elder Hanks. The gist of my talk was spiritual booby traps. Later at lunch, Elder Hanks questioned me in a friendly and encouraging manner about my experiences, and a lifelong friendship that had begun months earlier grew from the occasion. At 1930 hours I attended an LDS meeting at An Khe.

*

By reading my journal one might assume all was quiet on the Bong Son front between May 22 and 29. Tell that to Lieutenant Nathaniel Ward and Sergeant Oscar Draper of Charlie Company. Ward lost his foot to a mine on May 22. The same mine wounded Draper in the back. From Ward's journal, "Early this morning ... Mission ... Combat assault consisted of 46 ships — the largest one [combat assault] I've witnessed ... landed in tall grass ... in the center of my area and overlooking the ocean were a series of large rocks — natural lookout points. One of my men was crawling up the western face on a most difficult path. Seeing a somewhat natural path of rocks, I started out, leaping from rock to rock. There was a blast, confusion, blackness, nothingness and suddenly awareness. My first thought was that a mortar round had landed nearby, and I felt a multitude of sharp pains all over. Suddenly the stench of cordite and explosive penetrated, and I looked at my right foot only to see it wasn't. Instead I saw a splintered stump of bone, burned flesh and torn pants where a boot had once been. The realization was 'instamatic,' and I believe I accepted it at once. Immediately I began to feel myself over — to stick my fingers through the gaping absence in the palm of my left hand. Foolishly I tried to rise, unable to move my left leg which I could feel was shattered. ... I laid back. ... The thoughts of my army career, my wife, running, my traumatic loss, my life. ... Far away I could hear the Medevac chopper slowly approaching, working its way in to me. It had been a laborious four months only to discover a land mine at seven in the morning" (Wards journal pp. 88-89). Ward signed off his last journal entry, "Good Morning Vietnam," because he was wounded in the morning.

Retelling the story to me in 1997, Ward said, "I made a little run, intent on springing onto a large boulder to check it out. Apparently, I was almost in the air, reaching with my left foot, when a mine exploded beneath my right foot. The first thing I thought, as I lay there, much of my right leg gone and my left leg and hand mangled, was *how am I going to run marathons now?* Draper, who had been wounded on May 16, was hit by the same blast that got Ward.

Ward stayed on active duty for several years, then became an attorney and made several trips back to Vietnam. Later he said that he'd been informed that a command-detonated 105mm artillary round had gotten him and that the enemy blew up that hill that day.

In the life-is-stranger-than-fiction catagory, Ward, who spent two years of his youth in Indochina, said he was stranded in 1960 by a temporarily misplaced car key on the same little hill on which he lost his foot in 1967, and he had been at the hill during a nicer time in company with his sister and her friend.

About 0130 hours the next day, May 23, an enemy mortar killed Pfc. Clifford E. Kelsey and wounded Sgt. Albert C. Smith, Sp4 Harry M. Winnie, and Privates first class Kenneth Westmoreland and L. D. White, all of Charlie Company. Later the same day Sp4 John McGuthrey of Alpha Company fell from a chopper and broke his arm, and a mine wounded Pfc. Vincent K. Zummo of Delta Company — so went a quiet day in the battalion.

*

Alpha Company was again on the mountaintop west of the plain. After I joined the company, we swept down the east side of the mountain, under extremely hot and humid conditions. On the way, we discovered a VC medical aid station. The station was dug into the hillside.

In the heat, our water went fast. Fortunately we found a stagnant puddle of water near the bottom of the mountain, from which we filled our canteens with high-protein water — lots of microbes, polliwogs and such. Of course, we killed the little critters using water purification pills before consuming them.

A chopper came in the midafternoon laden with mermite cans full of hot food and cool liquids, plus essential supplies, of course. While the mermac cans were being lined up, I backed off into the trees on the south side of the clearing to wait until the enlisted men were all fed, and to take advantage of the shade.

From my position across the clearing I could see that three of the cans contained something very cold, ice tea as I later discovered.

Obviously those cans would be most welcome to the grunts.

One by one the troopers filed from the trees, keeping about 15 feet between themselves. Eventually, Sergeant Ralph Jensen appeared in the chow line — he didn't know I was with the company.

Well, I watched Jensen approach the last three cans, the cold ones, with a food-laden paper plate in one hand and an empty canteen cup in the other. At each can, he paused, looked in and moved on. Finally, Jensen hooked the empty canteen cup on his belt and disappeared into the trees. No doubt he washed his chow down with tepid, high-protein ditch water while watching his squad members down liquid so cold it formed condensation on their cups.

Jensen made me proud the way he obeyed the health code of his faith, even in these circumstances. Perhaps his behavior with the tea was no big deal to non-LDS folks — and to some LDS, those who called him foolish for passing up ice-tea under the extreme circumstances we were in. But in my eyes Jensen, far from being foolish, was a giant of faith.

By the way, Ralph Jensen had spent a month in hospitals in Japan since I first met him, recovering from being shot in the lower back and buttock by a helicopter door gunner.

*

May 29 was but the first of three very rough days, especially for Delta Company. I joined with Delta company at about noon, conducted a worship service and started mingling and visiting. A trooper, Neil K. Thomas, borrowed an Army field hymnal to learn songs so he could recall them for spiritual strength. I complimented Thomas for his spiritual maturity.

We set up for another night on the plain, with OPs all about and hunter-killer teams operating to our east. These teams, being free to move about a specified area, differed from ambushes. Ambushes stayed in place and covered a point within an area. Full darkness was barely upon us when the observation posts and hunter-killer teams began hearing movement on all sides. We went to full alert.

Reports of movement around our positions continued for an hour or so, but no attacks came. Then a hunter-killer team reported 15 to 20 enemy coming toward its position. Each member of the hunter-killer, on signal, tossed two grenades, fired a magazine of M-16 rounds, and dashed toward the nearest OP, assuming the OP was alerted to the arrival of incoming friendlies. But a trooper on the OP, out of fear, confusion, or because he didn't get the word, blew a claymore mine when the herd of shadowy figures came charging out of the night. Amazingly, the blast or hail of steel balls injured none of the team.

Reports of movement continued to come in, so we remained on full alert until dawn to the accompaniment of bursting artillery and the flickering light of parachute flares. For a first-time experience, I stood a watch in the night with a starlight scope and was quite impressed with how clear objects appeared its pale green glow.

We swept the area around the FOB at dawn on May 30 and found but a blood trail where our ambush had fired on a single VC during the night. No bodies, nothing to account for all the noises in the night. At 1040 hours, Delta Company air assaulted to an area south of LZ English. We met no resistance, so I remained on the chopper and returned to English and to mail from Helga.

Meanwhile, at 1206 hours one of the Delta Company squads, led by Sgt. Robert M. Eason, sustained six WIAs from an explosion, probably a claymore mine. Eason himself was wounded in both legs, the right wrist, the jaw and testicles.

Choppers extracted Delta Company at 1653 hours for another air assault, as soon as it finished evacuating the wounded. The company combat-assaulted into an area to the north of the central area of the plain at 1708 hours. The stage was set for more heroics and tragedy.

✳

As Delta Company approached its objective in choppers, the battalion received a classified message: "G-2, DTOC, from local civ. that there is a VC Battalion at coord, above ..." Sixteen minutes later, Delta Company, now on the ground in a rice paddy, took several rounds of small arms fire as it entered a hamlet several hundred meters north of where the enemy battalion was reported to be.

Two troopers were wounded as the company scrambled up the bank into the village. In the hamlet the troopers spread out for an orderly search and to establish a defensive perimeter. The enemy that fired on them moments before had apparently faded away.

This hamlet, the troopers discovered, was laid out in an east-to-west oval shape, about 40 yards wide and twice as long. It contained several huts, aboveground bunkers, palm trees and other ground vegetation, and a well.

It being near the end of a hot, humid and frightening day, the troops were low on water. The native well was very tempting, and shortly a trooper yielded to temptation. With the canteens of some of his squad members in hand, he went to draw water from the well, which he no doubt approached cautiously, but not cautiously enough. The NVA had removed the delay-fuse from an American fragmentation grenade, left the safety pin barely in place, and hid the grenade three feet from the well. An almost invisible fishing line connected the grenade's pin to a bucket on the rim of the well. The blast and sizzling, slashing shrapnel snuffed out the trooper's life almost instantly. This incident and casualty did not make it into the day's battalion or G-1 journals.

After 1800 hours, I was at the 15th Med with the remains of the grunt killed at the booby trapped well, Pfc. Daniel Nelson, I believe, when Medevac scrambled for another mission. A doctor, knowing the mission was to one of my companies, alerted me, and I accompanied the Medevac chopper to Delta Company. The time was 1830 hours.

As the Medevac chopper flew north, a smoke-enshrouded village came into view to the northwest, I saw that ARA rockets and heavier artillery rounds were exploding all around the village, except to the north. Moments later, approaching from the north, the medevac chopper swept in fast at ground level, nosed up, halted in midair, hovered a moment and settled on its skids. Grunts laden with their wounded buddies rushed the 50 feet from the village to the chopper. Hurriedly, I helped load the casualties onto the chopper, men I knew and with whom I'd spent the previous day and night. Moments later, the chopper skimmed the ground for a few hundred meters to the northeast, then gained altitude and headed for LZ English, giving the area to the east and south a wide berth.

*

The company commander updated me. At 1800 hours Delta Company had received orders to check out a village almost a klick to the south, where an NVA battalion was supposed to be holed up, according to military intelligence. Lieutenant Frazer's platoon got the mission. Without delay, Frazer moved his men from the village into the rice paddy and headed south across the rice paddy with two squads leading in a V-shaped or wedge formation. At the other side of the rice paddy, Pfc. George A. Sutt, the last man in the right wing of the wedge, had to choose between veering left or going straight ahead, climbing a bank and passing through the edge of a village. He chose to go straight ahead up the bank and directly into the muzzle of an NVA 30-caliber machine gun.

From about 10 feet, machine-gun bullets stitched Sutt at chest level, slinging him backward into the rice paddy. Instantly, bullets from other automatic weapons, interspersed with green-tracer rounds, began sweeping the remainder of Frazer's platoon, while other enemy elements took the company FOB under intense fire.

Quickly, the troopers dragged three grunts into the FOB who had fallen toward the rear of the platoon.

I learned Lieutenant Frazer and most of his platoon was still pinned down in the rice paddy. Those troopers who could, continued to low crawl back to the FOB under a rain of bursting artillery shells and shrapnel.

By the arrival of twilight, all but three of Frazer's men were back inside the FOB. The exceptions included a trooper who appeared dead and two grunts intent on recovering a buddy's remains.

Michael Daugherty and another trooper slithered forward when the last of the platoon broke for the perimeter. The two heroic grunts reached their buddy's body, almost under the barrel of the machine gun that had killed him.

Back in the company, aware of Daugherty and the other trooper's intentions, the company commander called in "Snoopy," an aircraft bristling with mini-guns, to keep NVA heads down. The grunts got ready, needing no orders, to give covering fire.

With daylight almost gone, Daugherty and the other trooper each grabbed the dead trooper near a shoulder. On signal, the pair leaped to their feet, raced across the rice paddy and delivered their buddy into waiting, willing hands, having dragged the body a hundred yards with NVA bullets kicking up dust at their heels and green tracers cracking all around. Daugherty sprained his ankle during the run; otherwise neither was hurt.

With the two troopers and the body inside the perimeter, we thought all the living were out of the rice paddy. Not so.

After full darkness, a grunt yelled from the paddy, "Give me cover. I'm coming in!" A shadowy figure charged the perimeter and collapsed among his buddies. The wounded grunt was Pfc. Thomas, who had recently borrowed a hymnbook from me.

Earlier, when the NVA machine guns first opened up, Thomas dived to the ground and buried his face in the soil, only to find himself the focus of unwelcome, undivided NVA attention. "The gooks shot at me every time I so much as twitched," he said.

Thomas tried to inch backward on his stomach toward the company perimeter, but a bullet tore through his helmet and another one tore a large chunk from one of his buttocks, from just below the waist. He played dead and waited for nightfall.

Thomas' tour of duty ended early. He kept the field hymnal. His

Dad answered my letter and asked for his son's bullet-riddled helmet, but it was long since lost in the system.

All night the darkness was dispelled by flares and fires in the village across the paddy, and the night was shattered by continuous artillery bursts and the ripping sound of mini-gun bursts as snoopy reached its fiery hands of death from the sky into the NVA positions. For a second or third night I had no sleep, though I tried off and on, protected and concealed, I thought, by a small palm tree near the south perimeter.

---

6 May 1967, G-1 Journal: 0600, C 2-8 WIA — Pfc. James Willis, frag hostile grenade. 0700, B 2-8 WIA — Pfc. Clifford R. Lundy, mulit-frag, both legs, booby trap. 1600, D 2-8 WIA — Sp4 Jerry H. Blond, gsw, left ankle, combat assault

8 May 1967, ibid: 1800, Pfc. James C. Loftis, frag chest and abdomen; Sp4 Peter Malacznik (medic, HHC), frag both legs, arm, buttock.

12 May 1967, ibid: 2045 (11 May), B 2-8 WIA — Pfc. Donald B. England, frag head.

15 May 1967, ibid: 2330 (14 May), B 2-8 WIAs — Sp4 Mirley J. Esprit, frag chest, hostile grenade; Sp4 Johnny R. Maze, same, chest and left leg; SSG R. Bernard, same.

16 May 1967, ibid: 2150, B 2-8 WIA — Pfc. George L. Jones, right hand, ps (punji stake). C 2-8 KIA — Sp4 George R. Arnos, frag neck, friendly fire, ARA, hostile action; Pfc. Brizzoli (A Co?), back of head and right leg (same as above). WIAs (same circumstances) — Sgt. William H. Anderson, frag from ARA, hostile action, contusion both feet; Sgt. Oscar Draper, frag neck; Pfc. Don H. Burrell, frag under left eye; Pfc. Willis W. White, frag. 2200, A 2-8 WIA — Sp4 Norbert Kuhle, frag right foot, hostile grenade.

17 May 1967, ibid: 0220, B 2-8 (0220 hrs) WIA — Ramond J. Cumba, frag back, hostile M79; 0245, Sgt. Riley Cleveland, gsw left arm, sniper; Sp4 Pascel Harrell, VC grenade hit shoulder, dud; 1200, Pfc. Frank M. Cordello, frag right eye, hostile grenade; 1400, Sp4 James J. Waters, hostile grenade.

19 May 1967, ibid: 1130, B 2-8 WIA — Sgt. Kenneth L. Stager, frag neck, hostile grenade; 1630, A 2-8 WIA — SSG Gnel (?). Burdett, frag, right thigh, hostile grenade; Pfc. James McGuire, left thigh (same).

22 May 1967, ibid: 0715, 1LT Nathaniel Ward, traumatic amputation leg, hostile booby trap; Sgt. Oscar Draper, frag back (same).

23 May 1967, ibid: 1159, A-8 WIA — Pfc. Jack L. Brammer, gsw, both feet, w/.45 pistol while drawing on VC suspects. 1700, D2-8 KIA — Sp4 Robert J. Bohmer, gsw chest, ambushed while patrolling river; WIA, Pfc. Willie P. Smalls, frag slight (same).

27 May 1967, ibid: D 2-8 WIA — Pfc. Vincent K. Zummo, frag left hand and arm, stepped on mine.

30 May 1967, Newby journal: 1200 hrs, 6 booby casualties brought in from D Co. Claymore? WIAs from Sgt. Eason's squad: Eason hit in testicles; Pfc. Francis P. Pepka Jr. hit in right arm; Sp4 Terry K. McComb multi frag wounds, left leg and hand, and face, died 5 June at Clark AB, Philippines; Pfc. Leland R. Pato, abdomen; Pfc. Freddie M. Ray Jr., abdomen; and Pfc. Michael A. Attrado, was hit in both legs. D 2-8 KIA — 1800, Pfc. Lonny L. Ehlers, gsw head. WIAs — Sp5 Wallace C. Dunn, gsw leg; Sp4 Emmett Doe (HHC, medic?), frag both legs hostile grenade.

30 May 1967, Honor Roll, D/2-8: KIAs. Pfc. Daniel Ivan Nelson of Rutledge, MN and Pfc. George Steven Sutt of Indianapolis, IN. Note: Veterans of the flight insist it was Sutt who was killed by the machine-gun, leaving Nelson as the booby trap casualty.

Chapter 18
Close Calls

During the hours before dawn on May 31, Charlie Company 1-12 Cav air assaulted to our north. At dawn it passed our lines on the east and took a position in the village east of the rice paddy in which Frazer's platoon had been hit. The NVA stopped shooting before dawn and our artillery ceased firing at daylight.

Immediately, Frazer's platoon swept the paddy to recover equipment — the dead and wounded were already off the field. During the sweep, a trooper made a chilling discovery. He kicked up a barely concealed double strand of black electric wire. One end of the double-strand wire led to a detonator (called a clicker or clacker) in the enemy machine-gun position, the gunner that had started the fighting the evening before. The other end of the wire was plugged into an American claymore mine that was hidden in the clump of bush I had used for concealment during the night. The mine was well placed. Had it been set off it would have decapitated me or wiped out the company CP group — the CP was set up within the effective kill zone of the claymore.

In awe and amazement, I stared at the claymore. *Surely, I've received divine protection. Why? Heavenly Father, I pray it is because my efforts to serve are acceptable unto Thee.*

The vagaries of war, how strange and unpredictable they are. Daugherty, with his sprained ankle, had sat just inches from the hidden, deadly claymore while I took his picture. Why had the claymore not been used against us? Because the detonator had been rendered ineffective when a strand of the wire was severed by shrapnel. The claymore mine, of such intense and emotional interest to me, merited this simple note in the battalion journal: "0630, D 2-8 found booby trap claymore type. Wire ran abt. 100 meters away. Destroyed."

✳

Orders came to saddle up and be ready to move out. I turned away from the claymore and started toward my rucksack, but turned aside to join some new guys huddled with some veterans about 30 feet away. The replacements looked very out of place and very scared in their fresh uniforms and bewildering loads of weapons and gear. Approaching the group, I introduced myself and tried to ease the new guys' obvious anxieties. Pfc. Charles W. Kreuger of Menasha, Wisconsin stood about 18 inches to my left while we visited. His slender body appeared especially overloaded. He carried an M-79 grenade launcher and a bag of M-79 grenades, in addition to his other gear. We'd visited only a couple of minutes, when hunger pains attacked me—very unusual, to feel hungery when we're getting ready to assault an enemy position. Always before, hunger had evaporated in anticipation of battle as the body automatically shifted into "fight or flight" mode.

Well, this time was different, so I excused myself and went to get some C-rations from my pack. The group with whom I had just visited with literally exploded after I'd gone 25 feet from it and rounded the corner of a Vietnamese hut.

Dashing into dissipating smoke under a rain of body parts and equipment, I found seven troopers sprawled on the ground. Kreuger's upper torso and lower body remained connected only by a small strand of muscle in his left side. Another trooper's right eye hung down to his chin. All but one of the casualties were in very bad shape, some of them having been in combat for less than an hour.

Assuming Kreuger was dead, we tended the other six men while we waited for the medevac chopper to arrive. Later, the medics and I were disturbed because Kreuger was still alive upon arrival at the 15th Med, but not for long. The doctors sent reassurances. Kreuger couldn't have lived no matter what we did, and he felt no pain. Still, logical or not, we wondered.

Wounded with Kreuger were Pfc. Roger L. Kennedy, arm and back; Pfc. Daniel H. Broetzmann, left eye and right side (right eye, as I recall); Sp4 James E. Taylor, back; Pfc. Ronald D. Ball, back; Pfc. Edward Tucker, back; and Pfc. Howard D. Jackson, back. Division G-1 incorrectly listed the casualties as having been hit by a grenade at 0700 hours while on a recon patrol. As M-79 grenades are quite stable until fired from a launcher, there being no pin to dislodge accidentally, we surmised a sniper's bullet exploded them in Kreuger's pouch — the crack of the shot would have been muffled by the exploding grenades.

*

The company moved out as soon as the wounded were in the air, and minutes later we passed lines — the Army term for moving one unit through another — with Charlie 1-12. As I passed through Charlie 1-12, I snapped a picture of a trooper in a telling position. In true infantry style he napped at the ready, lying on his right side in the depression between rows of some crop, his feet on one row and his helmet-covered head resting on his right shoulder on the other row. He held a hand grenade loosely in his right hand, and his left hand was in position to pull the pin if necessary. A .45-caliber pistol lay at the ready balanced on his left thigh. I wondered if all his precautions helped when Charlie 1-12 sustained from 25 to 35 percent casualties before the sun sat again.

*

Delta Company moved south another 500 meters after passing Charlie 1-12. There we stopped in and around a clearing that was obviously prepared for defense against American forces attacking along our route of approach; well-camouflaged punji stakes were strategically placed to impale all who threw themselves behind graves, tree trunks and in depressions for protection from cracking bullets.

From the sky came Lt. Col. Dashiell, the battalion commander, followed by the 1st Cav commanding general. I listened in while Lt. Col. Dashiell and General John Tolson discussed tactics with the company commander. Delta company would take a blocking position along the southeast side and lower end of the village into which the NVA had retreated and dug in. Charlie 1-12, would sweep through the village from the north. Delta Company wouldn't sustain casualties for a while, I guessed — correctly as it turned out. So, by hitchhiking on the general's chopper, I went to LZ English and from there to the hospitals at Qui Nhon.

*

While I was away, Charlie 1-12 sustained five killed and 22 wounded during unsuccessful assaults on the village. At 1800 hours, I rejoined Delta Company in its blocking position and trooped the line during the remaining daylight to update the men on the condition of their wounded buddies. With mixed emotions, I was saddened by the Charlie 1-12 casualties and relieved because Delta Company had sustained none during my brief absence.

I picked a spot on the line near the company CP and dug my foxhole in the gathering darkness. I intended to catch a little sleep within the protective embrace of the earth. But my plans changed immediately when I discovered I had dug into a termite nest.

Above ground, next to my termite-infested foxhole, I watched and listened for hours to the overhead rush, flash and blast of artillery as it rained on the village. The incoming ordnance included field and aerial rocket artillery and big naval guns, all targeted about 200 yards across a clearing from my position.

Like the men of Delta Company, I'd gone three nights without sleep. By midnight the tumultuous noise had lost its power over my groggy mind. The continuous crash of artillery actually took on a lulling effect similar to the pattern of rain on a tin roof. Soon I was sleeping so soundly that even a short round of artillery failed to awaken me. Minutes later, though, I jerked full awake at the gentle sound of cloth scraping against vegetation as a sergeant crept to my position. "Chaplain, McMillan is dead. Short-round," he said. A 105mm shell had exploded about 50 meters in front of our line and about the same distance from my position.

Battalion Journal, 0005 Hours, 1 June: "2345, D 2-8 ... 1 US EM KIA by [frag, scratched out] GSW wound in head and body. Serious. Medevac completed 0008." Though I wrote McMillan in my journal, the Division G-1 journal listed Sp4 James Taylor as the man wounded by the short round. However, G-1 also listed Taylor among those wounded with Kreuger, earlier. It is quite probable that Taylor, whose condition was listed as good on the earlier report, was treated and returned to duty. Whatever, I find no record of a McMillan being killed then. Nor do the records list Taylor as being KIA. So I keep looking for McMillan and anyone else who died then — one official source says the short round killed two troopers.

At 0335 hours, another sergeant captured an NVA lieutenant as he attempted to ex-filtrate the enemy position. The sergeant got the NVA officer's pistol for his efforts.

The U.S. Air Force air-dropped HE and napalm on the enemy position at 0730 hours, June 1, which strike I observed and photographed from a bomb crater. We assaulted the NVA position in the village at 0930 hours and met no enemy resistance. Then, hoping to overtake the evading NVA, we linked up with tanks and pressed on to the north, but we saw nothing more of the NVA that day.

After six hours of humping and hustling to keep up with the tanks, during which another Delta Company trooper was killed by a booby trap at 1010 hours, we left the tanks and we moved south about two klicks. Being exhausted, out of water and very thirsty, we set up for the night. At 1700 hours, I returned to LZ English and found a tape from Helga waiting to rejuvenate my shell-shocked body and soul. I recorded for Helga an answering tape before crashing for the night.

❋

After sleeping until 0800 hours on June 2, I arose refreshed. I let my bodily systems adjust to less stressful conditions, attended to administrative matters, and wrote letters to the children. Later in the day, I attempted to recruit Sp4 Paul Moody of Delta 2-12 for my chaplain assistant — no luck. I sought a replacement because Kirkpatrick had been transferred to the 173rd Airborne Brigade, still a chaplain assistant. I never heard from him again.

A month or so later an armored personnel carrier turned over and pinned Moody's legs into the ground. He was bruised, but not seriously injured. Still later, after I left Vietnam, Moody was seriously wounded by AK-47 fire. He survived to become a seminary teacher, my old job, for a year.

❋

At 1630 hours, June 2, I joined Alpha Company for the night. I'd been unsuccessful in reaching Charlie Company. During a one-hour period, beginning at 2000 hours, Charlie Company received 80 to 90 incoming M-79 grenades and some small arms fire — results, five lightly wounded. The M-79 fire came, we suspected, from the same individual who had been firing on our night positions for weeks. So far he had caused only minor damage to us for the most part. I nicknamed him *mad blooper*, mad for his determination and blooper for the sound an M-79 grenade launcher creates when fired.

Eventually my troopers killed the mad blooper. At least the troopers killed a VC who behaved like the blooper. At the time of his death the VC carried an American M-79 weapon and ammunition bearing the same lot number as that which we carried. The nightly attacks ended.

❋

On June 3, I operated for the first time north of War Zone 2 (II Corps) and the battalion entered a rare nine-day period of very light casualties. At 0730 hours, I accompanied Alpha Company on an air assault into the Quang Nhi Province in I Corps. We humped around in lower I Corps for a few quiet hours before I flew back to LZ English.

Between the time I returned to LZ English and that evening, when I joined Charlie Company in the field, I wrote several official and personal letters. I also read in the *Stars and Stripes* about Bau, the 16-year-old VC who surrendered to Bravo Company on April 15. The article about Bau bore a fair resemblance to facts as I knew them and added that he was serving as a Kit Carson Scout for an unnamed American unit (my Delta Company). Bau also got frequent mention in captured enemy documents. His former comrades tracked his every move, seeking revenge.

At 1830 hours I returned to Charlie Company, where next morning I held a worship service. Following the service, the company moved to the west side of the plains. There a VC surrendered to us, and we captured two VC women who had hidden in a cane field. On June 5, I returned to the division base camp at An Khe, where I spent the night.

*

Ammunition dumps, essential though they were, increased the hazards of life on firebases, as they had to be within the limited confines of the perimeter. Being at An Khe when the ammo dump went up, I missed the big bang.

At 0940 hours, the day before the ammo dump explosion at LZ English, Pfc. James P. Burns of Bravo Company sat in hiding on a slight rise, almost invisible in thick vegetation. From below, 200 meters away, a sharp-eyed trooper spotted him and, thinking him an enemy sniper, killed him with a single shot to the head. Subsequently, Burn's body was evacuated to LZ English and placed overnight in a refrigerator truck — the truck was parked by Graves Registration and the 15th Medical Clearing Company.

Near midnight an enemy mortar shell burst in the main ammunition dump at LZ English. The initial explosion created a fireball, followed by a chain reaction of explosions. Artillery and mortar shells were strewn all over the base and airfield — many had exploded on impact, while others lay about laden with potential death for the unwary. Some 500 meters from the ammunition dump, Kirkpatrick had huddled through the night beneath a stretcher and air mattress — small comfort in more ways than one.

Personnel and wounded troopers at the 15th Medical Clearing Company, less than 200 meters from the dump, hustled into culverts and bunkers. Two of my WIAs, who were being held there overnight, endured several hours of horror in an open-ended culvert. Unprotected Medevac choppers and the refrigerator truck melted in the fervent heat, along with the remains of my trooper.

At noon the next day I arrived at LZ English, the engineers having cleared the airstrip. From the airplane I went by jeep, weaving around unexploded ordnance past the 15th Med area to my battalion area. Nothing but black spots and bunkers gave evidence that the 15th Medical Clearing Company had ever been there. The black spots marked where Medevac choppers and the refrigerator truck melted down. Except for the two troopers in the culvert, the men of my battalion came through the ammo dump episode shaken, but unhurt. The battalion area was a mess, though.

∗

On June 7, I accompanied Alpha Company on an air assault to the top of the east-west running ridge that divides the Bong Son Plain from I Corps to the north. We landed without opposition and set up a larger than usual FOB.

After sunset, the troops gathered for a worship service in a clearing on the hillside, the congregation facing south. We worshiped with the troopers watching over my shoulder as twilight descended on the Bong Son Plain (the place of so many terrible memories). In the fading light, my friend, Lieutenant Miller, the artillery FO, stood forth and sang *How Great Thou Art*. Our souls vibrated and our bodies tingled — the hairs on the back of my neck snapped to attention. Under Miller's majestic voice, we were at peace. Even the plain seemed peaceful for just a flicker of time. Never had the song touched me so. "Oh Lord, my God, when I, in awesome wonder, consider all. ..." The special feelings and memories of this sacred moment in hell spring unbidden to my mind and lips whenever I feel especially worshipful and in awe of my God and his Christ.

Next day, I patrolled with the 1st Platoon into the Quang Nhi Valley in lower I Corps. En route the patrol fired on heavy movement in the bush, across a draw from the trail we were on. Out charged an angry, possibly wounded water buffalo. Fortunately, the beast charged away from us. Water buffalo generally didn't like American troops, perhaps because we didn't smell like their humans.

Except for the buffalo, nothing noteworthy occurred until we were about halfway back to the FOB, at which point we were ordered to secure an LZ so ice cream could be delivered to us! Eagerly we obeyed, to no avail. "Disregard," said a second message. Someone at LZ English or higher had decreed ice cream would be delivered no lower than the company. Suddenly, the troopers with me became upset and careless in their anger. Fortunately, the enemy forces we engaged minutes later were just as careless. In recent e-mail, Ray Bluhm said, "I ... decided not to deliver the ice cream to the platoon you were with, as I recall. ... even more serious was the real danger that the choppers ... would have given away the platoon's position and direction of movement back to the company. Bumping into the

VC squad shortly thereafter was a clear confirmation. ...."

Upon receiving Bluhm's message I reflected on what could have, probably would have, been. The enemy squad was near enough that a chopper would certainly have given the enemy our exact location. They could have attacked us while we were diverted — to our deaths — by the ice cream. In their place, I would have laid a hasty ambush for us and annihilated the platoon as it moved out, its members relaxed with their stomachs full of ice cream. Thanks, Ray Bluhm, for my life.

We bumped head-on into a squad-size element of VC. After a short, fierce firefight, the enemy faded into the jungle, leaving behind two rucksacks and assorted documents. We sustained no casualties and saw no sign that the enemy had. I stayed a second night with Alpha Company because we reached the FOB too late for me to fly out.

*

On June 10 and 11, I accompanied a chaplain, whom I shall call Fred, so he could provide communion services for all my companies. However, I came to regret using this chaplain because, following a service for Alpha Company, he embarrassed the troopers with his vile language — the men expected more from the chaplain than they did of themselves. I think this chaplain's disregard for sacred matters caused some troopers to be less certain about eternal things and, consequently, to be more scared about their fragile mortality.

*

Our casualty rates picked up briefly beginning on June 12. Delta Company moved into an area near the beach and at the base of a small, cone-shaped, single-canopy-covered hill. The hill was infested by VC and sown with mines and booby traps.

Within minutes of arriving in the area, Delta Company moved toward the hill and sustained a friendly KIA at its base, the first of several casualties the hill cost them — mostly to mines and booby traps.

Delta Company pulled back and I joined it for a quiet night — mines and booby traps don't move about in the dark. At 1035 hours the next day, while I visited hospitals in Qui Nhon, a mine blew off Sp4 Richard O'Brien's foot. At 1550 hours a grenade wounded 1st Lt Thomas M. Mancini of Alpha Company as he was engaged in destroying a VC complex.

*

The night of June 14, being unable to return to Delta Company, I remained on LZ English and visited with Captain (LDS) Tilton, commander of a 1-7 Cav company. While Tilton and I visited in the relative security of LZ English, the enemy probed the Delta Company FOB, wounding one trooper.

At 1300, June 15, I flew to Delta Company. At 1500 hours we crossed the beach and humped about two klicks northward, hugging the surf in hopes that fewer mines were there. Eventually we came to a rocky hill. The hill jutted a few meters beyond the beach and ended as a cliff.

Atop the hill we established a FOB. Soon two engineers arrived to check for surprises. They found and disarmed nine mines and booby traps before dark and four more the next morning. Amazingly, we set no mines off accidentally.

Next morning I had fun with a squad of grunts, searching cliffs along the shore. The surf below us was fantastically beautiful — almost made me forget where we were.

Later in the day, at LZ English, I learned the battalion was returning to An Khe with the promise of a month of easier and safer duty. I tried to reach Charlie Company for the night, but it was weathered in.

---

31 May 1967, 2-8 Journal 0644 "At 0630 D 2-8 ... found booby trap, claymore type. Wire ran about 100 meters away, destroyed.

0730, "D2-8 ... received 1 rd of s/a fire ... hit grenade on 1 indiv webgear causing it to explode. 1 US KIA, 6 US WIA."

2215, From 2-8 Journal: "Friendly casualties as of this morning: D2-8, 1 KIA, 6 WIA; C1-12, 2 KIA, 16 WIA, 3 MIA (bodies recovered the next day); A1-19, 1 KIA, 4 WIA; A-8 Eng, 5 WIA.

2255, D 2-8 1 EM wounded by frag hand ... HE arty."

31 May 1967, G-1 Journal: 0700, D2-8, WIA Pfc. Edward Tucker, Arty (short round), back; 2240, Sp4 James Taylor, (Same), right hand.

1 June 1967, 2-8 Journal, 0005: "2350, D2-8 1 US EM KIA by gsw (frag) wound in head and body, serious ..."

0350 2-6 D2-8 obsv 2 indiv, engaged, 1 escaped, other captured ... [a] 2nd Lt."

1019: "1010, D2-8 has 1 EM KIA by an unknown type booby trap, he was on hill setting up OP ... a B-3 can with M-2 grenade, no [fuse] delay."

2 June 1967, G-1 Journal: 2200, C 2-8 WIAs — 1LT Chester Collins, frag, hostile M79 fire; Sp4 Victor Sherman, left wrist (same); Pfc. Steven L. Leuga (?), frag left side (same); Pfc. Raymond J. Beckstead, frag chest (same).

5 June 1967, G-1 Journal: "0940, B 2-8 KIA — Pfc. James P. Burns, gsw head, mistaken for VC."

1000, D2-8 WIA — Pfc. Mark J. Carnevale, left arm, eye foot, booby trap, amputation right foot.

5 June 1967, Honor Roll, D 2-8, Internet: KIA Sp4 Terry Russel McComb, Lapeer, MI.

6 June 1967, G-1 Journal: 0410, B 2-8 WIA, Pfc. Dan L. Tanner, ringing in ears (ammo dump went up).

13 June 1967, G-1 Journal: 1030, D 2-8, KIA — Pfc. Clyde R. Houser Jr., gsw chest, frag, booby trap.

1040, WIA — Pfc. Richard M. O'Brien, mine, traum. amp, r. foot, left leg and hand frag;

1600, D 2-8 WIA; 1600 non-hostile, Pfc. Ronald C. Johnson, meningitis.

1600, A 2-8, 1LT Thomas M. Mancini, frag r. leg; Sp4 Michael S. Storey, frag, r. side and back.

14 June 1967, 2-8 Journal, 1052: "1035 D 2-8 received 1 US WIA from anti-personnel mine, lost foot…

15 June 1967, G-1 Journal: 0400 D 2-8 WIA — Pfc. Charles L. Vance, frag r. hip … hostile fire while on perimeter guard.

Chapter 19

"Light Action"

By June 18, all the battalion less Alpha Company had moved to the division base camp at An Khe in anticipation of a month of light action and low casualties. Alpha Company arrived on the 19th.

I was happy at the prospects of again regularly attending meetings with my LDS friends at An Khe for a month.

Following an evening Sacrament service, I did something unbecoming of an officer, but fun. How it happened I forget, but Sp5 Wayne Boring and I got into a brief friendly wrestling match, something a captain and sergeant shouldn't do. At least it was dark out.

For this indiscretion and violation of the solemnity of the Sabbath, I tried to excuse myself by making allowance for exuberance because of the fact that each day in the field, like every other, was the day to worship, given the chance. Besides, my hero, a prophet, liked to wrestle, too. Another besides, An Khe was much quieter than I was used to. Pretty lame excuses, but all I have.

✳

On June 22, Alpha Company lent me Sp4 Robiston, nicknamed "Preacher" by his buddies. He would be my chaplain assistant for a week or until Division sent me a new one, whichever came first. He was a licensed Baptist preacher from South Carolina and a good infantryman too.

✳

June 23 was a day for surprises. First, Lt. Col. Dashiell called me in. He'd found a tape from Helga in his ice chest. We had no idea how the tape got delivered to Dashiell.

Having planned to spend the day visiting and conducting worship services for the troops of Alpha Company, an all-day task as the company was dispersed over several miles along Highway 19 between An Khe and the Mang Yang Pass to the west, I borrowed a jeep and driver from battalion.

At the appointed time, 0900 hours, we headed out with Martinez driving and Preacher in the back seat. Obviously, my mind was somewhere other than on business, perhaps on the tape from Helga that I hadn't had time to listen to. For whatever reason, we were out the main gate and headed west before I noticed Martinez was unarmed and Preacher carried only a .45 caliber pistol. "I never draw a weapon for driving assignments," Martinez said. "My M-14 is in for repairs, and this is all I could get," Preacher said. *Turn around and get weapons. Nah, not enough time. The troopers need services today.* I ignored the prompting and we drove on.

Then came another ominous sign, which I also noted and discounted. The vehicle was so sluggish it barely made it up the first hill we came to — only three of its four cylinders were firing. *Oh well, there's plenty of traffic should we run into trouble.* On we went.

Our first worship service was at the farthest bridge to the west in the 1st Cav AO. At 1100 hours, a trooper was killed in Bravo Company, at another location. When the trooper died, I was preparing to start my third worship service of the morning, at Bridge 96.

Toward the end of my service at Bridge 96, a "Coca-Cola" girl arrived from the east — so called because she was one of several Vietnamese teenagers who peddled cold sodas each day to sell to the troops along the highway.

My combat senses set to tingling when the girl approached a rackety, beat-up civilian bus that had come from the west and stopped just short of the bridge. The girl immediately engaged in conversation with a military-aged male passenger on the bus, and the two of them kept glancing in my direction. Alas, for the third time that day I shrugged off the little warning voice. This time, though, I was distracted by an urgent message. A whole company of 173rd or 101st Airborne had been annihilated near Kontum. The 1st Cav was on alert to move to the Kontum area, and Dac To area.

So, shrugging off premonitions, we headed for Base Camp, intending to bypass the next Alpha Company position, which was co-located with an artillery unit some three miles to the east across a high ridge.

Near the top of the ridge, we passed through a dugway where clay banks arose above the road on both sides. Above the dugway the ground on both sides dropped below roadbed level. The road climbed and ran straight from the dugway for about 150 meters and then curved north and out of sight at the crest of the hill.

The jungle stood well back from the road on the north side and 50 to 100 meters on the south. Elephant grass grew from a few feet to 10 feet high wherever there was no jungle or roadway, the shorter grass being nearer the road.

I removed the .45 from my pocket, just in case still uneasy about the exchange between the Coca-Cola girl and the man on the bus. The jeep added to my concern. On three cylinders, we were doing no more than 20 miles per hour, and slowing. To a trained sharpshooter, we were almost as vulnerable as a sitting target.

Ambush! screamed my brain the instant geysers of dirt began sprouting up on the right shoulder of the road ahead of the jeep. A fraction of a second later, my ears confirmed what my eyes saw. An AK-47 on full automatic was kicking up those geysers. The enemy had hit us when we were about 200 feet from where the road curved left at the top of the hill.

One enemy gunner had opened up as we entered the kill zone, firing ahead of our jeep — leading us — and no doubt expecting us to try to speed away from the kill zone as quickly as possible. Had we sped up as expected, we would have driven straight into almost certain death. Martinez, however, reflexively slammed on the brakes and brought the chugging, laboring jeep to an instant halt, sparing our lives.

As Martinez hit the brakes, I leaped from the jeep and down a bank into the elephant grass. A fraction of a second later, Preacher landed almost on top of me. Almost simultaneously, Martinez threw himself down across the seat I'd just vacated, beating by a fraction of a second a burst of machine-gun fire from a second concealed position straight ahead, where the road curved to the left. Three bullets tore through the windshield and dash and passed on, missing Martinez. Other rounds punctured the radiator and a tire.

With the AK-47 and machine gun blazing away, Martinez slithered from the jeep and joined us in the grass. Hot lead cracked continually over our heads. My first thought was *the gunners will keep us pinned down while others sneak up and frag us. We've got to move away from the road!*

Ordering Preacher and Martinez to follow me and stay low, I crawled south into higher grass. We stopped about 70 feet from the road, though I wrote "50 to 70 meters" in my journal. Sitting back-to-back so we could watch for the enemy in all directions, we took stock of a bad situation.

"Let's run for the jeep," said Martinez, the driver.

"No, lets fade back into the jungle and work our way to bridge 96. We can do it," said Preacher, the infantryman.

"We'll stay here, because, barring a lucky shot, the VC can't reach us without maneuvering, and if the VC come for us, we'll capture the weapon of the first one who comes close," said I, the chaplain. I believed our best chance lay in avoiding our death or capture until better-armed Americans came along to rescue us.

The decision made, we waited with two relatively puny .45 pistols at the ready. While we waited, I considered the real odds, which weren't favorable. Our weapons — two pistols — were puny indeed against machine guns, and the traffic was too light for us to assume help would come in time. Sure, we could hurt the VC if they came for us, but we couldn't hold them off long if they were determined. I figured the VC were determined and would attack in the next few minutes, and we'd kill two enemies at the most before they killed or captured us. Preacher and I were unwilling to be captured. We remembered how Pfc. Jones died. And for a chaplain, capture by communist forces equaled death, I believed.

As I pondered our chances, peace and assurance suddenly flowed into my mind. Instantly, I *knew* we would escape. I shared this with Preacher and Martinez and assured them it was of the Lord.

For about 15 minutes we waited. The VC continually fired bursts into the grass in a criss-cross pattern, but the rounds no longer came close enough to crack the way near misses do.

*

Then I heard it — a truck was approaching from the east. Through the grass I saw an American five-quarter-ton truck come into view. Several well-armed soldiers were in the open truck bed. To my shock, the truck continued past where we'd left the jeep without giving the least indication of alarm or interest, neither slowing nor speeding up.

Thinking fast, I jumped up, fired a shot into the air to draw the Americans' attention, and yelled, "Americans over here. Ambush!"

In the back of the truck, heads swung our way and someone yelled. The truck screeched to a stop between the high banks where the road passed through the dugway. Soldiers leaped from the truck and formed a tight circle around it. *Oh no! The VC will frag them from the banks.* Leaping to my feet, I rushed toward the road, intent on securing the banks before it was too late. As I scrambled onto the road I saw why the truck had not slowed — our jeep wasn't there. *Why, they stole our jeep!* Angered at the thought, I raced toward the truck, yelling as I ran for the troopers to secure the banks. That's when I saw our jeep.

Martinez had left the jeep in neutral, and it had rolled backward off the road, down a four-foot bank into the elephant grass.

Preacher and Martinez had joined us by the time I got the security established on the banks. Then from the east came a deuce-and-a-half truck carrying an ARVN army band. Each band member was armed with an American M-16 rifle.

The truck stopped in front of the five-quarter-ton truck and the ARVN musicians leaped out. Immediately, and in good military order, they dashed up the banks and secured the area — I was impressed. An ARVN sergeant hurried up to me, saluted sharply, which I didn't particularly appreciate under the exposed circumstances. "Dai-ui," pronounced Diwee, "how can I help you?" he asked in pretty good English.

With the ARVN sergeant acting as my interpreter, I led about half the band in a sweep of the VC ambush positions. By then, of course, the enemy had faded away in the face of all our reinforcements and my valiant charge as leader of the band. Thus, I became the only American chaplain, probably the only American ever, to conduct an ARVN army band, not in making music, but during live combat maneuvers.

Soon after the sweep, troopers in another jeep stopped and traded a mounted spare tire for our shot-up one. We coasted the jeep down to Bridge 96, where we replaced the water in our radiator and radioed in our sitrep.

✳

While we were being ambushed and so forth, the division stood down from alert. So, no longer pressed to hurry to camp, we followed a large, heavily armed convoy past the ambush site and stopped at the artillery position. The jeep ran as well as it had before, despite the punctured radiator.

At the artillery site, we worshipped with some impressed, respectful Alpha Company grunts and redlegs who'd heard about the ambush and could hardly believe we had escaped. Redleg is Army slang for an artilleryman.

Back at Battalion, Major Iverson complimented us about how we had reacted to the ambush and to subsequent events. He stood by while Martinez and I received treatment for our minor wounds, then said, "I want you in the future to travel Highway 19 with convoys."

An interesting exchange occurred during General Tolson's evening briefing, as related to me by someone, Iverson perhaps. The operations officer concluded his remarks about the ambush with "one of the enemy weapons was an AK-47."

"How in hell does a chaplain know if he's being shot at by an AK-47?" General Tolson snapped, implying chaplains live too safely to distinguish between weapons.

"The chaplain was Newby of the Second of the Eighth," someone answered.

"Oh," said General Tolson and dropped the subject.

Three days later, a civilian bus — Captain Ray Bluhm said it was a truck — was ambushed at the same spot where we had been; a woman passenger was killed. Preacher and I passed through the ambush site several times over the next month, with me driving so Preacher could ride shotgun. We tagged along with a convoy when it was convenient.

In retrospect, my suspicions about the Coca-Cola girl were well founded. She fingered me for ambush, I'm certain. She probably assumed I was someone very important, perhaps the equivalent of a VC political officer, because the troops listened so respectfully to me.

*

Long before I went to Vietnam, Helga and I agreed to share everything, good and bad. Neither of us would withhold bad news out of concern it might cause the other to worry. Better, we agreed, to be assured one knows everything and need not fret about bad news being held back.

Thus, I opted, upon arriving in Vietnam, for Helga to be notified if I sustained wounds, no matter how serious. A few days after the ambush, before Helga got my account of the incident in the mail, a taxi driver delivered a telegram from the Department of the Army. The telegram caused Helga little concern because it described my wounds as minor and said I had returned to duty. However the telegram set the stage for a real scare two weeks later.

*

On June 24, I conducted a memorial service for our comrades who had died during the last operation. Representatives from each company marched into the 1st Brigade Chapel, which, like most chapels at base camp, gathered dust most of the time. I announced the purpose of the service, and an honor guard posted the national and unit colors (flags). Then, following airborne tradition — most of the fallen had been paratroopers — the company first sergeants, in turn, read the name and rank of each honored trooper. After each name was read, a trooper marched solemnly forward and placed a pair of jump-boots before the altar rail, highly shined toes toward the congregation.

Then, standing behind 29 pairs of boots, each representing someone I knew and loved, I tried to honor those who gave their lives and to bolster the faith and hope of their surviving buddies. Chaplain Dowd followed me with a sermon; a prayer was offered, *taps* was played, and the colors were retired. This was a very moving tribute, but so inadequate compared to the sacrifices these troopers had made.

On June 25, besides general Christian and denominational services I arranged a Baptist service and allowed Preacher to live up to his nickname, which caused a fellow chaplain's eyebrows to arc — he opined that enlisted men shouldn't be permitted to perform functions reserved for ordained clergy.

*

Combat for the battalion remained light during late June and most of July, with a few exceptions. As for me, my biggest problem was arranging ground transportation — the tote goat or gamma goat I'd used in February was long dead. Some days I worked Highway 19, other days the perimeter and Y-ring (part of the patrol area outside the perimeter), and visited hospitals and troops on Muc Non Mountain. In between, I went with companies and platoons on special operations. Casualties were light, with one major exception.

*

On July 1, I wrote in my journal, "Going home month after next!" The first two days of July were quiet, but busy. We had an especially spiritual meeting July 2. July 3 and 4 were notable exceptions to quiet duty around base camp.

*

I spent the morning of July 3 attending a farewell for chaplains who were near the end of their tours, those about to return to the "land of the big PX" or the "world." At 1300 Preacher and I accompanied Alpha Company minus its second platoon on an air assault and clandestine mission. We were to be inserted into the jungle several klicks from a suspected VC assembly area (where forces mass for battle). The VC, according to Intelligence, was preparing for an attack on the division base camp. Our mission was to find the enemy without being detected and then call in reinforcements, air strikes and artillery to wipe the enemy out.

For the mission, a tracker-dog team, two handlers and a black Labrador retriever augmented Alpha Company. To extend our

173

range, we carried several collapsible jugs of extra water. We were months into the dry season, and water would be hard to find.

We air assaulted about 15 klicks northwest of base camp and immediately set out under extreme heat, made worse by the necessity of traversing the first several hundred yards on hands and knees beneath bamboo. We humped until just before dark and then settled down for the night in and around a small grassy clearing (no digging in because of extra-stringent noise discipline).

Someone, a dog handler, I think, gave me a long-range patrol meal (LRRP ration) — dehydrated chili con carne, just add water. The LRRP meal was good, not as good as some C-rations, but many times better than the MREs (meals-ready-to-eat) that would replace C-rations in the late 1980s.

Most of the water we carried was gone, having been consumed to replace what we lost in heavy sweating. A little water yet sloshed about in my canteens and in a five-quart bladder in my pack, which water I shared with the troops, naturally.

---

23 June 1967, 2-8 Journal: "1100 B 2-8 reports 1 friendly KIA when he wandered [sic] off trail, wounded by friendly fire."

23 June 1967, 1st Cav Div Operational Summary: "At 1205, a 1/4 ton vehicle w/3 personnel from 2-8 HHC received automatic wpn fire, traveling east on Hwy 19, at BR333460. Fire not returned.

24 June 1967, Div Journal (AVDAGP): "HQ 2-8, Newby, Claude A02323895, Cpt, HHC/1st Bde, June 1205, laceration left forearm. Good. Bn. Medic. Vic An Khe. Passenger in jeep hit by small arms fire."

30 June 1967, G-1 Journal: 2030, A 2-8 WIA — Pfc. Gerald J. Roberts Jr., frag, l. leg, hostile grenade, pointman.

Chapter 20

Deadly Fourth of July

Dawn broke warm and muggy on July 4, with the promise of coming heat sufficient to rapidly sap our bodies dry unless we found water, quickly. But first, our mission objective awaited us, the suspected VC assembly area.

At 0700 hours we moved out toward the west along a distinct path through the jungle. The company CP and I were with the 1st Platoon in the lead. At the very front of the formation was perhaps the best point man in the whole battalion.

After moving about 500 meters, we came to a point where our path ended and intersected a well-used trail that ran generally north and south. I followed the column to the right on the new trail and had moved about 15 feet from the T-intersection when Herbert Fralix, the point man, called a halt.

While Fralix checked something out, I watched the unsecured trail behind us, south of the intersection. A trooper from the CP took it upon himself to back up and provide rear security. I relaxed when a trooper from farther back in the column moved forward to assist. But I didn't relax for long.

✳

Three rifle rounds cracked above my head and snapped me from my reverie. The shots were answered with automatic fire by the two grunts at the intersection. Three unsuspecting VC had approached nonchalantly from the south and, upon seeing us, recovered from shock a shade faster than the two troopers did. One VC pumped off three shots as he back-peddled up the trail and out of sight.

By the VC's casual manner, it was obvious Alpha Company had successfully accomplished its clandestine approach, but now we'd lost the element of surprise.

Captain Ray Bluhm, who took command of the company from Frank Yon, ordered an infantry squad and the team with the dog to pursue the three fleeing VC, while the rest of the company moved into the VC assembly area (which is what the point man had spotted).

The black Labrador quickly picked up the scent of the VC, and

175

we tracked them about 300 meters into an open field. There, their prints joined 18 other sets of "BF Goodrich" or "Ho Chi Minh" sandal tracks (nicknames the grunts gave footwear the enemy fashioned from car tires). A few meters farther on, all the tracks split, confusing the poor dog. We returned to the company empty-handed.

✳

We found the rest of Alpha Company in the middle of an impressive base camp. Under the jungle, the VC had constructed scores of hooches and other structures, eating and working tables, even sanitation facilities — all with materials taken from the surrounding jungle and arranged with casual military precision. These structures covered a circular area about 300 meters across — plenty of room for a battalion to bivouac. But, except for the three VC on the trail and heavy signs, the VC remained invisible. It appeared the new compound yet waited for its first occupants. The Military Intelligence people were correct, it appeared, about the enemy massing for an attack on something — and our base camp was the nearest, most likely target.

Captain Bluhm, in compliance with his initial orders, intended we not broadcast our presence in the area more than we already had. Consequently, we'd not call for choppers to resupply us with vitally needed drinking water.

After Bluhm studied the map with the lieutenants, the 1st Platoon, led by Lt. Richard Hostikka, went seeking ground water a kilometer to the northeast where there might be water, as indicated on the map by a line of blue dashes, the military symbol for intermittent streams. I accompanied the 1st Platoon on the water mission while the remainder of Alpha Company remained to search and burn the complex.

We took nearly three hours to work our way the thousand meters to the blue line, with Fralix doing most of the chopping and thrashing through bamboo and dense jungle. Finally, exhausted and bone dry but for sweat-soaked fatigues, we reached our objective. Yes, there was water, a small, filthy, stagnant pool at the bottom of a 10-foot embankment — glorious water all the same!

A trail ran along the west bank about 10 feet above the streambed, which was dry except for the stagnant pool. Being older and perhaps a little wiser, I stayed on the trail while several thirst-crazed troopers threw caution to the wind and rushed down the bank to fill their canteens. More than one of the troopers filled bellies and soothed parched throats without waiting for water purification tablet to take effect — thirst makes people crazy.

Nothing happened at first. No shots interfered with the grunts' reckless water-gathering efforts. Meanwhile, I sat next to a tree and ritualistically opened C-ration beans and franks and crackers, then wrapped a little "snake" of C-4 explosive around the base of the can of beans, the grunt's preferred food-heating method, and lit it.

At this point, Sp4 Boswell (Sp4 Lloyd Gratz remembers his name as Breland) climbed the bank carrying several full canteens — he carried no weapon, as he'd left it laying about three feet from me, its barrel pointed in my general direction.

Engrossed in meal preparations, I barely noticed Boswell as he dropped the canteens and picked up his M-16. Reflexively, I hit the ground when the rifle went off in Boswell's hand, seemingly into my left ear. On the way down, my mind registered blood and body matter spattering on me and my beans and franks. "Medic!" Boswell screamed, and took off up the trail, holding his face.

Doc and I and a couple of grunts caught Boswell. We had to tackle him to the ground before we could administer first aid. He'd shot himself in the face, with the bullet entering under the chin, passing through tongue, teeth, gums and jawbone, and exiting near the left ear. The bullet had then slammed into the tree inches above my head.

Within a halfhour of the shooting, Boswell was being strapped into a sling and hoisted via cable from the streambed into a hovering Medevac chopper. I never heard from him again.

*

Our canteens refilled with purification pill-treated water, with Boswell headed home and nothing pressing for a moment, four or five of us took a break and visited.

Like every soldier in Vietnam, I was aware of the passage of time, especially milestones like the halfway point, which had passed while I was in Hawaii. However, I never kept a short-timer's calendar — "362 days and a wake up" and so forth. I intended to count the days only after less than a month remained of my tour.

Fralix, Boswell and I had entered Vietnam about the same time the previous year. Fralix had six weeks left on his tour. So naturally, considering Boswell's fate and it being the Fourth of July, our thoughts and conversation turned to going home, to our chances of returning for another tour and to related topics of interest to short-timers.

"Man, I'm not coming back to 'Nam. I'll get up in them hills of

West Virginia [or was it North Carolina?], and the Army will have to send itself after me to get me back over here," a grunt declared. The other grunts, except for Fralix, agreed with these sentiments.

"How do you feel about a second tour?" I asked Fralix.

"I don't want to come back, but I'm very grateful for what my country has given me. No, I don't want to come back, but if my country asks me to, I'll come," Fralix said.

Fralix's sentiments would probably have ended discussion of the subject anyhow, had not new orders punctuated his last comment. Lieutenant Hostikka sent Fralix and another trooper to lead the rest of Alpha Company to the watering hole. So while we rested and waited, Fralix spent several more hours tearing through the jungle — he was too combat savvy to use the same trail twice.

About an hour before dark, Fralix returned at the head of the rest of the company. Soon afterward, our canteens full, we moved out eastward along the dry streambed, Fralix on point, followed by five or six others, then me.

New orders came up the line. "Hold up and about-face." Captain Bluhm was backtracking 300 meters to a small clearing to dig in there for the night. So we turned around and, for the first time in my memory, Fralix was the last man in a column.

A few minutes later, I broke into the clearing after most of the grunts had already entered it and spread out to defensive positions. Captain Bluhm and the lieutenants were clustered near the southwest side of the clearing. 1st Sgt. Catron, the tracker team and dog, plus a few others with no pressing duties, sat about the clearing, mostly leaning against their rucksacks.

*

I entered this scene, moved about halfway into the clearing, dropped my pack, sat and leaned against it, facing the direction I had come. A few seconds later, I had a strong, almost vocal impression to "get up and move."

Not knowing why I got the impression or if it applied to anyone else, I moved some 20 feet, entered the brush at the north edge of the clearing and turned. Fralix had entered and was crossing the clearing toward Captain Bluhm. He was almost to my rucksack when something exploded in a blinding flash about four feet in front of him, by my rucksack. Shrapnel hit me in the face and I went down.

Quickly looking across the clearing, through dissipating smoke, I saw a score of troopers sprawled about the clearing, some writhing in pain. Fralix's uniform was in tatters, his helmet gone. Blood poured from dozens of places between his ankles and his chin.

*

"Medic! Chaplain Newby's hit!" cried a trooper. I wasn't the only one. Nineteen others were too, in addition to Fralix and the dog. I felt only stinging and numbness in my right cheek. A medic slapped a bandage on me and I helped him treat the other wounded.

Sp4 Robert A. Woodrow had caught a BB-size fragment under his right eye, a quarter of an inch higher than the BB size fragment beneath my right eye — a quarter of an inch that was the difference between life and death. Woodrow's fragment passed through soft tissue and entered his brain. He died where he fell, despite all we could do. Cheekbone protected my brain and probably saved my life.

In heavy darkness a Chinook arrived to extract the casualties. Leaning into the rear-prop blast and hot exhaust thrown out by the chopper, we on-loaded the wounded, about a fourth of the present-for-duty strength of Alpha Company. The loading done, I backed to the edge of the clearing, intent on staying with Alpha Company as I felt no pain. "Hey, Chaplain Newby's not aboard," someone called from the darkness.

"Chaplain, get on the chopper," ordered Captain Bluhm, and I did, since it was his company.

*

Wonderful and sad events occurred later in the combination emergency/operating/triage area of 2nd Surgical Hospital at Camp Radcliff. First, a doctor confirmed what I already knew; my wound needed no further attention. So I went about visiting the wounded while the doctors and medics, some of whom wore flashy Hawaiian shirts and Bermuda shorts, plied their doctoring skills and griped because we had interrupted their Fourth of July celebration. "The booze and steaks will be gone," some moaned. It was easy to believe my ears — I'd become used to the disregard some support people held for the grunt.

Surrounded by griping doctors, Fralix was fully conscious and nude; the remnants of his jungle fatigues, boots and gear had been cut away. With my hand on his uninjured forehead — we'd just prayed together — I asked, "Fralix, remember our conversation today about coming back to Vietnam if ordered to, how you said you'd come?"

"Yes."

"Well, considering this," I asked, casting a meaningfully glance at the complaining doctors, "How do you feel now?"

"I doubt the doctors can fix me well enough. But if they can and if I'm asked to, I'll come back again," answered Fralix, in the best and briefest Fourth of July patriotic talk I ever heard — and the doctors never had a clue. To be fair, the doctors may have talked as they did, not out of disregard, but to rile Fralix up so he would fight harder to survive.

✳

The VC, I concluded, had been trailing us when Captain Bluhm gave the company an about-face to return the way we had come. Accurately guessing Bluhm's intentions, the VC set a surprise for us, which surprise they detonated just as the last man in the column — Fralix — crossed the clearing. This is in essence what I told Major Iverson when, at the hospital, he asked me "what really happened out there?" It is possible I told Iverson wrong, based on something I later heard in confidence — that earlier on the Fourth of July a trooper threw a hand grenade into the clearing, and it failed to explode until we returned.

From Bluhm's perspective, the enemy had no way of guessing where we were going, nor did they have time to set up a command-detonated claymore mine. He is convinced the explosion was one of our own duds. Still, why would one have been thrown into the clearing earlier?

✳

Later, a trooper brought me Fralix's pocketsize New Testament — Fralix wanted me to have it. Two shrapnel fragments had penetrated the little book before entering his body — the angle of the entry and exit holes showed Fralix was no more than four feet from the blast. The New Testament probably saved Fralix's life by slowing the fragments before they reached his heart. Recently I returned the New Testament to Fralix, to the joy of his wife, Delores, his mother, and her more than 60 grand children and great-grandchildren.

On the fifth of July I sported the only black eye I ever had, though many a boy and some men had tried to give me one.

✳

A few days later, back in Ogden, Utah, Helga was returning home with all the children from visiting an acquaintance in Roy, Utah. All at once from the back seat, three-year-old Brenda began chanting, "Daddy is dead. Daddy is dead."

Naturally, Brenda's chanting bothered Helga. It is hard to imagine Helga's shock when, upon arriving home, she found another taxi driver and telegram on her doorstep — her shock magnified by Brenda's chanting. With fainting heart, Helga opened the telegram. Yes, her mate was wounded again — but not dead! A flood of relief washed away the dread.

*

Back in Vietnam on the Fourth of July, Alpha Company remained in the ill-fated clearing overnight and continued the mission the next day, with a 15-kilometer hump to the east through very rough terrain and foliage. Of this hump, Bluhm said, "We were tasked to march 12 ks [kilometers] east and be in position before 0300 the next morning around a village. ... We moved all day through that thick brush and that night we made a night river crossing. ... It was a horrendous march, but my men did it well, and I was very proud of them."

An enemy grenade wounded SSG Donald Langston in the leg on July 7, and on July 11, Sp4 Sonny Youngblood, a tall, friendly black trooper, caught a VC spear through his upper thigh. The spear had been rigged to swing or strike when a trip wire (fishline) was released. A shorter trooper would have taken the spear in the groin or abdomen, with much more tragic consequences.

While Alpha Company and I were in most of the fighting that involved the battalion during early July, those nasty vagaries of war continued to take their toll in the other companies. For example, at 2200 hours on the evening of July 8, Pfc. George Potter died near his position on the base-camp perimeter. Potter had wandered off in the dark, probably looking to relieve himself. His buddy, hearing noises where they shouldn't be, blasted him in the stomach with an M-79 shotgun (double aught) round.

*

I spent July 8 trying to hold services along the highway, but threatening enemy actions limited me to just one, at Checkpoint 70. July 9 was a typical Sunday for me while the battalion was at Base Camp. Besides attending and participating in three LDS services, I held six general Christian worship services for the battalion. My most difficult duty of the day was counseling and consoling the trooper who killed Potter the night before. I reflected on how I was prepared for this kind of counseling when, back in January, I almost caused a helicopter to crash into my men.

*

On July 10, Chaplain Keene and I acted foolishly trying to reach one of my units so he could provide communion. We exited the base-camp perimeter on the northeast side through a concealed, carefully marked route used by patrols. Then we crossed the cleared or field-of-fire area and went afoot into the jungle and tried to find an element of Alpha Company, which supposedly was set up about 800 meters from the perimeter wire.

Several factors contributed to making this a foolish endeavor. First, going and coming, we risked destruction by friendly duds, left over 18 months by artillery and mortar barrages. Second, we might bump into a VC ambush or patrol. Third, without radio contact the Alpha Company element might blow us away as we approached, assuming we could find it, which we didn't. And finally, upon returning, we might have been blown away by the base-perimeter defenses, a high probability should we break out of the jungle at an unexpected point or if different troopers were on guard.

After an hour, we safely moved back across the kill-zone through the snares-and-flares zone and reentered the perimeter at the point we had exited earlier. I vowed to never again do such a foolish, unnecessary thing.

*

Back in March I had requested career status in the chaplaincy and an airborne assignment following this combat tour. In July, I was notified that career-conditional status had been granted me, and an airborne assignment would be granted. Consequently, on July 13, I combined a visit to the hospitals in Qui Nhon with an airborne physical examination.

The results of the hearing tests bode ill for an airborne assignment, and I was tempted to "doctor" my hand-carried medical records. Doctoring had worked once with a school report card when I flunked third grade, after all. But conscience prevailed, and I wrote a letter, instead, and spelled out why I thought high-frequency deafness need not interfere with jumping from airplanes.

I spent July 14-18 suffering and trying to recover from influenza and painfully swollen hemorrhoids. (The latter were a frequent problem for me during the years in Vietnam.)

On July 17, to start my blood circulating, I ran almost a mile to the shower point and a them back. Most of the next day I spent in bed suffering the residual effects of the flu and my "home remedy," plus about the worst hemorrhoid symptoms of my whole tour.

At 1845 hours, having dragged myself from my sickbed to conduct what I thought was to be a worship service for Alpha Company, I found the men expecting a memorial service. So we held one for Sp4 Woodrow, who was killed by the claymore on the Fourth of July.

*

After the memorial service I returned to bed. Meanwhile, on Highway 19, three troopers went AWOL from a bridge position and entered a village where one of them allegedly killed a woman, and for which all three were apprehended by the military police. They were rear-area troop, not grunts, as I recall.

To my knowledge, this was one of only two crimes against civilians committed by men in this battalion since I joined it. The other incident, which I couldn't confirm, allegedly occurred on the Bong Son plain. A trooper, during the interrogation of a female VC suspect, pulled down her black pajama top and bit off her right nipple. Of this alleged incident I heard disgusted comments, but no one admitted to seeing it happen or to seeing the injured woman.

*

On July 19 Captain Bluhm asked my advice on dealing with a trooper in Alpha Company, John Fontana, who had requested reclassification as a conscientious objector. "Should I require Fontana to bear arms, to go on ambush and so forth while he waits for a decision on his claim?" Bluhm needed to know. My advice was to relieve Fontana of any combat-related duties, immediately process his request, and send him to me for the required chaplain interview.

Later, I interviewed Fontana and reported that he was sincere and that the basis of his claim was wellfounded and thought out.

After the interview, impressed with his sincerity, I asked on impulse, "John, how would you like to read the earliest known record of conscientious objectors?"

"Yes," Fontana eagerly responded.

So I marked the story of the Anti-Nephi-Lehies in the Book of Mormon and gave it to Fontana with the warning that it was a religious book, and if he read beyond the marked section, he did so at his own risk.

4 July 1967, G-1 Journal: Alpha Company 2-8 casualties, KIA: Sp4 Robert A. Woodrow. WIAs — Privates 1st Class Stephen Overstreet, buttock and stomach; Larry L. Gilpin, left leg; Raymond Jones, leg; Prentice D. LeClair, leg and face; Cornelius Birth, leg, side and arm; Richard W. Bryan, leg; Bobby Sexton, leg; Thomas Houghton, stomach, face and both arms and legs, James G. Chavez, thigh and side; Robert Scheffler, leg; Herbert Tipton, leg and arm; and Herbert A. Fralix, face to ankles. Also wounded were 1st Sgt. James S. Catron, knee and thigh; Sgt. James P. Moore, leg, side and arm; Johnathan Kinder, arm; Specialists Fourth Class Carl Webb, leg; William Thelman, leg; and Andrew Greer, arm. Sp5 Jeremiah White. Headquarters Company: Cpt. Claude D. Newby, face.

7 July 1967, G-1 Journal: Sp4 Sonny Youngblood, crossbow arrow through thigh; Sp4 Bernard Cosmoski [date, company?].

Chapter 21

Premonitions

A few days before the Twenty-fourth of July, Wayne Boring, Scott Thereur, and several other troopers began laying plans for a celebration. On that date each year Mormons celebrate the arrival of the pioneers in the Salt Lake Valley in 1847 — it is an official holiday in Utah.

To add some pioneer, or at least Western authenticity to the occasion, Boring made a "bucking bronco" from a 50-gallon metal barrel. From somewhere, probably home, he came up with the necessary rodeo bareback rigging and plenty of rope to suspend the barrel between four trees to create the bucking effect. Boring shaped the sides of the barrel to resemble the back of a horse. Next he welded on eight metal eyehooks to which eight ropes would be attached, four for suspension and four to make the barrel "buck."

Administrative matters consumed Monday morning, July 24. After lunch Sp4 Robiston (Preacher) and I joined several others at the appointed time in a grove of trees, inside the base camp, near the river for our rodeo. I got good pictures of the event.

Next, we raced one another in rowboats at a recreation area of sorts. Then in the river we swam and conducted ducking battles for a couple of hours, after which we retired to my hooch/office and dined on tuna salad sandwiches and milk. For a finale to the great day, we held a chess tournament. Thus, the An Khe troopers and a Baptist preacher commemorated the 1847 entry of the Mormons into the valley of the Great Salt Lake.

Sometime during the festivities, one of the troopers told us a sad story about how his friend, whom I shall call Roger, had wrongfully and foully been shot by an Ogden police officer on this holiday a few years earlier. He was a little taken aback when I confessed that it was I who had shot his friend.

*

It was Wednesday, July 24, 1963, and I was on motor patrol in the central area of Ogden. I had spent most of the day on traffic control for the Pioneer Day Parade, followed by an evening of keeping the peace at the annual rodeo. We had expected trouble based on experiences the previous night, but were breathing easily because brawls, and perhaps a riot, had not occurred immediately following the rodeo. The quiet was deceptive.

The call came in at about 11:40 p.m. as I refueled my patrol car at the main fire station. A fire department dispatcher alerted me to fighting at Fowlers Drive-in on Washington Boulevard. I responded immediately, as the drive-in was in my patrol area.

At the scene, I parked by Bob's Bar B-Q, a half block south and on the same side of the street as the drive-in. Officer Richard DeVoe was already on the scene, and Officer Bill Stettler arrived about the same time I did. Other officers were nearby directing post-rodeo traffic. About 100 teenagers and young adults were milling about the parking area at Fowlers and on the boulevard. No one was fighting. The mood of the crowd was more rowdy than foul.

Trying to reinforce the light mood of the crowd, we moved through the area urging individuals and small clusters of people to keep calm and not linger too long.

For some reason DeVoe separated from Stettler and me before we reached Fowlers. Looking back along the path we had taken through the crowd, we saw DeVoe struggling with a white male and surrounded by several older, meaner males, the ones most apt to start trouble. I reached DeVoe, pulled a Hispanic male off his back and asked what was going on.

"He's under arrest," DeVoe said of the man he was holding.

We have to get him away before the crowd goes mad, I thought. No time to debate the merits or wisdom of the arrest.

We headed for my patrol car, with DeVoe and me each holding the prisoner, Roger (last name omitted), by the belt and an arm and Stettler protecting DeVoe's left flank.

The crowd moved in on us about halfway to my car; the mood had changed from rowdy to mean, like a rippling wave beginning where DeVoe arrested Roger. En masse, several adults jumped Stettler and DeVoe. Roger, suddenly freed from DeVoe's grip, swung across in front of me and tried to flee, with me holding on to him. So he turned and attacked me. Over Roger's shoulder I saw a swirling mob, kicking and shoving where I'd last seen DeVoe and Stettler.

Now more concerned for my fellow officers than with preventing Roger's escape, I tried to turn him loose so I could go to their aid. But Roger preferred fighting to fleeing. I knocked him backwards, but he barreled into me before I could get set. We went down with me on my back beneath him. Though I had my hands full, I had to help DeVoe and Stettler. So, still on my back and fighting Roger one-handed, I drew and fired a shot into the air, intent on drawing the officers on traffic duty to DeVoe and Stettler's aid.

Roger's continuing struggles prevented me from returning my weapon to the holster, so I switched the pistol to my right hand and knocked Roger off me with my left. Quickly I regained my feet and looked among the crowd for DeVoe and Stettler. Stettler was on his feet, pushing toward to the sound of my gun. He was about five feet away when Roger came off the ground and charged me, head down.

Simultaneously, Rogers's shoulder struck my right forearm and my weapon exploded — the muzzle flash appeared to leap straight at Stettler's stomach. Stettler stopped like he'd been hit hard and looked down at his mid-section. Meanwhile, Roger dropped on his stomach. Without taking my eyes off Stettler, I dropped astraddle of Roger to hold him down.

After a moment, Stettler looked up and shook his head. No, he wasn't shot. But in all that press of humanity someone had to have stopped my bullet. But no one was down or behaving as if he'd been shot.

Someone in the crowd said of Roger, "He's shot! Why did you have to shoot him?" *Who, me? Not possible. I know where my shots went, one into the air and the other into the crowd behind Stettler.*

Well, my eyes had deceived me. The gun is quicker than the eye. My second shot went downward, not outward, entering Roger's lumbar area and exiting through his buttock. No wonder he lay down.

The crowd had been momentarily cawed by the shooting, but quickly became a raging, riotous mob. After placing Roger in an ambulance, I returned and helped police of city, county and state break up the riot, helped by fire hoses. The rest of the night I spent answering questions and writing statements.

Reflecting back on the incident, certain elements in the crowd were intent on causing trouble, and there would have been some, even without the shooting. I thought DeVoe had used poor judgment in arresting Roger in the middle of the crowd. Firing my pistol would have been good judgment had DeVoe and Stettler been in as bad a situation as I thought they were, but was bad judgment in hindsight. To my mind, shooting Stettler would have been the worst possible outcome.

Having shot Roger accidentally, I was relieved his wounds

weren't serious. I regretted shooting him, but I felt no guilt, despite bad judgment calls. Had Roger not resisted illegally, he would not have been shot. My actions were vindicated by my superiors, the community, local media, and eventually by the courts.

The media were very kind to me. Headlines included, "Police Chief Thanks City Council for Endorsement of Riot Handling" *(Ogden Standard Examiner)*, "Teen Brawl Results in Shooting Injury" *(Salt Lake Tribune)*, and "Officer Injured, Youth Shot in Ogden Scuffle" *(Deseret News)*. The media spun the story in my favor, generally, by emphasizing points favorable to me and phrasing reports to justify my actions. For example, one article described Roger's gunshot wound as "in the lumbar area of the shoulder," as opposed to the more negative-sounding "shot in the back." The *Salt Lake Tribune* featured a picture of me behind a table laden with knives taken off youths during the riot — actually, the largest of these weapons had been taken off a youth at the rodeo grounds earlier, not during the riot.

Darrell Renstrom, Weber County assistant district attorney, said "No evidence has been received to date to warrant a complaint against Officer Newby." I returned to patrol the evening after the incident.

✻

About a month later, September 1963, I sat in a religion class at Weber State College while the instructor called the roll. He reached my name and called "Newby, Claude?"

"Here," I answered.

"Roger?"

"Here," answered the man I had shot a month earlier, from directly behind me. It was no coincidence that Roger and I frequently missed the same class periods during Fall Term, for whenever he appeared in court I was there to testify against him.

Roger was convicted of *Failure to Disperse and Resisting Arrest* and drew a monetary fine. About a year later, he invited me to attend his farewell when he was about to depart to fulfill a church mission.

✻

Back in Vietnam, the return of the battalion to "real" combat approached rapidly as July drew to a close. A month of low casualty rates had temporarily dulled leaders' and troopers' capabilities to shrug off the horrors and risks ahead. But the veterans couldn't shrug off the memories. We would deploy with many new, inexperienced troopers and a new battalion commander. Lt. Col. John E. Stannard replaced Lt. Col. Dashiell as battalion commander on or about July 27. Attendance at worship services improved as deployment drew near. Anxieties increased visibly in veterans and replacements alike, in veterans because we knew what was ahead, in replacements because they didn't know.

Anxiety among the leaders was heightened because we knew the battalion would enter unknown territory in the Marine AO, come early August. Reportedly, where we were going the enemy was too well entrenched for the Marines' resources, a situation suited for the 1st Cav.

Our combat trains would return to LZ English. The battalion would open a new firebase near the Song Re Valley, in lower I Corps. When we deployed, three companies of infantry would air assault into the mountains and valleys near the Song Re to find, fix and destroy enemy elements, while the other company secured the firebase. The risks would be high because we'd be almost out of range of supporting artillery, except for the 105mm-artillery battery, which would accompany us.

*

Sp4 Prentice Dale LeClair of Alpha Company came seeking help to get out of the field. This surprised me because LeClair, an American Indian from Tulsa, Oklahoma, was a fine, combat-tested infantryman, one of 21 that had been wounded with me on July 4.

"Chaplain Newby," LeClair said, "I'll be killed if I go on this mission. I know it."

My first impulse was to catalogue LeClair's concerns as normal pre-battle jitters, but, deep inside, I believed him. Perhaps LeClair's premonitions rang true because I'd grown up on stories of Indian warriors' uncanny mystic experiences and "visions."

However, I had few options. I might get LeClair out of the field, temporarily, for cause. But from the command perspective, premonitions did not equal cause. Oh yes, LeClair's wife was about to have a baby, but paternity wasn't sufficient cause to have him excused from the field, either.

Perhaps I could have convinced Captain Bluhm to find LeClair a temporary detail at base camp. But I had to be judicious in my recommendations, for a chaplain's ability to speak for the troops grows or shrinks depending on his demonstrated judgment. And LeClair was but one of several troopers who sought my help in obtaining a rear-area job out of fear he would be killed otherwise.

I reasoned with LeClair and offered what spiritual and moral reassurances I could. For two hours LeClair and I discussed his concerns. We tried to convince each other the chances were favorable, despite his premonitions. "LeClair, your odds are better than most because of your experience, barring the vagaries of war."

LeClair departed my office to face his fears, resigned to whatever happened, believing nothing he did would change the outcome this time. I hoped LeClair was wrong, but felt he was going to his death, as he felt. Naturally, for the sake of my sanity, I tried with less than impressive success to shrug off my foreboding.

*

Sunday, July 30, I taught a Sunday School lesson in the morning, conducted a general worship service in the brigade chapel, provided services to the men around the Y-ring all afternoon. At 1945 hours, I attended the Sacrament Meeting and spoke on revelation — LeClair was still on my mind. I met Major Smith, who was being reassigned to base camp, and felt impressed he should replace Scott Thereur as LDS group leader; it was time for Thereur to go home.

*

At 0400 hours on July 31, I accompanied Alpha Company on a 23-ship combat assault into Happy Valley. This was a rare international operation in which we cordoned a large village, and the civilian national police entered and searched it. The operation was uneventful. Being part of a 23-ship night assault was exhilarating, all those infantry-laden choppers lifted as one off the airfield, followed by a synchronized assault into the rice paddies surrounding the target village. Of course, the assault would have been even more impressive in the daylight.

By noon we were back at base camp, where I trooped the perimeter until dark talking to troopers, most of whom like me were trying to prepare spiritually, emotionally and mentally to return to the field. Perhaps command had had the same idea, a shakeout operation in Happy Valley to hone our combat senses for the upcoming months.

I stayed close to the flagpole on August 2, intending to participate in an aerial reconnaissance of our about-to-become new area of operations. For reasons I can't remember, the recon was called off. We'd go into unknown territory relying on others' observations.

Chapter 22

Battle of LZ Pat

By 0800 hours on August 3, the battalion was ready on the airstrip. We were to fly by fixed-wing aircraft into the Marines' AO, then air assault into the area of the Song Re Valley.

At 0830 hours, I held a worship service for Delta Company, with about 60 men attending — attendance always picked up the closer we got to combat. Almost all of Charlie Company, 125 men, attended a service at 0930 hours.

We lifted, mostly in C-130 cargo planes, at 1000 hours. My "seat" for the one-hour flight to Marine LZ Montezuma was the left caisson of a 105mm-artillery piece — not very comfortable. Riding with the artillery piece was more disquieting in some ways than the dangers on the ground. My imagination ran wild with images of what the heavy gun would do to my body in a crash.

At Montezuma I held a service for Alpha Company and then air assaulted with Charlie Company onto a mountain to the east of the Song Re Valley, a notorious NVA AO.

During the night I got acquainted with my new chaplain assistant, Sp4 Ken Willis. Willis had transferred from the Army Security Agency, electronic espionage, because he wanted to be closer to the combat. What Willis really wanted to be was infantry. I understood him. Obviously, I'd have no trouble getting Willis to stay with me in the field. With Willis' arrival, Preacher returned to Alpha Company. I would miss Preacher.

After a few hours with Charlie Company, Willis and I flew to the new battalion LZ, Landing Zone Champs. There, stranded for the rest of the day, we appreciated a little humor to break the monotony.

*

Chaplain (Lt. Col.) Parker Thompson had recently replaced Chaplain McGraff as division chaplain. Thomas' new deputy was a recent transfer to the Army from the Navy — why and how, I don't know.

Well, soon someone discovered that the former sailor had date of-rank on Parker Thompson. Just like that, the 1st Cav had a navy division chaplain. Of course, he knew nothing of Army ways, much less about cav operations in combat.

About 1400 hours, Battalion Operations alerted me to the division chaplain's approach. I went to the pad to meet the chopper, expecting Chaplain Thompson. Instead, a stranger alit and quickly explained how he had so recently become the "boss." Then came the funny part. "Chaplain Newby, in one hour, I want to conduct a Catholic mass here on the LZ for the whole battalion."

Uncertain if he were joking or for real, I explained the situation. Though we had part of the battalion, the TOC people and an artillery battery on the hill, everyone was very busy digging in and probably would be unable to break away for a service before dark. "Most of the battalion," I explained, "are in the jungle, and the mass has to go to them."

"I want to have a mass for the whole battalion. In the Navy, when I wanted a service, I simply announced over the public address speakers, 'Now hear this. Now hear this.' Why can't you simply announce the mass and have everyone take a break for it?"

"Come with me, sir, please." I led him to the TOC and introduced him the operations officer. The operations officer explained why preparing the LZ took precedence over everything, what with our being almost beyond the range of supporting artillery.

I pointed out the locations of the other infantry companies on the large operational map. The division chaplain pointed to the symbol for one of the companies on the map and asked how far the company was from the LZ.

"Eleven hundred meters," I answered.

"That isn't far. Couldn't the company come in for a service?"

Patiently, before the amazed TOC personnel, I explained that while the company wasn't far from us as the crow flies, it would take about eight hours of steady chopping, climbing and slipping to reach us. That wasn't going to happen, I assured the chaplain, because it would create unacceptable interference with the unit mission and undue hardship on the troops. Shaking his head, the chaplain got in his helicopter and departed.

I expect the new division chaplain was beginning to wonder what he'd gotten himself into by leaving the Navy. I wondered what we'd gotten ourselves into by letting him leave the Navy.

*

The next morning, August 5, was scary, not because of what we ran into, but by evidence of how rapidly combat skills had deteriorated. All morning, the company I was with manuvered through the jungle and occasional man-made clearings as we worked around the southern base of the mountain on which Alpha Company was helping establish a new fire base, LZ Champs. By early afternoon we had patrolled around the base of a mountain, from the west side to the east side of LZ Champs. Along the way I mentioned to the company commander that the men in the lead platoon were bunching up dangerously in a clear area. Nothing changed.

Farther north, now east of LZ Champs, we patrolled up a sparsely vegetated valley, hugging the hill and jungle on our left. I didn't care for our position because the valley was less than 150 meters wide, which meant we were quite exposed and well within small arms range from both sides.

Again, I held a little session with the company commander. The platoons' flank security was sticking too close to the unit; it needed to be deeper into the tree lines, especially when we halted on occasion. The company commander, perhaps in part because of my observations, reprimanded the lieutenants. Dispersions and flank security improved immediately, at least in appearance.

With better flank security, we promptly discovered an enemy complex inside the tree line on the west side of the valley. These bunkers were unusually well-constructed and reinforced. Judging by the size, layout and extensive engineering that had gone into the complex, I guessed it had recently housed an NVA division headquarters.

Without our improved flank security, we might have walked right past those bunkers. I shuddered to think what would have happened had their builders occupied them. Others probably shuddered, too, as latent combat skills began to resurface.

＊

The company was ordered the next morning to locate an NVA commissary and supply depot that reportedly sustained NVA operations for the whole area. We moved north about 500 meters to where our valley joined a river flowing from the east. The river was 100 feet wide and chest-deep on me at midstream. Several dead water buffalo were lying about and in the water — obviously, the 1-9th Cav had recently worked the area.

Leaving our packs with the company CP security, I accompanied a platoon across the river. We waded across just north of where the river curved from a west north-west course to a northern direction. As I waded ashore on the east bank, I remembered I had replaced the camera in the ammo pouch without enclosing it in plastic — I had used the camera before crossing the river. Sure enough, the camera was soaked. I quickly snapped two pictures — my last on this tour.

We patrolled east along the river for about a kilometer and came up dry. Again, I thought, *Military Intelligence doesn't know what it is talking about.* There was just no sign on our side of the river to suggest we were anywhere near a major NVA commissary and supply depot. We crossed the river and patrolled back to the west and found the NVA cache, on the side of the river we'd started from, 200 meters from where we'd first crossed to search on the wrong side.

The commissary contained 10 tons of salt in great, conex-size blocks, stashed in open-sided sheds that reminded me of my grandpa's corncribs. Another shed was packed to the roof with strips of cinnamon. Nearby was evidence that an American LRRP team had recently operated in the area — which explained the dead water buffalo and why we'd been sent there. Obviously, the LRRP team had identified the target and had been extracted, and the 1-9 Cav killed the NVA's walking transportation and commissary, the water buffalo, on the way out of the area.

The salt we found was too hard and heavy for easy removal and redistribution to Vietnamese farmers. So the grunts soaked it in JP-4 fuel, packed in a hefty C-4 explosive charge — and hardly dented it.

Early in the evening, we retrieved our packs, and I had a good bath and shave in the river. Meanwhile, like Bravo Company, the other companies in the battalion had now gone three days in the new AO without any significant contact with the NVA and without friendly casualties. Day by day LeClair's premonition of death haunted me less and less.

*

On August 7, at LZ English, the deputy division chaplain informed me I was selected to initiate a division policy of sending a chaplain to Japan each month to visit 1st Cav casualties. I was to go to Japan the following week.

Back to LZ Champs as quickly as I could go, I reported this development to Lt. Col. Stannard. "It is an honor to be selected for the trip, and I would love to see our men in the hospitals. But I'm concerned about leaving the unit just now," I explained. Stannard heard me out and said, "Go to Japan."

Right after I told division to cut me orders for Japan, the battalion got orders, which made me wish I hadn't made the call. Alpha Company was to assault onto a grassy ridgeline overlooking the Song

Re Valley. I knew this was a very bad place even before I saw it.

*

That evening Ken Willis announced he had quit smoking and wanted to discuss the LDS faith. My reaction was tempered by well-remembered counsel to LDS chaplains: never proselyte soldiers and their families unless specifically asked by them to do so, and when possible refer those who ask to missionaries or local leaders. We were instructed to never try to convert or participate in the conversion of other chaplains, under any circumstances. For me, chaplain assistants seemed too close, uncomfortably so, to this proscribed population.

*

At 1000 hours, August 8, I accompanied Major "Woody" Hayne, whom I remember as the Operations Officer — though Bluhm said a Major Olson held that position — and the battalion Artillery LNO on an aerial recon of the hills surrounding the Song Re Valley. Never before had I experienced so strongly what aviators called the *pucker factor* — a gross, but accurate description of those sensations one gets in anticipation of being shot at from beneath.

Later, on LZ Champs, I expressed to Major Iverson strong reservations about going to Japan and tried to enlist his help in convincing Lt. Col. Stannard to countermand the Tokyo trip. Iverson, though he understood my feelings, ordered, "Quit trying to get out the trip. Go to Japan."

So I went to An Khe to get ready for the trip. Some of the Alpha Company troopers beat me to Japan — as WIAs. My combat senses had been very accurate.

*

About 0940 hours August 9, Alpha Company air assaulted onto a south-running grassy ridge — designated LZ Pat — overlooking the Song Re Valley. The lead platoon hit the objective, right behind several minutes of artillery preparation (ARA only, according to several grunts). Sp4 Lloyd Gratz was among those leaping from the first hovering chopper to spread out and establish security for those still inbound. Gratz insists there was no shooting at first, as does Sp4 Joe Letarte, who was in the second inbound chopper. Sp4 Mark Y'Barra insists individual NVA soldiers were already shooting when he jumped to the ground from the second chopper.

Whichever was the case, from behind several anti-aircraft weapons and numerous bunkers and spider holes, hostile eyes watched the arriving choppers and the company's defensive preparations. The anti-aircraft weapons dominated the LZ from two nearby high points, Hill 450 at its north end and Hill 625 to the west. Apparently the NVA gunners' priorities were gunships and command choppers, then the choppers bringing in the last platoon and the troopers on the ground, in that order.

The anti-aircraft guns unleashed their hellish fire just as the choppers approached the LZ with the last of Alpha Company, the heavy-weapons platoon. Almost immediately, the AAA guns downed two 1-9 Cav gunships and an H-13 scout chopper and disabled the brigade commander's command and control bird.

To the sound of anti-aircraft fire, troopers in the last platoon began jumping to the LZ, seeking whatever sparse cover was available and hoping the slick ships wouldn't be shot down on top of them.

Most of the slick ships made it away from the ridge before the enemy shifted its anti-aircraft fire to the LZ, and each lift ship left the area under its own power. Already, from concealed spider holes and bunkers on and around the LZ, NVA infantry had opened fire at close range on the exposed, vulnerable troopers. Some were cut down even as they leaped from the choppers; someone said LeClair died that way. However, Shelby L. Stanton, in *Anatomy of a Division*, said LeClair was stitched across the chest by anti-aircraft fire as he ran into a more exposed area to retrieve ammunition for the heavy weapons. No matter which version of his death is closer to true, LeClair's premonitions had come true.

Joe Letarte said, "We in my position had almost no cover. If I moved even an inch I drew machine-gun fire." "It was the same where I was," said Gratz. "Then we started drawing fire from behind. I thought our guys were shooting over our head, too close, and yelled for them to stop. It was NVA shooting out of spider holes inside our perimeter."

The killing and maiming continued for about four hours, interspersed with miracles here and there, like Lt. Hostikka's narrow escape. Hostikka was hunkered low under intense enemy fire, trying to regroup his men, when a bullet killed his RTO and another bullet entered Hostikka's helmet and whirled around his head between helmet and helmet liner, said several grunts. Bluhm said it was Lt. Hostikka that this happened to. "It was Dick Hostikka who had the round through his helmet. I can still see him lying there with a grin on his face, wiggling his finger at me through the hole in the helmet," said Ray Bluhm.

✳

"Kelly's ruck pack was hit and literally blew up on his back," said Gratz and Letarte. "He didn't seem to be hurt too bad, but he never came back, though Roberts, who seemed in worse shape, returned in time to be killed before the month was out," said Letarte.

Jack Walton of Novato, California, jumped onto LZ Pat along with the Weapons Platoon. Moments after he jumped into hell, an NVA popped from a spider hole and shot him in the neck. The impact spun him about and flung him to the ground. After shooting Walton, the NVA turned his fire and attention elsewhere, probably assuming Walton was no longer a threat — a fatal error. With blood spewing from his neck, Walton killed the NVA who had shot him, then fell again, this time hit in the face, his jaw shot away.

Then, for about four hours, Walton, twice severely wounded and untreated, watched the battle rage. He said he saw a Medevac chopper explode in the air, and a Navy fighter go down in flames. "I saw Jerry Hodson get shot while he helped 'Pop' Theberge, who'd been hit in the head. I heard an LDS man, a real nice guy, became a killing machine after Song Re," Walton told me in 1995. After hours of excruciating pain and terror, Walton was medevaced. He didn't know the fate of some of his buddies until 1995, when he and I contacted each other.

Early in the battle, Alpha Company mortars and recoilless rifles were rendered ineffective because all remaining ammunition was out of reach and because these weapons made easy targets. SSG John Stipes, Weapons Platoon leader, tried to suppress the anti-aircraft guns with mortar shells, until the NVA guns zeroed in on him and forced him to take cover.

With the heavy weapons rendered useless, the M-60 machine guns were Alpha Company's main, almost only effective defense — and these were knocked out one by one.

At one machine gun, PSG Theberge, who had crawled to the position after breaking his ankle jumping from a chopper, was shot in the head and knocked unconscious (*Anatomy of a Division*).

From another precarious machine-gun position, Sp4 Michael Hotchkiss and his crew blasted away at the enemy. "Lysak was hit first, three times. Then Carl Gunter, assistant gunner, was shot in the head. After Carl was hit, a mortar round hit Hotchkiss in the back, killing him and wounding Mark Y'Barra, ammo bearer, who said, 'Then I lay there four hours. It seemed like half an hour, looking back,'" said Walton

The same mortar round wounded Lysak again, who, after getting his earlier wounds dressed, had returned to feed ammunition into Hotchkiss' machine gun.

"The battle at Song Re Valley was the worst I ever experienced, not excepting my Korean War experiences nor a later battle in the Aschau Valley when the NVA shot down 128 Cav choppers in a single morning," said 1st Sgt. Catron in 1969, who came late to the fight, according to Bluhm.

Captain Bluhm recommended Sgt. Theberge for the Distinguished Service Cross for his actions on LZ Pat. Bluhm heard that Theberge died in the hospital of secondary complications. Alpha Company received the Presidential Unit Citation for its action on LZ Pat — the equivalent of a Silver Star. Five Silver Stars and numerous Bronze Stars for valor were also awarded to the men of Alpha 2-8 for their action on LZ Pat. While these tokens of well-deserved recognition are a source of great satisfaction and pride to many aging veterans of LZ Pat, there was little comfort for the survivors on LZ Pat that horrible day.

*

LeClair's death hit me the hardest — and each death hurt sorely. My grief for LeClair was intensified because I hadn't gotten him out of the field. I didn't feel guilty, just deeply grieved, saddened and sobered.

The next day I was an emotional wreck during the flight to Hokado U.S. Air Base, Japan. Part of my turmoil resulted from intense awareness that in a month, barring death and injury, I'd be soaring from Vietnam again, not to Japan, but to my darling wife and adorable, *perfect* children.

My spirits should have soared at these thoughts, and they did, but only to limited heights. I was beginning to sense how difficult it would be to leave my grunts in combat for the last time — just how difficult it would be I couldn't imagine.

*

My orders to Japan included four days of R&R and five days of temporary duty. I went to Japan on an R&R flight and was to return to Vietnam via whatever transportation was available.

I'd received verbal instructions forbidding me to begin the hospital visits until after the R&R period, which I tried to obey, though I seldom enjoy sightseeing without someone special along to share the experience.

I arrived in Japan at 2330 hours August 11 and got to bed in the BOQ by early morning on the twelfth. Later in the morning, at the PX, I purchased a set of Nortaka china for Helga and a necklace for a Lieutenant Howard's wife. For dinner, I experienced the culinary delights in a Navy Chef's Club, followed by a movie at 2030 hours. The Tiptons, an Army family I'd met in April, took me to church meetings the next day, in which I spoke three times — in Sunday School, Priesthood and Sacrament Meeting. I enjoyed the rest of a pleasant Sabbath day dining and visiting with the Tipton family.

On August 14, I visited Chaplain (LDS) Jim Palmer and his lovely family. Sometime during the R&R period, I went horseback riding and spent a night with the Tiptons.

Captain Bluhm's Alpha Company casualties on LZ Pat (G-1 List — *KIAs:* (G-1 list) Sgt. Robert Maxwell of Fresno, California; also KIA Sp4 John Michael Beyraud; Sp5 Andrew Conrad, company medic of Millington, Michigan (with whom I often visited); Cpl. Joel Findley of Richmond, Texas; Cpl. Joseph Harrison of Thomasville, Georgia; and Michael J. Hotchkiss of Anaheim, California; Sp4 Prentice D. LeClair of Tulsa, Oklahoma. *WIAs, G-1 List:* PSG Frank Theberge; SSG Artis Wallace, Sp4s John W. Smith, and Raymond Snaders, Pfc. Chris Swensen, Pfc. Clarence Durham, Pfc. Kerry Holt, Pfc. James Collins, Pfc. Carroll Bartholomew, Pfc. James Bailey, Pfc. Dennis Kelly, Pfc. Mark Y'Barra, Pfc. Jack Walton, Pfc. Theodore Lysak [my self-appointed protector], Pfc. Carol Gunter, Pfc. Dwight Johns and Pfc. Edward Sammons, and three others whose names I don't have.

An incomplete list of non-Alpha Company casualties include Sp4 Ray E. Moran of Big Bear Lake, California; Pfc. Ceasar A. Pinto of New Bedford, Massachusetts (he may have been in Alpha Company), and pilot Francis A. Rochkes of Pana, Illinois.

Chapter 23

The Last Month

I spent all day, August 21, visiting troopers in the 249th Station Hospital. Among those I visited were four men from Alpha Company, casualties of the battle at Song Re on August 9. Sergeant Theberge was there with another head wound — despite which he immediately and happily recognized me; Pfc. Swensen (LDS), who had taken a gunshot wound in the shoulder while he tried to protect the wounded Theberge; Sp4 Campbell, shot in the right shoulder, going home; and Pfc. Lysak, my Catholic protector, shot in the arm and hit by mortar fire and going home, alive at least! With these latest casualties, most of the Alpha Company troopers whom I had met during late 1966 and early 1967 were wounded or dead, and so many were the latter.

※

After a day of hospital visits, I traveled by train and subway to dine and spend the night with the Price family in Tokyo. Price, a civilian, worked at the American Embassy, as I recall.

On August 23, I flew via chopper (with a Medevac pilot named Marks) and visited the troops in the 106th U.S. Army Hospital in Yokohama. There I found Pfc. Harry E. Kerrpash, the bulldozer operator who on March 1 couldn't destroy a bunker in the face of crying women and children. He'd lost a foot and perhaps an eye to a mine or booby trap. Kerrpash recognized me after I described our first meeting.

※

I found the 2-8 battalion signal NCO in another hospital where he was being treated for hepatitis. His story vividly shows the dangerous, destructive power in helicopter rotor blades. His weird, unusual accident happened like this.

It was a week before the sergeant came down with hepatitis. He sat on one hole of a two-seat latrine literally minding his own business. Fifty feet behind him, two choppers idled on the log pad, their rotor blades whirling. Beneath the sergeant was part of a steel barrel, partially filled with diesel fuel to better burn the human waste he and others deposited in the barrel.

Unfortunately, the pilots of the choppers didn't have their minds completely on their business, as slowly and unnoticed by them, the vibration of one or both of the choppers brought them nearer to each other.

With a crack of thunder the tips of the rotor blades met. About five inches of one of the blades broke loose and took off at supersonic speed straight for the latrine.

The sergeant's first hint of trouble came when the barrel beneath him took flight, knocking both his legs straight out in front and splashing diesel fuel and human waste all over his person.

The rotor blade, after passing through both sides of the steel barrel below the contents level and knocking it five feet forward, continued for another 50 feet.

The sergeant's only injuries were to his dignity and nasty bruises on the back of each calf. He didn't think the incident led to his developing hepatitis, but I wondered.

*

Following hospital visits on August 23, I spent the night with the Marks family, grateful for the hospitality of the Saints in Japan. Next day, August 24, I shopped in Yokohama, traveled via military sedan to Tachikawa, and spent a short night with Chaplain James Palmer and his family.

At 0230 hours on August 25, I arrived at Tachikawa Air Field for a return flight to Vietnam. That is when I learned I was supposed to have arrived at 0130 hours. An enlisted airman heeded my plea and got me on the plane, anyhow. At 1200 hours I landed in Saigon, via stops in Okinawa and at Clark Air Base, the Philippines — where I visited for 30 minutes with Chaplain (LDS) Robert Cordner. Finally, at 1730 hours on August 25, via Cam Ranh Bay and Pleiku I arrived at An Khe.

*

The next morning, August 26, I attended LDS services and visited with Sp4 Paul Moody. Before returning to the field, I reported on my trip to Chaplain Parker Thompson. Thompson said he and Lt. Col. Dashiell were writing a joint letter about me to the chief of chaplains, and together the two of them were working to ensure I received the awards for valor for which I had been recommended — nothing came of the promise.

As I arose to leave his office, Chaplain Thompson ordered me to "stay out of the field and relax for the remainder of your time in-country." Oh yes, he added, "You were reported AWOL for failing to return to Vietnam with the same R&R group you went to Japan with. Not a good career move," he joked.

It was raining and cold when I arrived at LZ English at 1710 hours. Lacking a dry place to sleep without imposing on anyone else, I wrapped up in my poncho for a miserable night.

✳

While I was in Japan the 2-8 Battalion had returned to the Bong Son Plain and the surrounding mountains and shore. Because of the weather, it took until August 29 to reach any of my companies. Meanwhile, during the night of August 28, a booby-trapped artillery shell killed Sp4 Julian Mendez of Bravo Company. He died near the beach, as did several other grunts, killed by similar booby traps. For example, a Medevac chopper landed about 70 feet from where several casualties were laid out. Each one of the casualties had been hit by the same booby-trapped artillary shell. The medic jumped off the chopper to help. Moments later, another booby-trapped 155mm shell exploded beneath the stretcher on which the medic and three grunts carried a casualty of the first explosion. The casualty and the four bearers were killed instantly and hardly recognizable as humans.

Back at English, I checked on Mendez at the 15th Med. His lower body was mostly gone, including all but a bare strand of cartilage where his genitals had been.

✳

On August 29, I accompanied Alpha Company on an air assault onto the mountain near the southwest sector of the plains. I'd tried very hard to reach Alpha Company, to pass on what I knew about the casualties in Japan. I also wanted to receive an update about the action on August 9, and to just be with the men again and to soothe the guilt I felt for having been away when the company took such heavy casualties.

After evening chow on August 30, I flew via LZ English to the 1st Platoon of Charlie Company. The company was operating along the north bank of a small river near the coast. A little later, the 2nd Platoon of Alpha Company arrived, OPCON to Charlie Company. The reinforcements were because we expected a strong force of NVA to cross the river in the night. After dark, the platoon split into squads and spread out about 20 feet from the riverbank to cover a section of the river.

*

At midnight I checked the squad I was with and found every trooper asleep. After awakening the squad leader, I decided to stay awake myself, just in case. Fifteen minutes later, we received sniper fire and M-79 grenades. The grenades missed our position by 30 feet. We didn't respond because we suspected the NVA were trying to draw our fire so they could pinpoint our position.

*

The platoon from Alpha Company wasn't so fortunate, scattered as it was in squad- and team-size blocking positions along the river to our west, facing south. About 0100 hours, NVA soldiers sneaked within striking distance of one of the positions, and tossed home-made hand grenades — beer or soda cans packed with C-4 explosive. Ralph Jensen sustained a shoulder wound that earned him about 10 days in the hospital. The grenades killed three Alpha Company troopers in a nearby position: Marvin L. Franklin Jr. of Oklahoma City; Sp4 Lawrence G. Grass of Belleville, Illinois; and Cpl. Gerald J. Roberts Jr. of Torringtron, Connecticut.

In yet another of the 2nd Platoon (Alpha Company) positions, Joe Letarte and his exhausted squad succumbed to sleep. Letarte had earlier received a sedative for bad sunburn. Consequently, he had completed the first watch and was fast asleep in the wee hours.

"I awakened to the sound of the grenades and the shots that killed Grass, Franklin and Robert, less than 20 feet away," said Letarte. "A moment later, I was sitting up when up the bank came a figure wearing a steel helmet, which detail I could make out from his silhouette. At first I thought the approaching figure was one of us, until he placed a hand on each of my shoulders and spoke in Vietnamese as though he were instructing someone. All the while I was feeling for my weapon. The figure fled when I swung my M-16 in his direction. A moment earlier, the figure had stabbed Buddy Braakefield in the shoulder."

At 0900 hours on August 31, I attended to the three KIAs from Alpha Company and tried to visit Jensen, but he had already been evacuated to Qui Nhon. About 1000, back in the field, I held a worship service for the 2nd Platoons of Alpha and Charlie Companies. I intended to spend the night with these elements, but was recalled to LZ English, something about a GI prisoner.

*

"I go home to Helga this month!" This was my first waking thought the morning of September 1, at LZ English. But my tour wasn't over yet. Though I recall no details, the prisoner matter kept me at LZ English until 1700 hours, at which time I finally joined the 2nd Platoon of Charlie Company on a hill near the Bong Son River, nearer the coast. Soon after I arrived, we worshiped together, then started preparing for a platoon-size foray down the mountain.

*

At 2000 hours, well after full dark, we headed down the very steep north face of the mountain, slipping, sliding, holding on to limbs and whatever to maintain our place in formation and avoid falling into the abyss. Pfc. Michael McCord fell into a depression at 2130 hours, after we'd "progressed" perhaps a third of the distance toward the valley. The medics and I feared McCord's back or neck might be broken — he had no movement from the neck down.

A few minutes later the Medevac chopper crept into the extremely narrow draw and performed one of the hairiest, most heroic extractions I ever witnessed — and I had an unenviable bird's eye view.

The pilot moved his chopper very carefully into the draw, until the main rotor was chopping grass a few feet above my head, to its front and on both sides the draw. Hovering there, the pilot held the chopper steady in the air while the crew chief lowered a litter on a cable. Below, disregarding the whirling blades over their heads, the platoon medic and grunts immobilized McCord in the litter. After hoisting McCord up, the pilot eased his chopper backward until it had space to bank and drop toward the valley to pick up speed, almost too late.

Naturally, McCord's rescue operation required use of the chopper's landing lights, and these attracted the enemy. Fortunately, though, the rough terrain slowed the enemy's efforts to get into position to shoot down the hovering chopper. Their first shots came just as the chopper banked and dived, at 2230 hours. Our presence given away, we climbed back up the mountain, assuming our mission was over for the night — not so.

*

We had barely regained the mountaintop when the platoon was ordered down the mountain by a different route. The Lieutenant didn't like the orders and neither did I, but orders were orders.

At 2345 hours we began our descent, along a spur of the hill and down a trace of a trail through erosion washes.

A sniper opened fire on us 45 minutes into our descent. The incoming wasn't even close enough to crack around us in passing. Still, we called in artillery, which was as ineffective as the sniper's fire, exploding as it did far from his position. This time, the company commander aborted the patrol mission, having concluded we were not going to reach the valley undetected. At 0200 hours, I rolled into my poncho liner to sleep.

*

At 0700 on September 2, we humped down the mountain and took a position along the river nearer the rest of Charlie Company. Soon afterward, we got orders to cross the small, slow river and search both banks. The first trooper into the water sunk instantly over his head — the bank went straight down. Quickly, I helped pull the trooper out and then did something very foolish, which I think I'd never do again. I swam across and secured the opposite bank so the squad could cross over, floating their gear on inflated air mattresses.

Our search came up dry, but we didn't, having searched the riverbanks from a leaking boat, one weaved from palm fronds. A few minutes later, we rejoined the company to help search a village, and a chopper was hit by small arms fire as it came into the village. The enemy fire came from the banks we'd just searched.

*

On September 3, I held a worship service at 1000 hours, my last on LZ English. At 1330 hours I conducted a memorial service in the field for Mendez of Bravo Company. And at 1600 hours I conducted a hilltop memorial service for Grass, Franklin and Roberts of Alpha Company.

On September 4, I left the Bong Son battlegrounds for the last time, I thought. As part of my farewell efforts I traveled by jeep with Moody and Willis and visited wounded troopers in the hospitals in Qui Nhon, where we stayed the night.

*

About 1330 hours, September 5, I arrived back at LZ English, intending to retrieve my rucksack and say goodbye to the battalion commander and staff — which plans changed because of what had been happening in Bravo Company.

Five troopers had been wounded, including Sergeant Earl W.

Fernandez (LDS), SSG Roosevelt Williams, Sp4 Lloyd Gabriel, Sp4 George Jones, Sp4 Jefferson Lewis and Sp4 Gary Stene.

✳

In late afternoon, I joined Bravo Company on the rocky east side of a mountain spur, due west and over a hill from LZ English. I wasn't supposed to go, but I couldn't *not go.*"

Arriving at the Bravo Company position, I found the company CP radios atop a clear knoll about 50 feet above some cliffs. Troopers were all over the cliffs. Below the cliffs, a cave entrance slanted upward to where several VC had taken refuge. To the left of the cave opening stood a rock about the size of two CONEX containers, and, strangely, much of the bottom of the rock stood a foot to three feet above the ground. Two crevices extended upward from the cavity under the cliff, one to the top and the other between the main cliff and the big rock. Another part of the cliff rose 20 feet above the big rock.

Captain Root updated me. So far, he'd failed to get all the cornered VC out of the cave. Five VC had come out, but one scooted back into the cave at the last moment and rolled out the fatal hand grenade that wounded Sergeant Fernandez and the other five troopers.

Consequently, Root's men tried unsuccessfully to burn the remaining VC out with JP-4 fuel and to force them out with CS gas. When I arrived, the troopers were pushing 250 pounds of C-4 explosives into the cave — to blow the VC out.

---

1 September 1967, 2-8 Journal: "C 2-8, 2-6 element at 2130, 1 EM fell in hole...possible broken back ... medevac complete. At 2220, received 3-5 rounds s/a fire."

2 September 1967, 2-8 Journal: "0115, C 2-8, 2-6 element received 4 rd s/a fire, came from w ... neg assess."

5 September 1967, 2-8 Journal: "0923, B/2-8 fd cave complex while searching. 3 x VC threw 2x grenades, 1 was dud. Results, 5 US WIA, 1 serious, all medevaced ... VC trapped in cave. Trying to get them out."

1030 "B 2/8 captured 5, 4 det from cave wearing shorts. Neg equipment. Believed to be more in cave. Trying to talk out."

1930 "B 2-8 Readout Detainees...Hamlet guerrillas. One states 2x guerrillas left in cave. Man who was killed was a guerrilla, also a secretary to the hamlet chief. No grenades left."

1830 "Cave blown at 1828, found 1 male, 1 female, found 6 enemy KIA ... one of enemy WIA died on way to med."

Chapter 24

The Last Day

To get out of the way of the anticipated explosion, I climbed above the cave and cliff and joined an RTO, who was monitoring the company radios. I moved about 15 feet from the RTO, squatted down under rapidly darkening, rain-laden clouds, and waited for the blast in the cave, which I expected to be soft because of the earth and stone beneath me.

Suddenly there was a blinding flash accompanied instantly by a tremendously explosive clap of noise. *That was a lot more than 250 pounds of explosive* was my first rattled thought.

Then I saw the RTO standing in a daze several feet from his smoldering radio. Fortunate for him, he'd put down the radio handset and stepped toward the cliff for a better view of the action a moment before lightning struck his radio. We were both shaken and momentarily dazed, but unhurt. The blast from the cave, when it came, was very tame by comparison to our near miss.

*

Moments later, having descended to the cave entrance, I looked upward when a lieutenant at the top of the cliff yelled that someone was climbing up the larger crevice.

"He's American," yelled the lieutenant. "Those (expletives deleted) made a GI go through all that (another expletive)!"

Enraged beyond reason, the adrenaline-charged lieutenant and a sergeant pulled the man from the crevice, only to discover he wasn't American after all. Enraged anew at the VC because his unusually tall, "cave-pallored" body had deceived them, the two leaders rushed the VC to the edge of the cliff to fling him headlong to the rocks below, I thought. But upon seeing me looking up at them, the two hesitated. Slowly, the wildness drained from their eyes countenances, and they turned and led their prisoner away from the precipice.

As the first VC was being hustled away, another soldier, situated on the rock by the other crevice, called, "One is coming up here!"

As I scrambled up the rock, I saw a female arm extend from the crevice to the soldier.

"Don't touch me, you bitch," the soldier snapped. Slapping the girl's hand aside, he lifted her from the crevice by the hair of her head.

"Stop it," I snapped, as I pulled the young woman away from him.

"I'm just trying to help her, Chaplain," he mumbled.

"She doesn't need that kind of help," I retorted, harsher than was necessary under the circumstances.

Turning from the soldier, I studied the young woman in my arms. She was 16 to 18 years old. Her clothes were partly burned away as was much of her skin — some of which came off on my hands and uniform.

Hoisting the girl as gently as I could across my left shoulder, taking off more skin and flesh in the process, I prepared to take her up the cliff to the medic.

A medic tossed down a rope. Grabbing the rope in my right hand, I walked the cliff face with the girl on my shoulder, while the medic and two troopers pulled up the rope.

About halfway up the cliff, the girl emitted a sound, something between a grunt and a gasp. Coming over the top of the cliff, I lay her gently on her back.

"She's dead, Chaplain," said the medic after examining her.

"No, her heart's beating!" I insisted.

"It's your own pulse, Chaplain, from climbing the cliff with her on your shoulder." Yes, she was dead, probably since that last grunt halfway up the cliff.

"Sergeant Fernandez died at the aid station," someone whispered in my ear, as I knelt over the girl's body.

Fernandez had returned recently from R&R, or leave, with his wife. I recall that he returned that day from leave, but Lt. Alfred E. Lehman says differently. According to him, Fernandez was a close friend of his and had been his platoon sergeant during infantry advanced training, prior to Lehman's going to officer candidate school and becoming an officer. "I bade my wife a final farewell when I left her to return to Vietnam because my Hawaiian kuhuna told me I would be dead in three months," Fernandez told Lehman.

"Fernandez was killed three months to the day his kahuna told him that," said Lehman to me.

In the deepening twilight, I joined Captain Root above the cliffs. While Root expressed his regrets over Fernandez's death, a trooper pressed a quart-size container of ice cream into my hand. Choppers had brought ice cream in while I was beneath the cliff, and the trooper had set the portion aside for me.

A few days later, in a different world, it seemed unimaginable that I ate ice cream under those circumstances, reeking as I did of charred flesh and death, but I had. Sleep didn't follow, though.

For my last night in the field, I never bothered setting up a rain shelter. Instead, I inflated my air mattress about halfway, donned my poncho and slipped the back of it under the top of the air mattress, and settled down into a rock chute of sorts, facing downhill. Thus I spent my last, long, wet night in the field with the Bravo Company, 2-8 Cav.

All night long I pondered my mixed emotions about leaving the troopers and going home. I thought about the noble traits so common in these grunts, and regretted the flashes of cruelty like the ones I'd just witnessed. And I was awed that the RTO and I had escaped harm from the bolt of lightening. I loved these wonderful troopers, who in my opinion were the best and the brightest of young Americans. I wondered how I would be able to leave them come morning. I knew I had to leave; I just wasn't sure how.

*

Vague, unreasonable guilt is probably the most common trait among Vietnam veterans. So it was with me, only my unreasonable quilt wasn't vague. I arose the morning of September 6, cold, soaked to the skin and stinking of burned human flesh. I was still torn between overwhelming desire to go home to Helga and the children and almost overwhelming guilt — like I was deserting these men. My guilt feelings were compounded because I also felt disloyal to Helga and the children for feeling guilty about leaving here. Such emotional chaos as I was going through can't be described, only experienced. *One year is all that's required* I told myself, but it didn't help right at the moment.

*

My problem was settled for me. At 0700 hours, an H-13 helicopter landed. Colonel Stannard climbed out, marched up to me and after brief greetings said, "Get in my charlie-charlie and go home, Claude." He added a few words of appreciation for my services and promised to do everything he could to see I got all the medals for valor I deserved, those I'd been put in for and more.

I climbed in the right seat of the two-seat H-13 chopper and began my homeward journey. Colonel Stannard stayed on the ground with Bravo Company to be sure I got out.

*

Later, I learned mine was the first and only official chaplain visit to hospitals in Japan. An insider told me the whole Japan-visit thing had been a ruse, used by command and Chaplain Thompson to keep me out of the field during my last month, lest I be killed — I'd used all my numbers, they believed.

At An Khe, someone handed me an Army Commendation Medal with V device for valor. I headed home with this, the lowest of all combat decorations, plus the air medal, another purple heart, and the "general issue" bronze star for service.

A few days would yet pass before I left Vietnam behind, presumably for the last time. But for me, my tour of duty ended about 0704 hours on September 7 when I climbed into Colonel Stannard's Charlie-Charlie chopper and flew out from the Bravo Company AO.

On the trip to An Khe, before boarding the Caribou, in a symbolic act of finality, of closure, I took from my left front pocket an item of government equipment. After rendering it harmless, I placed it in my rucksack — an action that could have brought me considerable embarrassment and some expense. At base camp, I landed at the alternate airstrip nearer An Khe and hitched a ride in the back of a two-and-a-half-ton truck to the division administrative area. From there I walked to the battalion area.

Unknown to me, the item I'd placed in my pack fell out when I jumped from the truck, which fact I discovered about an hour later as I prepared to turn in my gear to the supply room. With great anxiety, expecting to miss my flight home, I reported the loss to the battalion adjutant.

Captain Spiegelmeyer, after calling the supply sergeant, informed me a trooper had found and turned in my lost item — quite a coincidence, if true.

By long odds, someone other than a member of my battalion found the lost item and kept it. *Was the lost item really found, or are the supply sergeant and Spiegelmeyer conspiring to protect me by writing the item off as a combat loss?* Being one who gives little credence to coincidence, I'm left with benevolent fellow soldiers, divine intervention, or both. I can live with that.

On September 10, I talked for the last time in an LDS Sacrament Service at Camp Radcliff. Two days later I flew eastward toward home from Cam Ranh Bay, two days short of a year from the day I left the states for Vietnam.

Chapter 25

"But There Is No Peace"

I'm lying in a prone shelter. Suddenly, a chicom grenade — a potato-masher type — hurdles from the darkness and lands against my leg. Frantically, I grab the grenade in my left hand and fling it across my body to the right. The "grenade" emits a blood-curdling scream — I wake up lying in bed at home. It's Helga that I hurled toward the window, not a grenade.

The word *world* means many things. To God, it is a degenerate human condition that we must be in, but not a part of; to scientists, a celestial sphere; and to some, a collection of possibilities. To soldiers in Vietnam, the world was America, home, sweetheart and family, the land of plenty, the land of the big PX.

Constant reminders of the war and the men I left behind dampened considerably the wonders of being home — in the world — with Helga and my family. And try as I might, I could neither adjust to the business-as-usual civilian world nor to the garrison military.

Glorious reality awaited me at the Salt Lake International Airport. My mind, heart and spirit caught up with my body the moment I glimpsed Helga and the children at the terminal gate. In an instant the faces of war were behind me, beyond the greatest ocean in the world. At least, they were temporarily.

Helga got the first hug and kiss; then came the children. A few minutes later, with our emotions under tight rein and my war-worn civilian rucksack on John's back, we went to our rented home in Ogden. However, feelings of disloyalty dampened the occasion. Surrounded by home and family, the faces of my grunts grew dimmer, and I feared I might forget those I'd left behind, especially the dead. Little did I know.

✳

That I wouldn't, couldn't forget and put Vietnam behind me became quite obvious during the two short weeks we lingered in Utah. Awareness began with a telephone call from a former seminary student of mine.

The call came just before noon my second Sunday back.

During the morning session of a conference in the Ogden, Utah Tabernacle, Elder Gordon B. Hinckley had asked that anyone who knew how to locate me please do so and invite me and my family to attend the afternoon session of conference. Naturally, I accepted the invitation.

We were not surprised when Elder Hinckley invited me to take a few minutes of his time to address the conference. I don't recall speaking especially well, but I vividly recall the reawakening of feelings about Vietnam — and these have remained close to my consciousness ever since.

*

We arrived at Fort Bragg, North Carolina, in our new American Ambassador *lemon,* where we quickly learned that housing was very scarce and so were airborne assignments — there would be no jump pay to augment our meager income. Chaplain (Colonel) Jim Skelton said, "Sorry, but the chief of chaplain gives me my assets. I manage them, and I need you in the basic training center. So that's where I went to work under the technical supervision of Chaplain (Major) Virgil Hill, a Baptist and easy man to work for. Chaplain Hill assigned me religious support responsibility for a training battalion in a brigade commanded by Colonel John P. Barker, with Lieutenant Colonel O'Brien as his executive officer.

*

All the while, the nightly news and my surroundings pulled me back to Vietnam and made quite unpleasant many of the things I had to do in this peacetime, garrison environment. For example, I found it especially difficult to attend social functions, especially the formal ones. The crowds made me very tense, and I felt shamed to be surrounded by such elegance while the grunts fought and died far off in Asia. Though I attended to my social duties, my unease must have shown through because the problem soon showed up on my efficiency reports.

The same nightly news that infuriated the populace served to make me angry with my surroundings and to feel increasingly guilty for being safe in the world while the grunts fought on.

One day during the TET offensive, 1968, I stood in for a battalion commander in the reviewing stand while his battalion of trainees — several hundred strong — practiced passing in review. It occurred to me that before me were almost enough young men to replace those who were killed in Vietnam during the past week. This observation did not help me adjust.

Another incident in April 1968 created a spike in my maladjustment. It happened in Salt Lake City, where I had taken a C-130 load of soldiers to attend a church conference.

It was Sunday afternoon, as I recall, and Helga and I were wandering around Temple Square between conference sessions — I was in uniform. A couple tentatively approached us. "Are you in the Army?" one of them asked.

"Yes, I am."

"We wonder if you can tell us how to get information about our son. He was killed in Vietnam."

"Gladly. What is your son's name, his unit in Vietnam and when did he die?" I asked, after expressing condolences.

"Our son was Pfc. Danny Hyde," said his Mother.

Maintaining careful, superhuman control of a flood of emotions, I shared with the couple all I knew of Danny Hyde's last days with David Lillywhite, how he quit smoking and declared his intention to get his life in order. I told of my futile attempt to visit Danny earlier on the day he was wounded and related to the couple Danny's last words as I'd heard them from buddies and medics. Finally, I shared the details of my visits to Danny in the hospital — holding back only the gruesome details about his wounds — and how I finally commended their son to God's will. The pull of Vietnam became increasingly difficult to resist.

On December 12, 1968, while in Washington, D.C. with a carload of soldiers for the groundbreaking for the temple there, I dropped into the office of the Army chief of chaplains. "I'm here to volunteer to return to Vietnam," I said. With those simple words, I was on my way back to Vietnam for a second tour that made the first one seem easy by comparison.

The next day, I arrived home to find Helga in the hospital suffering with pneumonia. At her bedside, I broke the news that I was returning to Vietnam. She chose that moment to break the news that she was pregnant with our sixth child.

✳

The author returned to Vietnam in 1969 for a second tour. He'd been in field less than an hour with a year stretching before him when blazing fire from an enemy machine gun cut down the trooper in front of him and pinned Newby to the ground. In that moment a new parade of heroes marched forth. Newby's forthcoming book will tell that part of his story as it continues his tribute to those valiant, faithful sons of an ungrateful nation. These were the same men he had tried to leave behind in 1967 — only the faces, names and military identification numbers had changed. The men were the same, but the war was different, harsher. Political defeat was in the air.

Glossary

A/C:	Air craft.
Air Cav:	Air Cavalry; 1st Cavalry Division, Airmobile.
AK-47:	Standard Russian Assault Rifle, used by NVA and VC.
Alpha:	Letter A in Army phonetic alphabet, as in Alpha (A) Company.
Alpha 2-8:	Thus used, *Alpha* refers to company, the numbers to the battalion and regiment the company belongs to.
AO:	Area of operations.
ARA:	Aerial rocket artillery.
Arc light:	B-52 strategic bomber strike (raid); carpet bombing of an area one-quarter-mile wide by one-mile long; often ineffective because enemy had advance warning — USAF registered B-52 flights with international agencies favorable to Hanoi.
Arty:	Abbreviation for artillery.
ARVN:	Army of the Republic of Vietnam.
B-40:	Rocket propelled grenade, a nasty weapon used by the NVA and VC against armor and personnel.
Barrier:	Primary base defenses; used at the An Khe Base Camp, 1965-68.
Battery:	Basic unit of artillery, personnel, guns and equipment; comparable to a company in non-artillery organizations.
Beehive:	An artillery round containing steel flechettes, or tiny steel arrows; see *Flechette Round.*
Berm:	Earth barrier around defensive perimeters and bunkers.
Bird:	A helicopter; see chopper, and Gunship.
Bubble:	OH-13, a light observation helicopter; a deathtrap.
Blues:	Infantry rifle platoon, one-each in each Air Cav Troop in the 1st Squadron, 9th Cavalry.
Bravo:	Letter B in Army phonetic alphabet.
C-130:	Air Force hercules transport aircraft.
CA:	Combat assault; also *Charlie Alpha.*
Cav:	(1) The 1st Cavalry Division (The Cav); (2) Troopers of the division; (3) Infantry battalions in the division; (4) First Squadron, 9th Cavalry (the "real" Cav).
C and C:	Command and control; also, *Charlie-Charlie,* the commander's command and control helicopter.
Canister:	Rounds containing steel ball bearings for tank and artillery cannon and the M-79 grenade launcher,

CG: Commanding general.

Charlie: Letter C in Army phonetic alphabet; short for Viet Cong.

Chieu Hoi: Vietnamese for "open arms," a program to entice enemy soldiers to change sides in the war.

Chinook: CH-47 tandem-rotor transport helicopter; also, *Hook.*

CIDG: Civilian Irregular Defense Group. Natives recruited to serve with U.S. Special Forces.

Chopper: Helicopter; see Huey, and *bird.*

Claymore: Anti-personnel mine. The American version spews out hundreds of steel balls in a fan-shaped arc, lethal at 50 meters.

CO: Conscientious objector.

C.O.: Commanding officer.

Combat Trains: Battalion forward support site, usually on a firebase during the Vietnam war; see Field Trains.

Company: Basic unit of infantry and other non-artillery personnel, weapons and equipment; usually with between 100 and 200 personnel — Infantry companies, about 140.

CONEX: Metal shipping container with double doors on one end. Utilized for "jail." Inner shell for tactical bunker, etc.

CP: Command post.

CS: Tear gas.

DaisyCutter: Ten thousand-pound bomb used by USAF to cut instant LZs.

Delta: Letter D.

Det-cord: Explosive fuse-like cord used to explode multiple charges simultaneously.

DivArty: Division Artillery, may mean headquarters or all artillery organic to the division.

Division: The major maneuver element of the Army, ranging in strength (during Vietnam era) from 18,000 to 24,000 personnel.

DoorGunner: Machine-gun operator on a helicopter.

Echo: Letter E.

EM: Enlisted man (men); later, EP for enlisted persons.

FAC: Forward air controller; an officer who directs air strikes.

Field Trains: Rear-support area, usually located at a major base camp; see Combat Trains.

Fire Base: Site of artillery battery(ies). Battalion combat trains usually co-located (called landing zone or LZs during most of the war).

FIX: To entrap or confine an enemy so he can be destroyed.

Flak Vest: Body armor.

Flare: Illumination device (noun); or the landing attitude of an aircraft (verb).

Flechette Round: Small steel arrows or darts in canister or beehive shells.

FO: Forward observer. Usually artillery officers attached to infantry companies to call and adjust artillery fire; also, individual members of mortar platoons in support of rifle platoons.

FOB: Forward operating base for an infantry company, often called an NDP, especially during 1966 and 1967.

Fougasse: Home-made napalm used for defense around American firebases.

Frag: Fragmentation grenade (noun); part of an operational order or *frago* (verb); criminal act of attacking one's own leaders in a war zone, usually by hand grenade, but the term expanded to include other attacks against one's own leaders during the Vietnam War.

FSB: Fire support base; usually a battalion-size operational base that included the battalion combat trains, TOC and a battery of howitzers; also, called an LZ during most of the Vietnam War.

GI: Term for American soldier, carried over from World War II.

Grease Gun: Simple and reliable .45 caliber automatic weapon that resembles a devise for greasing vehicles.

Green Line: The generic term for the outer defensive ring of bunkers, wire, towers, etc., at most base camps.

Grunt: American infantryman; popularly believed to have arisen from the infantryman's grunting as he hoisted his heavy rucksack.

GSW: Gun shot wound.

Gunship: Helicopter armed with mini-gun, machine guns, rockets, and some with 40MM grenade laundchers.

Hooch: *Make shift accomodations.*

Hotel: The Letter H.

HE: High-explosive ammunition.

Hoi Chanh: VC or NVA soldier that joins South Vietnamese; see Chieu Hoi.

HQ: Headquarters.

Huey: UH-1 utility helicopter. Also, *HUEY.*

IO:	Information officer; also PIO (public information officer).
KIA:	Killed in action.
Klick:	Kilometer, slang.
Leg:	A non-airborne infantryman; also *straight leg.*
LNO:	Liaison officer.
LP:	Listening post.
LRRP:	Long-range reconnaissance patrol unit; *LURP,* to grunts.
LZ:	Landing zone; any place designated for aircraft to land, one or more times. See also FSB.
M-14:	U.S. Caliber 7.62-mm, predecessor to M-16 and in use in Vietnam.
M-16:	U.S. Caliber 5.56-mm, the basic U.S. forces assault rifle.
M-60:	U.S. Caliber 7.62-mm machine gun; platoon and company weapon, also used on Hueys and Armored Personnel Carriers (APCs).
M-72:	LAW (Light Anti-tank) weapon. HE round fired from a throwaway tube; used in Vietnam to attack bunkers.
M-79:	40-mm grenade launcher, breech-loaded, shoulder-fired.
Machine gun:	Crew-served automatic weapon
MG:	(1) Machine gun; (2) Major general — two stars.
Medevac:	Aerial medical evacuation, 1st Cavalry term.
Medic:	Medical aidman; also, affectionately called Doc by many grunts.
Mini-gun:	Multi-barreled machine gun with firing rates of 2,000 and 4,000 rounds per minute, every fourth round a tracer.
NDP:	Night defensive position, usually called a FOB or forward operations base in 1969.
Net:	Short for radio network. All tactical radios operated within a defined network on a designated frequency.
OP:	Observation post; see LP.
OPCON:	Operational control.
Picket Line:	The defensive area several kilometers beyond a base camp barrier line or perimeter; also, *rocket belt.*
Pink Team:	Two-helicopter team, Gunship and scout ship.
Police:	(Verb) To clean up or search an area.
Pony Team:	Fire man patrol.
POW:	Prisoner of war.
PRC-25:	FM radio, back-packed; basic communications for nearly every level of command within the division.
Prep:	Short for preparation of an LZ by artillery, ARA and, occasionally, by air strikes.

Prone Shelter: One-man position; shallow, body-length trench used frequently early in the war in place of foxhole.

PSP: Perforated sheets of steel that joined together to provide a runway for fixed-wing aircraft; also used to reinforce overhead cover on bunkers.

Punji Stake: A small sliver of bamboo, stuck in the ground and in punji pits to impale "enemy" forces; sometimes tipped with feces and other matter to cause the wound to fester; used by VC forces.

Quad: Four guns, M-60 machine guns, 40-mm launchers, etc., configured to fire together.

R&R: Rest and recuperation.

Recon: Reconnaissance.

Roger: Formerly, the letter R and radio language for "yes" or "affirmative." Grunts often shortened it to "Rog."

Rome Plow: A standard D7E tractor, equipped with a heavy-duty protective cab and tree-cutting blade. Rome-plowing was carried out to deny the enemy sanctuary by removing jungle and to enhance base defense by clearing around bases.

RPD: Soviet 7.62-mm machine gun (NVA).

RPG: Soviet 82-mm rocket-propelled antitank grenade; used by NVA as an antipersonnel weapon; see B-40.

RTO: Radio telephone operator.

RVN: Republic of Vietnam.

S/A: Small arms or small arms fire.

Sapper: Soldier (originally an engineer) who attacks fortifications. VC and NVA used sappers extensively and effectively.

Satchel: Explosive package fitted with a handle for ease of handling arming and throwing; favorite weapon of the NVA sapper.

Sitrep: Situation report.

SKS: Soviet carbine.

Spider Hole: Small, easily concealed NVA and VC foxholes.

TOC: Tactical operations center.

Tracer: Bullet that burns as it moves from weapon toward impact, leaving a *trace* of fire in its wake. Our tracers burned red; NVA tracers burned green.

Tube Arty: Tube artillery. Also field artillery and naval guns.

USAF: U.S. Air Force.

USARV: U.S. Army Vietnam.

VC: Viet Cong, also Vietcong, Victor Charlie or Charlie.

WIA: Wounded in action.

XO: Executive officer, "first officer" at echelons below division.

37-mm: Soviet anti-aircraft weapon, electronically aimed and fired.

40-mm: Projectiles or rounds for the M-79, for a four-barrel launcher and launchers on gunships.

Index

225